Working the Spirit

Joseph M. Murphy

Ceremonies of the African Diaspora

BEACON PRESS / BOSTON

Beacon Press
25 Beacon Street
Boston, Massachusetts 02108–2892

Beacon Press books
are published under the auspices of
the Unitarian Universalist Association of Congregations.

The author would like to thank Judith Gleason for permission to use material from her film *The King Does Not Lie*; song from *Life in a Haitian Valley* by Melville J. Herskovits, copyright 1937 by Alfred A. Knopf, Inc., renewed 1965 by Frances S. Herskovits, reprinted by permission of Alfred A. Knopf, Inc.; songs from *Voodoo Heritage* by Michel Laguerre, copyright 1980 by SAGE Publications, Inc., reprinted by permission of SAGE Publications, Inc.

LIBRARY OF CONGRESS CATALOGING-IN-PUBLICATION DATA

Murphy, Joseph M., 1951–
    Working the spirit : ceremonies of the African diaspora / Joseph
M. Murphy.
      p. cm.
    Includes bibliographical references and index.
    ISBN 0-8070-1220-3 (cloth)
    ISBN 0-8070-1221-1 (paper)
    1. Afro-Americans—Religion. 2. Blacks—Latin America—Religion.
3. Voodooism. 4. African diaspora. I. Title.
BL2490.M87 1994
200′.89′96—dc20   93-3929

99 98 97 96 95 8 7 6 5 4 3 2

Text design by David Bullen

to our African ancestors

Contents

Preface

When I began planning this book in the winter of 1989 I had in mind a kind of handbook of religions of the African diaspora. The book would organize basic information about the traditions and show something of their spirit. As the research and writing continued I began to realize that it was this spirit that interested me, especially the special ways that the spirit was "worked" in the communal ceremonies of each tradition. After years of attending *santería* drum and dance ceremonies, I started to see, hear, and feel many of the same "workings" during visits to African American churches. The book began to focus on what an outsider might experience at services of the spirit in five diasporan communities, and how these experiences might relate to the communities' own interpretation of their actions.

I've discovered that while it is difficult enough to relate basic information about the traditions, it is quite something more to presume to understand their spirit. As a white, North American, middle-class male, I've continually discovered new limitations in my understanding of religions of the African diaspora as I have projected my own interests and issues on people with very different ones. As I have grown in my understanding of their traditions, I have experienced a continual correction of these projections, a challenge to my prejudices by diasporan realities. Yet further on the road of understanding, I have found new commonalities of material and spiritual values. At each level of understanding I've learned that I am more like and more different from the people whom I have been getting to know. I hope that I have been able to give an account that is acceptable to them and intelligible to outsiders.

One of the highest hurdles to overcome in interpreting diasporan traditions to outsiders is the deep-seated popular image of them as "voodoo," malign "black magic." Hundreds of books and scores of films have portrayed the spirituality of millions of people of African descent as crazed, depraved, or demonic manipulations of gullible and irrational people. These images have their origin in the French colonial reaction to the revolt of Haitian slaves whose motive in liberating themselves from grinding and brutal enslavement was thought to rest in *vaudoux*. The success of the Haitian revolution sent shock waves through the white world that are still being felt today. I think that the relegation of "voodoo" to the horror genre reflects mass America's real horror of independent black power. If voodoo was powerful enough to free the slaves, might it not free their descendants?

Whenever I present this liberating view of diasporan traditions I will be reminded that there are genuine practices of malign sorcery within them. Yet I have grown tired of answering calls to present the less-salutary dimensions of diasporan spirituality in the interests of "balance." I take it for granted that peoples of African descent are as venal as anyone else, and charlatans and spiritual sadists might be readily located among them. I see my task in presenting the traditions to outsiders as practitioners might wish them to be presented, concentrating on the spiritual depth and beauty that practitioners find. As this spirituality is almost never reported by outsiders, this book may be a corrective toward a "balanced" view.

This entry into the cultural fray of outsiders representing African American traditions presents another, allied, difficulty. Just as outsiders have sought to marginalize diasporan spirituality by blame, they have served much the same end by praise. The opacity of black culture to whites, and the desire of some whites to appreciate the sufferings that black peoples have endured, lead them to imagine a black culture more authentic and noble than their own. In the portraits of diasporan religions that follow I run this risk by presenting ideal versions of the traditions, interpreting their spirituality as unwaveringly authentic and profound. Again I think that the neglect by outsiders of what is extraordinary, beautiful, and grand in the lives of members of the diasporan traditions warrants this emphasis.

Outsiders are drawn to what is different about others, and so the distinctiveness of the spirituality portrayed in this book is based on an outsider's view. In the traditions of my European ancestors the spirit was not "worked" through the human body in ceremonies of rhythm, music, and movement. Though this way of worship may be found in many places in the world, I have found it distinctive of diasporan traditions when it is interpreted through their experience of exile and their hopes for deliverance. This spirituality has struck me as different, distinctive, and profound. I hope in these portraits that the tension between what I, the outsider, see as distinctive about the traditions and what the practitioners themselves see will produce an accurate portrait.

Of course, growing up in America, this spirituality is not really alien to me. It has crossed over to shape all Americans' lives in its more secular forms of blues, gospel, rhumba, samba, and even rock and roll music. When the beat is right we all know that there is something that makes us want to shout. Though the music is popular among people who don't understand the heavy burdens these songs represent, I don't believe that this form of diasporan spirituality is necessarily inauthentic or compromised. It is a great gift of peoples of African descent to all Americans, but it is a gift that could not be freely given. How are we to acknowledge the freedom, spiritual depth, and energy which most of us have felt through the syncopations, blue notes, and gospel flights of African American music? I think it is their service to the spirit which has brought the power of that music down to us. How do we thank them, praise them for their faith that sustains us?

I can only thank them by dedicating the book to our African ancestors and thanking their descendants for their contributions of body, mind, and spirit. Among the many teachers and students who are named at the end of the book, I want to thank the people who most directly made the completion of this book possible. Thanks to my colleagues in the theology department at Georgetown for their friendship and support; to Deborah Chasman of Beacon Press for carrots, sticks, and unfailing good advice; to Mary and Anna for patiently waiting for apple juice; and most of all to Jane for working so hard and making me laugh.

Finally I thank the spirit, particularly in her road as Yeyekari, who graces the book's cover, for the charmed life she has given me.

Note on Orthographies

Orthographies represent communities of writers. Often orthographies have a complex political significance which might be lost on the naive outsider. Since I find myself more often than not in that category, I have had to make a number of rash decisions about the ways to render terms from Haiti, Brazil, Cuba, Jamaica, and the United States. I have been torn between the goals of de-exoticizing the traditions and of rendering them most closely in the multiple orthographies in use in the literature of their nations of origin.

I have adopted the Créole spellings of most terms from Haiti except where their francophone spellings are familiar to a wide circle of readers of English; for example, *petro* instead of *petwo*. For Brazil, I have gone with the renderings of the most recent Brazilian literature on candomblé; for example, *iaô* and *orixá*. Even the name *santería* is controversial, and I have reluctantly continued to use it, along with anglophone renderings such as *orisha*, in order to be consistent with my own publications of a few years ago. In general I have constructed plurals with the letter "s" where I have heard communities of speakers do so (Brazil, *orixás*), and I have avoided the "s" where it is not heard (Haiti, *lwa*).

For these and many other decisions I ask the indulgence of the writers in all the communities of the African diaspora.

1

Introduction

This book is an attempt to understand a spiritual tradition from the outside in. It begins with the premise that there is a distinctive spirituality that can be identified and appreciated in a variety of cultural settings throughout the Americas. This spirituality has its roots in Africa and was developed in the slave and emancipated societies of the Western hemisphere. It flourishes today wherever people of African descent have worked to pass it on to a new generation.

The religions of the African diaspora are different from each other in that each possesses a unique heritage from African, European, Native American, and still other sources. Yet they are like one another in that all recognize the special priority of their African roots. The founders of diasporan religions came from Western and Central Africa where certain conventions of worship obtained over wide geographic areas.[1] Each diasporan tradition shares this heritage, and the similarities and differences of their worship styles can be explained, at least partially, by tracing the history of their transmission from Africa. Each tradition was presented with unique challenges in its fight for survival, which in turn shaped the development of its cultural heritage. Haiti achieved independence as a black republic in 1804, while slavery was not outlawed in Brazil until 1888. In pre-abolition Cuba free people of color made up nearly one-third of the colony's black population, while scarcely one-ninth of antebellum Virginia's black people were free.[2] Yet the religious traditions of the African diaspora are alike in that each shares a social history of enslavement and racial discrimination. Each tradition became the focus for an extraordinary struggle for survival against and triumph over brutal systems of exploitation. They share an elevated sense of solidarity against injustice and a commitment to the protection and advancement of their communities.

Yet the subject of this study is something different from cultural heritage or social history. While these are vital to a full appreciation of the religions of the African diaspora, I am concerned with the similarities and differences among the traditions in a more limited way. I am interested in the way in which each tradition constructs and develops a code of relationships between human beings and "spirit," however this word may be defined. These activities toward the spirit are the tradition's "spirituality." Each tradition "shows" these relationships, enacts its spirituality, in community activity, that is, in ceremony.[3] Each diasporan community celebrates the spirit in ceremonies, and shows in various ways, through the arrangement of symbolic objects and actions, a spirituality of interdependence between the community and the spirit.

Like the spirit that animates them, religions of the African diaspora are at once one and many. Because I have some personal experience of five of these traditions, and because the literature on them is plentiful, I have chosen to to concentrate on the spirituality of five diasporan religions: Haitian vodou, Brazilian candomblé, Cuban and Cuban American santería, Revival Zion in Jamaica, and the "Black Church" in the United States. By offering separate portraits of each of the five traditions, I hope to show the distinctiveness of each in its own community. By placing these portraits side by side, I want to show that they are related to each other: that they share a distinctive spirituality. In as much as the spirit is one, so is the spirituality which brings it to the community. By using the singular noun "spirit," I only wish to indicate, at this point, that the participants' description of their own behavior is accurate, that the spirit is a real and irreducible force uplifting communities throughout the African diaspora.

A "portrait" is necessarily an impression, an outsider's selection and arrangement of elements to produce a "true image" of its subject. As we move toward the subject from the outside, we recognize a constant dialectic of similarities and differences between the subject and ourselves. At one level the subject is like us, at a deeper level unlike, and deeper still, like us in an unsuspected way. The levels seem to have no end.

The portraits of the religions are constructed to emphasize their similarities to each other and their differences from European-derived traditions. The first emphasis runs the danger of supporting an erroneous idea that all black religions are alike. They are indeed very different from each other, and I hope that through the individual portraits presented in the chapters to come, the reader will be able to see their uniqueness. In fact it should be noted that the very idea of *vodou* or *candomblé* as a single tradition in Haiti or Brazil reveals the problem of generalizing interpretation by outsiders. These words represent categories created by outsiders to label by one term a vital, diverse, and ever-changing variety of religious traditions. Those familiar with what we call *vodou* or *candomblé* take regional, lineal, and personal differences very seriously and in some cases reject these umbrella terms entirely.[4]

Nevertheless I think the emphasis on the similarities among diasporan religions is well placed. If we remain cautious to overgeneralizations, some generalizations offer us insights into underappreciated hemispheric and global connections. North Americans are notoriously insular in their cultural outlook. We have laid claim to the word "american," and it does us well to think about the cultural heritage that we share with other Americans. Since the book is written in English and published in the United States, the emphasis on the similarities among diasporan religions allows North Americans in particular to see black religion in the United States in a larger context, a context which may challenge certain assumptions and illuminate new meanings. Once we know something about vodou and Revival Zion, the spirituality of the Black Church of the

United States is revealed in a new context. From a "hemispheric perspective," black religion in the United States can be seen as a special articulation of a spirituality which has kindred expressions throughout the Americas.[5] The religions of the African diaspora become a family of traditions, cousins sharing common ancestors and set apart by the "intermarriages" made in the line. They remain many traditions, yet reveal one tradition.

The second emphasis of the book, the difference between religious traditions derived from Africa and those coming from Europe, raises special problems that bring us back to the motives and perspectives of the outsider. When the central concern of understanding is the distinctiveness of the spirituality of the African diaspora, it becomes important to recognize how outsiders' presuppositions affect the grounds for the presentation and comparison of the traditions. "Distinctiveness" is a category of difference. When religions of the African diaspora are construed to be distinctive by an outsider, we need to ask from whom or what are they different? If we build a typology of African-derived religions around their differences from European-derived religions, are we saying that the basic orientation of these traditions is "other" than European? If so, do we make the religions of the African diaspora dependent upon European-derived ones in that they can only be understood by contrast? What avenues of understanding, elements of commonality and ordinariness, are lost by this decision? On the other hand, can it be legitimate for the outsider to ignore this difference, to presume the ability to understand people with different histories and living in different social and material circumstances? The very decision to "study" religions of the African diaspora presupposes a privileged economic and social position, a comfortable ivory tower to venture from and return to.

It has been a persistent tendency of Westerners to think that "other" traditions are alike because they are different from "Western civilization." Categories like "heathen" may seem antiquated, but the equally inclusive "primitive" still grips the popular mind, and "developing" continues to be seen as a descriptive category for a society. If the religions of the African diaspora are alike in their contrast with "Western civilization,"—whether this difference is seen as a justification for their marginalization or as a hallmark of "primal" authenticity—they have life only as an instructive contrast to European-derived religions.

It seems to me that the way for the outsider to proceed is to begin with what is "outside" as a vehicle toward understanding what is "inside" a religious tradition. It is the easily observable elements which strike the outsider as distinctive. Percussive music and physical movement in time with music are not central features of European-derived religious worship in the United States. Yet they are important characteristics of all of the religions of the African diaspora considered in this book. It has been my decision as an outsider to make these features central to the interpretation of diasporan spirituality, not only because they appear distinctive, but because they are shared by so many people of African descent. The linkage of music and movement with the presence of the spirit, while neither an exclusively diasporan way of worship, nor inclusive of all black people, is a distinguishable, important tradition among a great variety of people of African descent in the Americas. If all black people do not worship through music and movement, very many do, and they do it in comparable ways in such diverse places as Haiti, Brazil, Cuba, Jamaica, and the United States. It is the genius of their way of worship which is the focus of this book.

The outsider begins to understand a diasporan religion where he or she first encounters it, in the external expressions of the tradition that can be seen in public ceremonies. This is where the tradition presents itself to itself and to the communities beyond it. In public ceremonies the community shows what it wants its members to know, and what it wants known about itself. The knowledge of the community is compressed into limited space and limited time. It is understood at different levels by different participants as they recognize different layers of interconnection among symbolic objects and actions. The outsider participating in the ceremony understands one thing; the devotee, that and something else; and the initiate, those and something else again. Each object and action can be seen as an endless line of metaphor radiating out to form new webs of meaning with other objects and actions. In public ceremony these lines are visible to the outsider, and if the subtle connections known to the initiate are unknown to the outsider, the main lines are still available to be followed. This process will, of course, lead the outsider to cul de sacs and false conclusions, but if these are acknowledged and checked, the main outlines and directions of the tradition can be discerned.

The interplay of symbolic actions and objects in ceremonies, the showing of the relationship between human and spirit, forms the basis from which this interpretation of diasporan religions moves from outside in. Each portrait begins with an overview of a diasporan community, a brief history of its experience in slavery and emancipation, and an outline of its constitution as a community of worship. The portrait then proceeds to a description of representative ceremonies conducted by the community. From this base of a community and its services, we can begin to discern a spirituality, a way of making the spirit present among a people. In the diasporan religions portrayed, the spirit is recognized as present by means of the actions of the community in ritual time and space. It is this "ceremonial spirituality" that concerns us, and the explication of this spirituality forms the line of interpretation linking the portraits and leading us to conclusions about a distinctive diasporan spirituality.[6]

I believe that what is distinctive about the spirituality of the religions of the African diasporan can be found in the way that the relationship between human beings and spirit is worked out in community ceremony. The etymology of the English word "liturgy" contains some clues to the role of ceremony in the religions of the African diaspora. "Liturgy" has its origins in the Greek *leitourgia* which might be translated as "work" or "service" of the people. In its Hellenistic context the word indicated any kind of work required of people for the public good, what we might call "public service." Theologians built upon this notion of service to express attendance on God, and the English usage of "religious services" coveys something of this original meaning. Recovering the sense of "liturgy" as "work" and "service" from the ancient Mediterranean can help us understand something of the ceremonial spirituality of diasporan religions.

For diasporan liturgies are seen by their practitioners as both works for the spirit and works of the spirit. The reciprocity between community and spirit is expressed in physical work as the community works through word, music, and movement to make the spirit present. The spirit in turn works through the physical work of the congregation, filling human actions with its power. Diasporan ceremonies are thus services *for* the spirit, actions of sacrifice and praise to please the spirit. And they are services *of* the spirit, actions undertaken by the spirit to inspire the congregation. Thus the reciprocity of diasporan spirituality is affirmed: service to the spirit is service to the community; and service to the community is service to the spirit. Service is revealed to be the central value of communal life. Service shows the spirit, in ceremony, but also wherever one member serves another. It is "service," in all its elegant multiple meanings, that shows the active quality of the spirituality of the African diaspora. The spirit is "worked" in the service to empower the community and praise the spirit. We will be looking at services, human and divine, liturgies of "working the spirit."

I have been using the singular noun "the spirit" throughout this introduction to bring together a number of different ideas in diasporan religions. It will become apparent that practitioners of vodou or candomblé or santería venerate a number of distinct "spirits," while members of black Christian congregations in Jamaica and the United States quite definitely worship only one Holy Spirit. This theological difference is an important one to which the long history of debates on the unity and multiplicity of the Christian trinity attests. We will see that each of the traditions portrayed has an idea of a divine unity in which the multiplicity of spiritual and human beings participate.[7] So when we say that Haitians accept many spirits while Baptists believe in one Spirit, are we comparing entities at the same level? Can the ideas of multiplicity and unity held by each tradition be fruitfully compared?

I am interested in the ceremonial context in which these spiritual entities are invoked, and I think that the structures and styles of the ceremonies are crucial to the idea of the spirit invoked within them. By concentrating on the ceremonies of the African diaspora, I want to give equal stress to the actions of worship as well as the beliefs. I am interested to see if the actions of ceremony are at least as important as the words of interpretation in developing the distinctive ceremonial spirituality that characterizes the religions of the African diaspora. It seems that some white and black Christians may quote the same scriptures to interpret their actions, but experience very different things by them. When Irish American Roman Catholics, for example, refer to the presence of the Holy Spirit at a ceremony they are likely to be referring to a different experience from that of black Pentecostals when they use similar language. I am wondering if the converse might be true among different diasporan traditions. When African American Pentecostals affirm the unity of the Holy Spirit and *santeros* speak of a variety of spirits, could they be saying different things but experiencing something much the same when "the spirit" descends? I do not intend to discount their differing interpretations. I only want to suggest the idea that the experience of "the spirit" in diasporan ceremonies may share important theological qualities without the traditions having to agree on the singularity or multiplicity of "the spirit."[8]

At this stage of the discussion I find that the phrase "the spirit" is useful in bridging the gap of theological explanation among the different diasporan traditions. I mean it to be evocative of connections rather than evasive of differences. "The spirit" can, at once, refer to God in the person of invisible power, to one power among other powers that emanate from God, and to the spirit of a diasporan people, the *geist* that characterizes and inspires them. In the biblical tradition "the spirit" connotes images of breath, wind, and power. It is a genderless, nonanthropomorphic force, the breath of life, *pneuma*. Its iconic representation is the soaring, unpredictable energy of a bird in flight. These biblical images can help us toward understanding "the spirit" of nonbiblical traditions. The suggestion of invisibility and power, of motion and action, leads us to look at human activities which express these qualities of the spirit. The biblical tradition seems to be deliberately trying to de-objectify the idea of spirit, to thwart discursive reasoning about spirit, and to promote direct interactions between the devotee and the spirit. The living spirit cannot be

8

shown except in activity, and this activity makes it present in the ceremony to be experienced and shared by all "in the spirit."

The actions of the spirit and their relationship with human actions express the spirituality of the religions of the African diaspora. Within the borders of the ceremony, the relationship between the human and divine is shown in its full clarity to the community. Within the ceremonial "work" lies the diaspora's resource for developing relationships of wisdom, power, and freedom.

2

Haitian Vodou

Vodou is a dance of the spirit: a system of movements, gestures, prayers, and songs in veneration of the invisible forces of life. Vodou was created in Haiti in a revolutionary struggle against slavery and continues today as the religion of most of the Haitian people. It is the oldest, most famous, and least understood of all diasporan religions. To enter the world of vodou we must know something of the community that has created it, the services that express it, and the spirit that animates it. What follows is a portrait of vodou: its community, its services, and its spirit.

COMMUNITY

In 1797 a Martiniquean traveler, Médéric Louis Moreau de St. Méry, described a dance that he had observed among the slaves of the French colony of St. Domingue, soon to be independent Haiti. His is the first use of the word *vaudoux* in literature about Haiti and likely the reason why the word has come to describe in a single term the variety of the African-derived religious traditions in Haiti. Moreau speaks of a dance led by slaves from Arada, a town in present-day Benin, dedicated to an all-powerful being known as Vaudoux. Vaudoux, he says, is a kind of serpent which possesses oracular powers and communicates them through the mediumship of a priest or a priestess. Led by these "kings" and "queens," the community begins a vigorous dance. Moreau writes: "Each makes movements, in which the upper part of the body, the head and shoulders, seem to be dislocated. The Queen above all is the prey to the most violent agitations. . . . Fainting and raptures take over some of them and a sort of fury some of the others, but for all there is a nervous trembling which they cannot master. They spin around ceaselessly."[1]

Moreau is quick to see the revolutionary potential of this ecstatic worship:

> In order to quiet the alarms which this mysterious cult of Vaudoux causes in the Colony, the affect to dance it in public, to the sound of the drums and of rhythmic handclapping. They even have this followed by a dinner where people eat nothing but poultry. But I assure you that this is only one more calculation to evade the watchfulness of the magistrates and the better to guarantee the success of this dark cabal.
>
> In a word, nothing is more dangerous . . . than this cult of Vaudoux. It can be made into a terrible weapon—this extravagant idea that the ministers of this alleged god know all and can do anything.[2]

Moreau speaks of a black man of Spanish origin named Don Pèdre who gave his name to a dance "analogous" to the *vaudoux,* but with more precipitous movements.[3] The *danse à Don Pèdre* seemed an alarming plot to colonial authorities, and folk tradition maintains that it was at such a *petro (petwo)* ceremony that Haitian slaves began their role in the revolution. On the night of 14 August 1791, slaves gathered in the Bois Camain in the north of Haiti, sacrificed a wild boar to the gods of Africa, and swore an oath to overthrow the French slavemasters.[4]

The success of the twelve-year war of independence begun that night set the image of vodou as the spirit of resistance: a rite of liberation for the Haitian people and a dangerous subversion to slaveholding authorities.[5] The memory of the revolution is renewed and the spirit made present today in many vodou songs. Alfred Métraux attended a mid–twentieth-century vodou ceremony where the Revolutionary general Dessalines came in spirit to join the dancing. The congregation sang:

Oh Emperor Dessalines o,
You're a fine fellow,
What do you think that they did to us,
This country is already in our hands.[6]

Michel Laguerre recorded this song reenacting the sacrifice at Bois Caiman at a *petro* ceremony in Port-au-Prince in the 1970s:

Members of the family,
Come to drink the pig's blood.
Come to the ceremony.
And drink from it.
Come to this feast
And get a drink from this blood.[7]

The Haitian revolution is very much alive in vodou ceremony and symbolism, and it is this revolutionary spirit which gives vodou its critical force and fearsome image. While not all of what we shall call vodou is characterized by what Robert Farris Thompson calls the "spiritualized militancy" of the *petro* rite, this spirit of resistance and challenge forms the basis for our portrait of vodou.[8]

When the revolution was won, the plantation economy and the slave society that supported it were destroyed. Former slaves became peasants, tied to their new property of small plots. The Haitian economy turned to subsistence farming with a rural Créole-speaking peasantry and an urban Francophone élite. Laguerre argues that it was Dessalines's land grants that eventually settled vodou into the countryside. Given the opportunity for an independent life, liberated slaves established extended family compounds called *lakous*.[9] Vodou became the religion of the *lakous*, honoring African spirits that had been preserved through slavery, and venerating the reconstellated family ancestors of the *lakou*. Laguerre speculates that it is from the base of the *lakou* that charismatic and entrepreneurial vodou priests and priestesses established more or less public vodou temples with congregations that spread across family lines.

James Leyburn believes that a major reason for the growth of vodou was the absence of Roman Catholic influence during the first sixty years of the Haitian republic.[10] Allied with Napoléon, the Catholic Church broke relations with the Dessalines government in 1805. The "great schism" continued until 1860 by which time only a handful of Catholic priests lived in the country. Unopposed by the Church and grounded in the lakous and temples, vodou became the religion of the Haitian folk.[11]

A Concordat of 1860 between the Vatican and the Haitian government of General Geffrard reinstated Papal support of Haiti's schismatic Catholicism and led to a re-Europeanization of her parishes and missions. This hiatus and return of orthodox Catholicism created a complex set of relationships between Catholicism and vodou which would endure until the Duvalier governments of the twentieth century. True to its West African roots, vodou had developed by the ritual inclusion of new elements. Vodou rites required Catholic prayers so that all the elements of the Haitian religious experience were present. A special vodou priesthood arose in the pre-Concordat years to fulfill this role. A *prètsavann*, a "bush priest," came to ceremonies to offer Catholic prayers in French along the others in Créole and African *langay* (*langage*). Thus Catholic belief and ritual came to be seen as a special element in vodou rites, a necessary invocation toward the veneration of the spirits of Africa.

After the 1860 Concordat, French Catholic priests returned to Haiti, ready to reinstitute opposition, in varying degrees of hostility, to vodou practices. Not until the 1920s did Haitian intellectuals see in the disparagement of vodou an imperialist echo of the 1790s. The United States Marines occupied Haiti from 1915 to 1934, and the reputation of vodou as an "alarming plot" was just as disturbing to them as it had been to Moreau de St. Méry's French colonists. Haitian writers recognized in vodou the spirit of resistance to the values of Europe and white America.[12] Poet Roussan Camille looked to the vodou spirits for a second victory against foreign powers:

> O surely the gods
> who know that our sorrows

are as long as the way
from Africa to here—
our black gods—now
can foretell again
the victorious colors
of tomorrow's dawn.[13]

Contemporary Haitian writers lament what Laguerre calls the "Duvalierization" of vodou, the co-option of vodou priests into the secret police of the late regime.[14] As early as 1966 Rémy Bastien wrote that vodou "has lost its original revolutionary impetus. It has turned into a conservative institution which condones and feeds upon the backwardness of the peasantry."[15] While championing the "noirist" values of vodou, Duvalier used the beliefs and networks of vodou congregations to enforce total loyalty to his government. When Jean-Claude Duvalier was overthrown in 1986, among the first targets of the people's rage to uproot Duvalierism were prominent vodou priests who had collaborated with the regime.[16]

Vodou has been a potent force for organizing the disenfranchised majority of Haitian society, and if it has not always opposed tyranny, it has always remained a critical force against external authority, particularly when that authority has come from imperial powers, be they French, American, or Roman.

A further result of the Duvalier era is the creation of a large Haitian community in diaspora, and the founding of vodou centers in New York, Miami, and Montreal. Here the revolutionary spirit of vodou is taking new forms as non-Haitians are discovering the gods of Africa. Vodou is part of the new cultural mosaic of many North American cities where the majority of citizens share an African heritage and are seeking non-European models to integrate their experience.

The nearly universal adoption of some form of Moreau de St. Méry's term *vaudoux* by writers both inside and outside Haiti might lead to mistaken ideas of uniformity or orthodoxy that the single word connotes. While there may be informal ties among neighboring vodou communities, each congregation sets its own standards in matters of ritual and belief. Practices of one congregation may be unknown in another, and what is kept rigidly separate in one community may be brought together in another. This variety is further complicated in literature about vodou when writers choose to call very different things "vodou," or more commonly, "voodoo." It is worthwhile to make some basic distinctions.

Moreau states that Arada blacks were the "true followers" of vodou, and he speculates that it was carried from Juida (Ouida or Whydah) on what was then called the Slave Coast of Africa.[17] In its many spellings, "vodou" means roughly "spirit" in the Adja-Tado family of languages spoken in Arada.[18] If we choose to follow Moreau and use the term in its most restricted sense, vodou refers only to the Arada rites and stands in distinction to other rites of African derivation that are practiced in Haiti. Eighteenth-century slave traders distinguished at least seventy different African ethnicities present in Haiti, of which the Arada were but one.[19] If we choose to use "vodou" in its widest sense, all the African-derived elements of Haitian religion might be considered vodou. Harold Courlander organizes the definitional problem of vodou into three interlocking sets of usage: (1) vodou as only the rites derived from the Arada and Nago; (2) vodou as a complex of rites including others clustered around the Arada and Nago, such as the Ibo; and (3) vodou as all Afro-Haitian rites including those of the Congo and Petro.[20]

The variety of African-derived rites in Haitian religious life is understood by believers through the concept of "nation." The African origins of different spirits, dances, and drum rhythms are remembered as those of different "nations," and any particular ceremony will usually offer some service for several different nations. Each vodou community will have arrived at its own constellation of nations to be invoked, and this will also vary according to the type of ceremony involved. In the 1930s Melville Herskovits was told that there are "seventeen and twenty-one classes" of spirits, but could elicit the names of only eight: Rada; Petro;

Dahomey; Ginen (Guinée), Congo, Nago, Ibo, and Wongol.[21] Forty years later Ira Lowenthal also was told that there were twenty-one nations of the spirits worshipped in Haiti.[22]

Two centuries have passed since Africans first came to Haiti in numbers, and the colonial-day sense of African ethnicity has been lost. Membership in a nation has become a matter participation in its dances. Thus the idea of "nation" is not an ethnic, geographical, or political concept, but rather a means of classifying the variety of spirits by the kind of rites that are offered to them. The nations of vodou have their roots in the multiethnicity of colonial Haiti, but they have since been brought together as a single constellation of rites maintained by individual congregations. Each congregation has chosen among the ritual traditions which may "walk together" and has integrated them into a liturgical "mosaic" that represents its own history and aspirations. So the African rites, no less than the Catholic ones of the *prètsavann*, are brought together into the "vodou" of each congregation.

What emerges from this definitional problem is that at whatever level one chooses to use the word "vodou," one is referring to practices derived from a variety of African ethnic groups and integrated into a whole of an individual community's making. Even for those communities committed to the Arada or Rada ceremonies, other rhythms, spirits, and prayers, including those of European Catholicism, have been organized around the Rada rites in a conscious and intricate arrangement. This portrait of vodou will focus on these Rada rites as the core of vodou, while feeling free to generalize from that core to refer to vodou as the folk religion of Haiti.

It is helpful, finally, to distinguish these Rada rites from the infamous sorcery that "voodoo" usually connotes to outsiders. Haiti is full of *wangas* and *gardes*, objects which channel invisible forces in aggressive or protective directions. The spirits which are venerated by the Rada rites, called *lwa*, may even be the driving forces of these objects. Yet what we are calling vodou is concerned with the development of a personal relationship with the lwa. Vodou initiates look with disdain on individuals who have "bought" their lwa and who now seek to direct them for personal advantage at the expense of others. Maya Deren, the most acute of all writers concerning the spiritual dimensions of vodou, writes: "A magician's apprenticeship consists of exchanging his services for secreted, concealed information, whereas the religious neophyte, by virtue of experience and ordeals, matures spiritually to an understanding of things which have been frankly evident in public ritual all along."[23]

This does not mean that vodou devotees never practice sorcery, but that the people and spirits that are the center of vodou are bound together as a spiritual community. This shared spirituality is expressed in the communal ceremony of dance, and so vodou is, first and foremost, a dance, a system of movements which bring people and lwa together in a progressive mutual relationship of knowledge and growth.

The vodou community is organized around the development of spiritual power, marked by stages of initiation into a special quality of mind called *konesans* (*connaissance*), which might be seen as both ritual knowledge and spiritual insight. Vodou recognizes a three-part hierarchy of involvement in *konesans*: ordinary devotees who are more or less active in the service of the lwa; the *ounsi* or "spouses" of the lwa who have made a lifelong commitment to the spirits; and the *oungan* and *manbo*, respectively the male and female leaders of a community who have the power to make new *ounsi*. Thus the oungans and manbos control the patterns of authority in their communities and can assure the proper transmission of *konesans* to their initiates.

The ordinary believers of a vodou community might be either family members connected by blood to a particular compound, or unaffined neighbors drawn to a *ounfo* (*hounfor*) or "temple," headed by a manbo or oungan. For the family members, vodou is a way of remembering the dead and the lwa which have incarnated themselves in their family. These ceremonies usually take place at the family lands or *heritage* in the countryside and are seldom an affair for nonfamily members. Unless a family member is a oungan or manbo, these specialists are brought into the compound as experts to assist in the veneration of the family spirits. The urban ounfo, on the other hand, is a family by initiation, a *société* with its own traditions and very much dependent on the gifts of its presiding manbo or oungan. In their own ounfo they organize the liturgies, discipline and instruct initiates, and offer consultations to clients in need of spiritual advice. For the ordinary devotee, the urban ounfo is a supplemental family of like-minded individuals, or even a surrogate family when one's own is lost through emigration or dislocation.

The sign that a person is called to be something more than an ordinary participant in the services often, but not always, occurs when a lwa manifests itself in his or her body. This experience of "possession" by a lwa indicates that the spirit is calling the devotee to its service. The initial call is often "wild," and the called one is termed a *ounsi bosalle*, whose manifestation of the lwa must be instructed and "civilized" by trained initiates.[24] The *ounsi bosalle* is brought along the path of *konesans* in the ways of the spirit as they are prepared to be more precise receptacles for the presence of the lwa. Their heads must be "washed" to open them to the lwa without impurities or resistance. These *hunsi lave tèt* then may embark on what may be years of instruction in ritual knowledge. Finally as *ounsi kanzo* they take on all the privileges and responsibilities of a marriage with the spirit and become true *serviteurs* of the lwa and permanent members of the hierarchy of the ounfo. The most accomplished of the *ounsi kanzo* is selected to be the *oungenikon* or "song master" of the congregation who leads the other ounsi in their invocation of the lwa.

The oungan and manbo are the ultimate human authorities of the ounfo. They demand total obedience of their ounsi, and it is their *konesans* which guides the progress and health of their spiritual family. They have achieved the highest levels of *konesans* and are bound to use it for the benefit of their congregations. They must know every nuance of vodou ceremony, the proper drum beats, songs, and prayers to invoke or direct the presence of the lwa. At their initiation oungans or manbos are said to "take the *ason*," the sacred rattle which is at once an emblem of office and a ritual tool. The *ason* is positioned in certain ways and shaken in certain rhythms to control the direction of the energy of the lwa's presence. In his or her ceremonial setting, the oungan or manbo is thus conducting the

WORKING THE SPIRIT

invisible energies for the instruction and edification of the congregation.

Oungans and manbos are also experts at *féy* (*feuillages*), the herbalist arts of physical and psychic medicines. They must be able to recognize hundreds of plants and be able to prepare them for infusion or ingestion in proper dosages. They must also know the symbolic properties of plants and how these allegorical meanings may be multiplied by their combination to produce powerful statements in *ouangas* or "charms."

The oungan's or manbo's *konesans* must ultimately be toward an insight into the invisible causes and ends of things. They must develop a second sight which allows them to understand the hidden meanings of human and divine actions. The culmination of the oungan's or manbo's *konesans* is a ceremony called *prise des yeux*, where the eyes of these leaders are fully opened to the invisible world of the spirits.[25]

SERVICE

Membership in the vodou community is defined by service to the lwa and to one's fellow initiates. In fact, one is not a "member" of vodou, but rather a "serviteur" of the lwa.[26] Service to the spirits is based on a hierarchical path into *konesans*, in which the heads of the devotees are gradually cleansed so that their eyes may be opened. Because of the enormous variety of vodou rites, it is helpful to look at the details of one such cleansing process as a key to understanding the spirituality of vodou. Then we can examine this spirituality in action in drummed dance.

Kouche

In the early 1940s the American dancer Katherine Dunham was in Haiti doing anthropological research for the University of Chicago. While she was attending rites at a ounfo in the Cul de Sac region, the *manbo*, Téoline, persuaded her to undergo a *lave tèt* ceremony called *kouche*. In her account of this experience, Dunham doesn't say what motivated her to participate other than to explain that an initiate does not choose to join a vodou community, but responds to a call from the lwa.[27] The call might take the form of a powerful dream or an unsolicited *bosalle* mediumship experience at a drum dance. For many the call is a series of ordinary misfortunes interpreted by a manbo or oungan to be divine interference and to be relieved only by committed service to the lwa. Many initiations are the results of promises to the lwa in thanks and payment for cures of serious illnesses. The disruption of the ordinary life, particularly when it is a matter of life and death, at once causes devotees to seek divine solutions and puts them in a psychological and social state where major changes can occur.

Dunham tells us that her continual presence over many months at vodou ceremonies won her greater confidence from her teachers, and eventually she was advised to cleanse her head in preparation toward a spiritual marriage with the spirit Danbala. She tells us of busy days of preparation she spent amassing the ingredients necessary for the ceremony. For the *lave tèt* she needed special kinds of clothes, food, liquors, and lotions. She offers us a list which includes: a new nightdress, a new ceremonial dress, a necklace of blue and white trade beads interspersed with snake vertebrae, a pair of white roosters, florida water, barley water, strawberry soda, sugar cookies, eggs, herbs, roots, powders, a picture of St. Patrick and another of the Virgin Mary. Many of these items are coded to prepare her for receiving Danbala as her *mèt tèt* (*maît' tête*), the master of her head.

Danbala is perhaps the most powerful of all the vodou spirits. He is likened to a great snake undergirding and encircling the world, whose coiling movements trace the path of the sun and the rotation of the earth and stars. The ingredients of the *lave tèt* for Danbala would be sure to be special to him, assuring his presence in allegorical colors and numbers. The foods would be chosen to entice him to come to feast with the initiate. Eggs, for instance, since they are a favorite food of snakes, are Danbala's ritual food, and he will demand them through his medium in his ceremonial manifestation. Danbala's symbolism takes another form in the picture of St. Patrick, who because of his association with snakes, is often considered to be an anthropomorphic representation of Danbala. The Virgin Mary has the same relationship to the lovely vodou spirit

Ezili, who, Dunham says, is Danbala's wife and is present so she will not be jealous of her husband's new wife. The meticulous coding of all the ingredients sets up a sacred space and time for initiates. Even their very selection produces its own effect. Dunham writes: "I began to feel in the personal care and effort in the choosing of each object, its "mana," its mystic power, as different from the object next to it—similar in appearance, but utterly profane and unmystic.[28]

Dunham says that no money is exchanged in vodou ceremonies, but much is spent. For the poor of Haiti who make up the bulk of vodou serviteurs, the outlay for these ingredients can be onerous. It may take years to amass all that is required. The spirits themselves may modify the basic ingredients and often ask yet more of the initiate, accepting promises for offerings, and sometimes administering cruel punishments when they are not fulfilled.[29]

Once the ingredients are collected, the initiates are led off to isolation in the *djèvo*, a sanctuary room within the ounfo. Dunham writes of a three-day *kouche* ceremony, where she and eight other initiates were "put down on the floor" of the *djèvo* on a Thursday only to rise before the community on Saturday as *ounsi lave tèt*. They were confined to the floor on their sides, spoon-fashion, for most of the three days and allowed only the most minimal movements. Every few hours the officiating manbo Téoline would appear in the doorway to shake her *ason* and call *"ounsi lave tèt,* rise up and turn." Then the nine novitiates would merely roll over and fit themselves together on their opposites sides. They ate only the unsalted sacrificial foods of their *mèt tèts*, and they could wash and relieve themselves only at morning and at night. Dunham describes the ordeal of leaving ordinary life behind.

> Perhaps it was the physical need for some change, if only to turn over
> on the dirt floor and bring momentary relief from the cramp of our
> awkward positions. Perhaps the fasting, the incessant subdued drum-
> ming, the intermittent ring of the bell and the rattle of the ason, the
> smell of burning charcoal, fresh and dried blood and incense, the
> intoned instructions at our departing "selves" and entering "loa" were
> gradually effecting hounci out of bosalle."[30]

Lying on the damp floor of the houngfor in a cold chill, probably because I had forgotten a supply of quinine, aching from head to foot, I condemned all mysticism, all research, all curiosity in the ways or whys of other peoples, all "calls," all causes. . . . With aching knees tucked under the buttocks of the woman in front of me I even wished I were back in Chicago or in Joliet, which indicated a state of total eclipse.[31]

She began to see that this discomfort was a necessary ingredient in the instruction that she and the others received from manbo Téoline and her manbo colleague, Dégrasse. During breaks in the "flooring," she was instructed in the elaborate and esoteric salutations of the ounfo. The initiates have different greetings appropriate to their rank and years of service. And each lwa has his or her proper greeting which varies with the rank and spiritual patronage of the human initiate. She writes that manbo Dégrasse

seemed determined that I would pass my examinations with flying colors. We began the ritual of the crossed and recrossed handclasp, the bow with knees flexed, turn underarm, hounci of the highest protocol guiding the other. Then the turn to all four directions of the compass, hand gripped tightly in hand, with sacred words spoken in each direction, the approach to the altar, the recognition of each grade of protocol by obeisance and word. I was not required to prostrate myself before the mambos as is the practice, flat on the ground, face down, bracing oneself by toes and hands, body rigid, touching each cheek to the ground, swaying side to side. It was up to my instructors to decide what to do, and I followed them, asking no questions.[32]

Together with these elementary social competencies, Dunham was also instructed in the service proper to her *mèt tèt*, Danbala. She was required to memorize long lists of Danbala's ceremonial clothing, foods, dances, and emblems. She was instructed in the character of Danbala, and in the import of the wedding of this character to her own. She remarks that she believes that Danbala's famed capacity for jealousy has been particularly relevant to her in understanding her own feelings.

WORKING THE SPIRIT

Finally she was given the history of the rites and told the nations of Africa from which the ancestors had come.

This instruction, received in the altered awareness caused by sensory privation, was only one element of the "head washing." The novices' heads had to be prepared to manifest their *mèt tèts* as mediums for the spirits. The head of a human being has special meaning in vodou, explained by Maya Deren as a harmony of visible and invisible elements.[33] The physical head is seen as a container for two invisible elements which might be translated in English as "souls," but are likened in vodou to angels. The *ti bònanj* (*ti bon ange*), the "little good angel," is the conscience of a person, the impersonal element of the self which observes and permits self-reflection and self-criticism. The *gwo bònanj* (*gros bon ange*), the "big good angel," is the "psyche," the source of the memory and intelligence that defines the personhood of a human being. When the head is washed, the gwo bonanj is prepared to become separable from its visible receptacle and allow a spirit in its place.

At the beginning of their confinement, the heads of the novitiates are anointed with a poultice of ritual ingredients and then tightly wrapped with a white handkerchief. For her *mèt tèt* Danbala, Dunham's head was anointed with cornmeal, feathers, orgeat, blood, herbs, and raw eggs. By being bound on the fleshly container of the *gwo bònanj*, these ingredients are thought to feed it directly. The anointment strengthens the head in its vulnerable state and prepares it for the rigors of a direct relationship with its master. The poultice had to remain on Dunham's head for a full week after the *lave tèt*, until it was removed without ceremony by the manbo.

At several points during the "flooring," the mèt tèts of Dunham's co-initiates manifested themselves in their new receptacles. Dunham writes of the first such manifestation:

> The woman fitted into the curve of my lap began to tremble. Softly at first, so that it might have been a chill from the damp earth, then violently, so that all of us were jarred by her cataclysmic tremors and knew that her god had entered. To me it was a great relief because it meant that I could move, even stretch without attracting attention,

without breaking that somber expectancy that we had lived in for twenty-four hours.[34]

The woman was named Alliance, and she began to speak *langay*, the sacred African language of the spirits. Manbo Téoline came in from the outer room and, shaking her *ason* over the woman's head called, "Alliance, open up and let Papa Gede come in. Come, my child, you are one of us now, let Gede talk to us."[35]

After some time in an in-between state of manifestation, the lwa Gede established himself in Alliance and was brought to dance with the senior ounsis attending the vigil. Téoline brought in Gede's ritual accoutrements, a black coat, top hat, and cane, and Gede performed his ribald dance of death before the hierarchy of the ounfo.

The other novitiates, in turn, received these manifestations of their *mèt tèts*. Dunham writes with some ambivalence that she was not to experience this usual confirmation of the "baptism" of spirit. Whether she thought this was due to her lack of Haitian cultural experience, her own stubborn personality, or the character of her Danbala, we are not told.

As the heads of the novitiates are being prepared to receive their *mèt tèts*, so receptacles are prepared to receive the displaced *gwo bònanjs*. These *pot tèts* act as containers for the new selves of the initiates, their newly baptized *gwo bònanjs* together with their *mèt tèts*.[36] The pots are described by Dunham as large, white, china apothecary jars which are often hung with bead necklaces or decorated with ribbons. They contain ingredients symbolic of the new union of spirit and human being: bits of hair from the center of the initiates' head together with the sacrificial foods, drinks, herbs, and oils identified with their *mèt tèts*.

The initiates sat cross-legged before these *pot tèts* and were instructed in their meaning and use. Dunham writes:

Facing our head pots, we were given the meaning of what was in them; why a sacrificed animal was considered fortunate to be allowed to take messages to the god to whom this animal represented an approach; how the prayers that were said to this fowl or goat or pig or beef and the prayers for its safe conduct to the god made it indeed superior and privileged beside others of its kind who were butchered without care or rite. How the offerings of foods which had come from Africa could carry a certain part of our spirit back to Africa . . .[37]

After this instruction, the final investment of the *pot tèts* was carried out by the manbos.

We were permitted to speak to our pot tèts through a small crack as the mambos [manbos] held the covers lifted before the final sealing. All of our hopes, aspirations, troubles were confided in whispers to them. . . . The head pots were passed around our heads three times, then emphatically closed by the mambo, with orders from her to each of the pots, which orders were, I presume, to grant us what we had requested, carry out our wishes, and act as intermediary between hounci lavé tête and our gods. Then we chanted in unison and sang in unison, ason and bell the only accompaniment.[38]

A song fragment shows the relationship between ounsi and spirit in the *pot tèt*.

> The saints want something to eat
> Kneel down
> A loa in a pot is incapable of eating
> You must eat instead of him.[39]

When the *manbos* finished with the *pot tèts*, there followed a promenade of the *ounsi lave tèts*, their *pot tèts* balanced on their heads, before the senior members of the ounfo. The pots were then placed on the altar of the ounfo with the other accoutrements of their *mèt tèts*. Eventually these pots would become the property of the initiates to be kept with them at all times. When Dunham returned to Téoline's ounfo a week later to have her head wrapping removed, she believed that the dried bits of ingredients remaining on her head were taken by the manbo and placed in another head pot. This would be kept on Téoline's altar as a permanent sign of Dunham's presence in her ounfo.[40]

Though Dunham often returned to live in Haiti, she never assumed the duties of an ordinary ounsi in Téoline's ounfo. Her career as a dancer led her all over the world, and the mundane tasks of assisting the manbo in all her secular and sacred activities could not be expected of an such a peripatetic figure. While she did not serve Téoline as a ounsi, Dunham's emotional and spiritual bonds to her manbo, fellow initiates, and ounfo were never considered to be less real than those of the ordinary *ounsis lave tèt* who would continue to serve in the day-to-day life of the ounfo, and would develop their *konesans* from assistance and service at ceremonies. These ounsis place themselves in the power of a stern teacher who demands from them the unconditional devotion of a parent. It is to be hoped that a manbo or oungan is not an abusive parent, but the social world of Haiti is harsh, and family life is never easy. A well-run society is a happy place, but authority is rigid, and the progress in *konesans* is ruled by the manbo or oungan. As vodou has no civil sanctions to preserve discipline, only the moral and spiritual powers of the oungan or manbo can insure the proper transmission of *konesans*.

After the elementary education of the *ounsi lave tèt*, the path leads to *kanzo*, a rite where the head is once again prepared and the ounsi shows self-mastery by dancing in fire. The *boule zen* (*brulé zin*), the ceremony of the burning pots, closes the seven-day flooring of the *kanzo* initiation. Three pots are filled with oil and sacrificial ingredients and set on nails over three flames in the ounfo. One is of iron, representing the lwa Ogou, while the others are of clay representing the dead and the initiates' *mèt tèt*. The novitiates, "possessed" by their *mèt tèts*, are individually led from the *djèvo* under white sheets. The pots are set alight and the sheeted initiate is placed over each so that he or she "breathes fire." This will "heat up" the lwa in manifestation so that it will allow the initiate to handle the burning contents of the pot and to dance over the flames. The pots eventually break or are overturned, and all the ounsis, inspired by their *mèt tèts*, dance in the flames. This "trial by fire" confirms the ounsi as a possessor of formidable *konesans* and a fully mature member of the vodou community.[41]

Danse Vodou

The emphasis on the preparation of the head, on the development of *konesans*, and on the opening of the eyes reveals vodou's concern with a spirituality of human consciousness. The old *bosalle* self must be tamed to become a vehicle for a spirit that has been born anew within it. This new "amalgam" of consciousness is prepared for service to the spirits in the *lave tèt* and *kanzo* initiations. It is then realized in songs, dances, and rhythm.

Moreau de St. Méry was right to see "vaudoux" as both a deity and a dance. It is through the movement of dance that the lwa are able to be fully present to the congregation. The ritual orientations of the initiates, the rhythms of the drums, the songs of the ounsi, work together to create a kinesthetic medium for the lwa to manifest themselves in dance. The lwa "mount" the dancing ounsi and bring their immense *konesans* for the disposal to those present. This is the purpose of vodou service: the "center toward which all the roads of Voudoun converge."[42]

A vodou service might be held for any number of reasons. Some are feasts set by the calendar: to honor a lwa on the day of the equivalent Catholic saint, or to mark the anniversary of an initiation, or to celebrate the postfuneral rites of an ancestor. Vodou service is also occasioned by critical problems in the life of the ounfo. A service may be prescribed for the special intentions of a serviteur: in thanks or hopes of a cure, securing a job, or finding a lover. A service may be necessary to remove evil influence or guard or strengthen a devotee against harm. Many services are the results of delayed promises to the lwa for help rendered. Often as not, the impetus for a service is the result of a demand from the lwa themselves, who might appear at one service and extract a promise from the congregation or an individual to sponsor another ceremony, usually more lavish. The lwa are quick to resent what they consider to be stingy service, and they can keep the cycle of ceremonies going indefinitely.

But it is not only the hunger for service that the lwa have to communicate. They offer all the *konesans* of Africa for the disposal of their serviteurs. If they are satisfied with their service, they bring healing power and sage advice to those who approach them. "Tell my horse," say the lwa. Give a message to the person who is acting as the "horse" of the spirit, whose personality has been displaced and cannot be there to hear the words of the lwa. The messages may be anything from medical advice to news of the departed to biting social commentary, but they have the divine advantage of always being true. Thus the dances seek the truth, and the capacity of the lwa to speak the truth and offer it to their serviteurs is a valuable, if volatile, gift.

Finally, and most practically, the lwa comes to the service to eat. In a country where most people do not have enough to eat, the importance of sharing food cannot be overemphasized. The lwa are fed, and so the serviteurs are fed. The mounts of the lwa benefit from the lwa's appetites, and those attending may share in the feast. The lwa are brought into a community of shared food, and thus shared responsibility. Vodou is a society that feeds its serviteurs.

Vodou service begins with the consecration of space in order to orient the visible world of human beings to the invisible one of the lwa. The focal point of this spatial relationship is a center post supporting the roof of the vodou dance area or *peristil* (*peristyle*). To "have a center post" is to have a vodou community which offers the protection of the oungan, manbo, and lwa. The ounsi sing a song that speaks of the protective power of this arborial link with *konesans*:

> You, the no-good Haitians, Loko Davia knows me.
> You, the no-good Haitians, Loko Davia knows me.
> You do not know which father trains me,
> You do not know which mother cares for me,
> You do not know who has helped me all my life.
> You the no-good Haitians, Loko Davia knows me.
> If I did not have a center-post,
> You would have tried to kill me.[43.]

The center post, or *poto-mitan*, acts as a vertical link between the sky, earth, and underworld, and thus the worlds of *lwa* and human beings. It is a great tree with its branches above and its roots in Ginen (Guinée), Africa. It draws up the spirits from their homes in Africa, which is seen to lie on the "other side" of this world, among the waters below the earth. Ginen is the sacred world of Haiti's past that is present in the dances oriented to the *poto-mitan*. The ounsi sing to Agwé (Agoué), the lwa of the sea, to come from his home below the waters in Dahomey:

> Agoué in Dahomean clothing
> Agoué, you are coming from your villa.
> Agouétaroio, you are coming from your villa,
> All dressed up in Dahomean clothing.
> All dressed up in Dahomean clothing.[44]

As the spatial representation of access to Ginen, all ceremonial activities take place in the shadow of this great tree. Reinforcing and particularizing the point of connection with Ginen are line figures of cornmeal called *vèvès*.[45] At the beginning of most vodou services, to the accompaniment of special songs and drum rhythms, a oungan dribbles the cornmeal between his thumb and fingers to trace a number of the *vèvès* on the ground below the *poto-mitan*. Each *vèvè* is dedicated to a particular lwa, and its placement around the *poto-mitan* indicates the organization of the liturgy to come. The *vèvès* call for the specific lwa to be invoked and drum rhythms to be played. The ounsi sing a song of anticipation as the *vèvès* are drawn:

> When they arrive, the spirits will carry me on their backs.
> This ceremony will be fascinating.
> I am about to draw a vèvè in front of my temple.
> I am about to draw a vèvè, Papa Atisou Legba, in front of my altar.
> I am going to draw a vèvè on my back
> So that they can say something good about me.
> When they arrive, the spirits will carry me on their backs.
> This ceremony will be fascinating.
> They will have news for us.
> It might be good or bad news, depending on what we have been doing.[46]

Libations of water or alcohol are made into the *vèvès*, and the animals which have been consecrated and slaughtered as food for the lwa are also lain on them. The *vèvès* become the first point of reception for these gifts, the pictorial face through which the lwa may eat. Once fed through their *vèvè* gateway in the earth, the lwa are energized to come up and mount their human horses.

Most vodou services begin the invocation of the spirits with *actions de grace*, Catholic prayers led by the *prètsavann*, the "bush priest." God and Catholic saints are honored in French by the recitation of the Lord's Prayer, the "Hail Mary," the Credo, and the Confiteor, with appropriate signs of the cross and genuflections. The invocation of the Catholic spirits provides a kind of frame around vodou, a transition from the exterior world of Haiti to the interior world of Ginen. The responses of the *actions de grace* are rote and solemn, a mask of respect in official French. When the Catholic prayers are over, the service moves to Créole and progressively "heats up."[47]

Katherine Dunham was our guide through the psychic preparations of the *lave tèt*, and we can turn to another American visitor to Haiti to open us to vodou dance. Maya Deren was a filmmaker who first went to Haiti in 1947 to record Haitian dances for an art-film project. As her knowledge of vodou grew, she somewhat reluctantly began to hear the call of the lwa. She describes such a service which began with the first invocations to the lwa Legba, the spirit at the intersection of our world and Ginen.

> Open the road for me,
> Legba, I want to pass through.
> Open the road for me,
> Papa Legba, I am here.
> Open the gate for me,
> Master Legba, I want to get in.[48]

Deren writes:

I can remember an evening when it was as if, with those initial salutations, the drums flung the enormous snare of their sound into the night, across the still landscape, and from every direction drew captives across the threshold into the peristyle. I was among these latecomers. The singing, which might have been desultory at first, became warmer as the stream of arrivals gradually filled the benches, the space near the walls, flooded into the corners and finally overflowed into the court.[49]

The oungan then began a series of salutations to the cardinal points of the *peristil*, once again affirming the orientation of the community to Ginen. The drummers took up the rhythms for the parade of the flags of the *société*, and two flag bearers, led by the oungan's assistant, the *la place*, began their procession around the *peristil*. The *la place* wields a machete and with his flag-bearing attendants recalls the military dimension of the *société*. His name is an abbreviation of *commandant général de la place*, and as the *actions de grace* anchor vodou to the religious life of official Haiti, so the showing of colors in the flag and iron root vodou in its revolutionary past. Deren describes her salutations to the *la place* and flag bearers:

> . . . the trio balances in place before me, stepping side to side in rhythm with the drums. As I rise in answer, a sense of nervous self-consciousness overwhelms me, although I have done this many times. (I am not at all alone in this; I have seen the lips of even mambos and houngans quiver nervously in such moments.) Curtsey turn left, two three; curtsey, back right, two, three; curtsey, now left, two, three—mirroring the trio before me. I walk west, crossing between the la-place and the flags, as they walk east. I turn, curtsey, then left, curtsey, right, then back, then north; then south. We approach each other and suddenly I cannot remember what I am supposed to do, but no one can perceive this, for the la-place kneels, holding the hilt of the sabre high. I touch it with my lips, the two flags cross over it, and I salute these also. Then with an enormous feeling of relief at having accomplished this act properly, I return to my chair.[50]

The oungan then began his invocations to the spirits. Although Deren does not tell us the words of the songs sung during this particular service, Laguerre offers a popular song of orientation often sung at this point in the service. In it the ounsi ask Agwé, the lwa of the seas, to bring the lwa to the service from Ville-aux-Camps, the land beneath the seas in Ginen.

> We are announcing to you, Voodoo spirits
> That a ceremony is about to begin.

We are inviting all the spirits of the Ville-aux-Camps,
We are asking Agouétaroio to bring them in his boat.
Please do use Agouétaroio's boat
And do come to the temple.[51]

After the initial salutations to Legba, each lwa is invoked in an order determined by the manbo or oungan presiding over the service. The order of invocation becomes a critical point of protocol in the progress of the liturgy, and disagreements about procession are frequent. Katherine Dunham wrote of this important ritual responsibility:

I have tried to find out, with no real success, what decides the order of the rhythms, how a mambo or houngan decides which loa is dominant at a given ceremony, why some are allowed to stay for the evening or until the next day, while others are sent away—if possible—shortly after their arrival. The answer must lie in a maze of extrasensory perception, personal taste, custom, and the multi-theistic mysticism that makes the vaudun what it is.[52]

Directed by the manbo or oungan, the songs are "launched" by the *oungenikon*, the song master, who knows the entire repertoire of the ounfo. Each spirit is offered at least three songs, although a lwa-in-manifestation will likely begin to demand certain songs for itself or other lwa. The tension between the lwa and the oungan for control of the service is summarized by a proverb cited by Ira Lowenthal: "You may invite the ouga [oungan] as you would invite anyone, but it is the lwa who make the sèvis."[53] In manifestation, the lwa take command, or attempt to take command, of their own liturgies. They teach new songs and dances to the ounsi and instruct the drummers in rhythms.

Deren give this powerful description of the song launched for Danbala by the *oungenikon* Titon:

Over the demanding, compelling rush of its syllables, the tight staccato Yanvalou beat of the *petit* [drum] sets in; now the rounder tone, the more rolling rhythm of the *seconde* slides in under it; and then one feels a vibration beneath one's feet even before the beat of the *maman*, which rises as if from some unfathomable depth, as if the very

WORKING THE SPIRIT

earth were a drum being pounded. Hardly has hearing plunged to encompass this dark dimension, than the high clang of the iron *ogan* [bell] sets in, its wind-filled resonance abruptly flinging open all the upper reaches of sound, and the very air vibrates as if with tones above and beyond the reaches of the ear's intelligence. For a brief moment this towering architecture of sound, stretching solidly from the abyss below to the heavens above hearing, seems to advance without movement, like a tidal wave so vast that no marker exists to scale its progress for the eye. Then the chorus of voices, having, it would seem, accumulated its force in the trough concealed behind the towering crest, hurls forward over that crest, and the whole structure crashes like cosmic surf over one's head.[54]

The surge of seas is an apt metaphor for drumming to Danbala, the snake coiled in the waters around the earth. The serpentine motion of water is expressed in the most famous of vodou dances, the *yanvalou*. Deren feels the pull of the seas and is brought to her feet to join in the ounsi's *yanvalou*.

Before me the bodies of the dancers undulate with a wave-like motion, which begins at the shoulders, divides itself to run separately along the arms and down the spine, is once more unified where the palms rest on bent knees, and finally flows down the legs into the earth, while already the shoulders have initiated the wave which follows. The eyes are fixed on the ground, and although the head is steady, the circular movement of the shoulders seems to send it forward, to draw the body after it, over and over; and as the bodies, which began in a posture almost erect, bend toward the earth, the undulation becomes more and more horizontal, until all figures blend into a slow flowing serpentine stream circling the center-post with a fluency that belies the difficulty of the movement.[55]

The service is in full swing now, and ounsis are receiving Danbala and his consort, Ayida. The lwa appear and eat eggs on the floor of the *peristil*. The ounsis' songs show the shifting perspectives of the deities' presence:

> Watch out, I am Damballah Ouédo [Danbala Wèdo].
> Watch out, I am Danbala Ouédo.

Watch out I am Aido Ouédo.
Watch out I am Aida Ouédo.
When I saddle my horse, some people will be upset.
When I saddle my horse, some people will be upset.[56]

Deren begins to feel lightheaded, disoriented, and oddly directed by the beats of the *maman* drum. She begins to recognize these sensations for what they are, the "warning auras of possession." The invocations for Danbala conclude, and the rhythms for the lwa Agassou, Agwé, and Badé are played with little incident. Then, with the first beats of the invocation for Ogou, the presiding oungan, Isnard, receives his and the ounfo's patron lwa.

He is barefoot, the legs of the trousers are rolled up, so that the abrupt movements of the feet do not catch in them and trip him, and he wears a bright red handkerchief. He is pacing up and down, in a kind of anger. It is impressive. Isnard is, to begin with, tall and powerful in body; now that sense of stature is enormously reinforced by the psychic projection of the heroic loa which has infused that body. The loa walks to the drums, and, laying his hand on the skin of the *maman*, orders them silenced. He stands and waits. Titon approaches, turns in ritual salutation, kisses the earth at his feet and would withdraw, but Ogoun extends his hand in ritual greeting. I see Titon stiffen, as one might prepare to endure an onslaught.[57]

Deren is concerned that when it comes time for her to greet Ogou, the ritual hand-to-hand contact with the mounted lwa will lead to its transference to a new "horse." Already vulnerable from the Danbala rhythms, Deren fears the loss of control should Ogou choose her for a *bosalle* manifestation. But Ogou is not calling her, and though she feels a shock at the touch of the lwa's hand, she returns to her place.

The service proceeds in these fits and starts. Rhythms are frequently interrupted by a lwa, and alternatives suggested. Grievances between the lwa and the congregation are often in the air.

What did I do to Féray
To make him so angry at me?

To make him so angry at me?
I have previously told you about what I was going to do.
You are angry at me.[58]

Ogou tells the congregation that he is satisfied with his service and that he will now leave them. Deren writes: "He stands there a moment, then a great spasm shakes the body, jerking it off balance. But already there are several to catch Isnard as he falls, to drag his limp body to a chair where, in a moment, he slowly raises his head, looks about him with the puzzled concentration of one who wakes in a room not yet habitual and familiar, and would orient himself."[59]

Everyone takes this moment to rest. The drummers get snacks, and people mill about the *peristil* and outer court exchanging greetings and gossip. But the *oungenikon* calls the ounsis back to the *poto-mitan*, and the drummers take up the rhythms for Ezili, the loveliest of the lwa. The ounsis move to another *yanvalou*. Deren follows the drumming and the "breaks" in the rhythm of the *maman* which reorient the dancers and quicken the movement of the law: "When, following a "break" and having resumed the erect posture which would slowly sink earthward again, they may face each other and briefly mirror each other's movements, even then the pairs seem less to duplicate each other than to be, both, mirrors which, face to face, doubly reflect some invisible figure who dances between and who knows reality only in such mirrors."[60]

The invisible figure that Deren begins to perceive in the mirror of the dancers is the lwa Ezili herself. As the drummers take up a vigorous Mahi rhythm, Deren is pulled up to dance and mirror the lwa herself.

As sometimes in dreams, so here I can observe myself, can note with pleasure how the full hem of my white skirt plays with the rhythms, can watch, as if in a mirror, how the smile begins with a softening of the lips, spreads imperceptibly into a radiance which, surely, is lovelier than any I have ever seen. It is when I turn, as if to a neighbor, to say "Look! See how lovely that is!" and see that the others are removed to a distance, withdrawn to a circle which is already watching, that I realize, like a shaft of terror struck through me, that is no longer myself that I watch."[61]

She is terrified at her loss of control, at the way the *maman* drum can hold and release her leg movements. The harder she struggles against its control, the more firmly she is rooted to its power. Her consciousness thins into a paradox of glory and terror, a flow of "white darkness."

There is nothing anywhere except this. There is no way out. The white darkness moves up the veins of my leg like a swift tide rising, rising; is a great force which I cannot sustain or contain, which, surely, will burst my skin. It is too much, too bright, too white for me; this is the darkness. "Mercy!" I scream within me. I hear it echoed by the voices, shrill and unearthly: "Erzulie!" The bright darkness floods up through my body, reaches my head, engulfs me. I am sucked down and exploded upward at once. That is all.[62]

The first *bosalle* manifestation of Ezili is terrifying to Deren because she has not undergone the *lave tèt* preparation. Her head had not been made ready to receive Ezili as Katherine Dunham's had been for Danbala. Deren's *bosalle* experience was fearful and awkward. If she had become a ounsi her *gwo bònanj* would have been fluid and she could have manifested Ezili with ease.

When the lwa mounts its horse, the ridden remember nothing of the activities of the lwa. Their *gwo bònanjs* are displaced to Ginen, and ounsi characterize the consciousness of the horse as that of dreamless sleep. In the long process of coming back to her former self, Deren remembers nothing of the rest of the ceremony. She does not tell us what witnesses saw of her manifestation of Ezili. It is considered unlucky and dangerous to speak to the horse of the activities of the rider except in the most oblique ways. Messages may be relayed, but it must be strongly emphasized that the horse is innocent of the ways of the rider.

Most vodou services end with the invocation and appearance of Gede, the rude and hungry spirit of the cemetery. Gede is in fact a whole family of the spirits of the dead, objectified into a ribald clown who delights in tricks and crude jokes. His antics close the ceremony for he symbolizes the sunset of death that brings all activity to an end, and he calls for the *banda* dance, a lighthearted mime of sexual fun. The congregation laughs and teases each other with sexual jokes in *banda,* and so Gede leaves the services on the somber note of death together with the laugh of erotic play.

> I am not a sheet, if I were one,
> I would let them use me as their cover.
> Someday they will need me,
> Someday they will need me,
> I am Guédé [Gede] Nibo, I am not a sheet.
> When they are sick,
> They all love me.
> When they are healthy, the say Guédé is no good.
> When they are healthy, the say Guédé is no good.
>
> Praise the Guédés.
> Praise the Guédés.
> Papa Guédé is a strong spirit.
> Praise the Guédés.[63]

SPIRIT

The spirit of vodou grows out of the service which manifests it, which in turn grows out of the community that performs the service. The lwa depend on the rites for their sustenance; without these rites, the lwa would wither and die. So the living community holds the responsibility for the definition and maintenance of the divine. If we are to understand the spirit of vodou, we must examine the rites which manifest it. Without rites the spirit is inchoate, remote, an impersonal and unpetitionable fate. It would be dead to particularity. The rites focus the spirit, bring it into dialogue with the human world in an illimitable variety. Each specific spirit is called to a specific role in balancing the never-ending imbalances in the hard life of the Haitian poor. Individuals require a constellation of spirits to arrange their own "heads" with the particular problems which their path in life has given them. So too, the community of the ounfo trusts in the oungan or manbo to orchestrate extraordinarily complex arrangements of spirits in order to ensure the health of the collective.

We can see vodou spirituality as a progressive focusing of the spirit into spirits. The rites focus an unformed *Grand Maître*, a *Bondye* (*Bon Dieu*), into tangible forces, who may assume personalities through the gift of service from their horses in vodou dance. This growth of service from rites can be seen in three ways: in the ritual orientation to Ginen; in the development of *konesans* through the rites of head washing, handling fire, taking the *ason*, and attaining "eyes"; and in the collective dance of incarnating the lwa. We can examine each in turn.

Haitian proverbs say: "Haiti is the child of Dahomey"; "Haiti is the child of Ginen."[64] Followers of vodou remember the different African nations of their forbearers as long lost children remember stern parents. They have been given a harsh destiny by the spirits, but the lwa have come to their aid again and again. Ginen lies over great waters, and it is a memory of crossing waters that underlies the liturgy of vodou. It is Agwé, the lwa of the sea, who is asked to carry the lwa to the ceremony in his boat. And Loko, the great tree with its roots in the waters beneath the earth, draws the lwa up from the cities beyond the seas in Ginen. So the *poto-mitan* is a tree that draws the spirits up to be present at vodou ceremony. The liturgy begins with a series of exacting orientations to the *poto-mitan*. Offerings and libations are made to the cardinal points with the *poto-mitan* as the center of their raidants. *Vèvès* are drawn to channel the flow of the lwa into the particular *lwa* to be invoked. The ounsi dance around the *poto-mitan* and greet it with songs and dances. All this is ritual focus on the source of the center, Ginen. To dance the lwa is to remember the ancestors who came and who didn't come to Haiti. To serve the lwa is to "serve Ginen."[65]

To understand the spirit of vodou, then, is to see that it is an orientation to a historical memory and to a living reality. The memory is of the ancestors and their lands of origin, and of the great gulf of space and time which divides Haitians from them. This memory provides the precedent for all action. Things are done because "cé commandment l'Afrique."[66] Africa becomes the criterion of harmonious and moral action, and authority derives from fidelity to the traditions of Ginen.[67]

But Ginen is not only a historical memory, a veneration of past power and precedent. It is alive and present in vodou ceremony. As the orientation to the *poto-mitan* allows the lwa to come to Haiti, so it allows the Haitians to live in Ginen. Legba is the first spirit to be invoked in vodou ceremony. Legba is an old man who walks with a stick, his own "poto Legba." He is the first person in vodou history and hierarchy, an original trickster, with his mind in two worlds. And so he becomes a gatekeeper between the worlds of Ginen and Haiti. When he opens the gate, the two worlds can interpenetrate.

> Papa Legba,
> Have patience
> At your service,
> Ago, ago-e!
> Papa Legba,
> Come from Guinea
> That we may pass.[68]

The power in this contact needs the controls of orientations, songs, and the secret directions of the *ason*. In short, contact with Ginen is through *konesans*, the knowledge of the rites, and the insight that accompanies progress through them. From the spirituality of orientation we move to the personal growth of developing the spirit in one's head.

The lwa differ from human beings by the level of their *konesans*.[69] In a sense they are more developed human beings, having gone through initiations unavailable to living men and women. The lwa are human beings whose *gwo bònanjs* have been preserved after the death of their original bodies and are now capable of riding the corporeal horses of the living. Because of their extraordinary *konesans* when they were alive, it behooved their communities to preserve their *gwo bònanjs* through a complex series of rites of spiritual dissolution and reclamation. The *gwo bònanj*, detached from the body of the living, is sent to join the lwa in Ginen for a year and a day. Thus re-Africanized, it is then recovered to reside in a *govi* jar on the altar of the ounfo. If petition to this spirit should prove particularly successful, it may join the families of spirits venerated in the ounfo. It may become a great lwa on its own, or become a new dimension of an established lwa, a new refinement of a more basic lwa energy. Thus the great lwa develop "surnames," like Danbala Wèdo or Ezili Freda or Ogou Feray. These indicate a particularization of the lwa created by the special rites offered to them.[70] Thus Ezili Freda is a Rada "surname" indicating a Dahomean lwa that may be invoked by Rada rites. Ezili Dantò is a Petro designation indicating her origins in more recent times in the fire of the Haitian revolution. Ogou Panama recalls the hubris of Ogou as it was manifested in the early part of the century when a Haitian president lost his panama hat as a prelude to a tragic end.[71] Each of these designations represents a new refinement of a lwa, another "side" to divinity, that continually reveals itself in the historical experiences of the vodou community.

The road to participation in this living history is the preparation of the head. Through divination or luck or, most usually, critical misfortune, a lwa reveals itself as the master of one's head. While one may serve many lwa, it is the discipline of one's master which will lead the serviteur to spiritual progress. So, too, neglect of the discipline will lead to peril. Katherine Dunham's fellow initiates were tortured by their *mèt tèts* until they agreed to open their head to their lwa's service. But once committed, the faithful serviteur is brought along a path of ever deepening under-standing of the world and its ways. When Dunham married Danbala, she took on a marital responsibility of mutual service. She would honor and obey as Danbala would protect and guide. She and Danbala had joined in mystical union, and the quest to understand the mystery of their unity and separability became her spiritual path. She writes: "The ring of Téoline's bell and the subdued clatter of her ason were in my ear. It was as though she had sensed my self-doubt and, probing beyond the houngfor and the initiation, regarded my entrance into the vaudun as a personal need and quest, and wanted to assure me that all that I had seen and experienced would take its place to be interpreted in its symbology through the years."[72]

This process of self-discovery lies behind vodou spirituality. Maya

Deren quotes a vodou proverb, "Temperament mun, ce temperament loa-li" ("The character of a person is the character of his lwa").[73] The lwa is the key to understanding one's own character, and the relationship with the lwa represents a knowledge of self. Dunham uses the metaphor of electricity to describe her relationship to Danbala: "It was as though an electrodynamic pattern were at work, loa choosing abode because of qualities of himself already latent in the abode, or abode gravitating to loa and discovering itself on some polar current."[74]

The relationship between spirit and person, for Dunham, is like that between electrical poles. They are at once the same thing and opposites. The lwa is both the "other side" of the personality of the serviteur and the same energy in another "direction." Thus the lwa makes the person whole. Later Dunham likens the manbo and oungan to psychoanalysts seeking to uncover a "dominant personality hidden under the social layers" of a client's psyche. Here again the same/other quality of the lwa is affirmed. Like a lwa, the layers of the personality are both "me" and "it." Self-consciousness at one stage cannot recognize the self at the other as itself. "Tell my horse," command the lwa. Deren writes: "To understand that the self must leave if the loa is to enter, is to understand that one cannot be man and god at once.[75]

The other within, the "dominant personality" is to be recognized as a teacher, the other side of the person which shows the person to itself. This is one of the reasons why the mirror is such a pervasive vodou symbol. The mirror shows an "other world" which is this world. It shows the serviteurs themselves. Deren describes the dances as mirroring the lwa, that the serviteurs' actions in the *peristil* are showing Ginen back to itself. So too the lwa are showing their children themselves by their actions. Their kindness and chastisements are what their children lack to be fully themselves. If the lwa are trusted, they are the keys to the serviteurs own spiritualization, their path to Ginen.

Beyond an orientation to Ginen and the development of *konesans*, vodou spirituality requires a sharing of the spirit in dance. The ounsi's relationship to the *mèt tèt*, so carefully cultivated in the *lave*, *kanzo*, and *ason* "floorings," is not for the ounsi's benefit alone, but for the entire community. The ounsi are called to service not only for the lwa but also for the ounfo. Deren sees the communal ethic to be so strong that she finds that the "horse" benefits least by its riding.[76] It is often exhausting work to allow the lwa the use of one's body, and most serviteurs at one time or another are reluctant to make this sacrifice. Yet vodou requires that the initiate share his or her *mèt tèt* and its *konesans* at the dance services of the *peristil.*

The serviteurs share the spirit in the dialogue between lwa and humans when a rider speaks through its horse. The community and the lwa speak to each other in one-on-one consultations and confrontations, and in communal songs and prayers. The sharing of spirit is evident in the shifting perspective of the songs. At times it is the lwa speaking; at other times, an individual petitioner; at still others, it is the community.[77] The lwa can even address each other in song. The fact that these shifts occur in a single song suggests that the usual differences between the human and the lwa community are in some way overcome. Look at this new level of identification in this song of sacrifice to the lwa Bosou:

> Before killing me, judge me seven times.
> Before killing me, judge me seven times.
> Before killing me, I shall ask God why.
> Before killing me, judge me seven times.
> Before killing me, judge me seven times.
> Before killing me, Bosou, ask them why.[78]

Here is the sacrificial animal consecrated to Bosou singing with the voice of the community. Who is being judged and who is being killed? The community, lwa, and offering are swept up in a single ritual action. The spirit is shared by all the actors in the service.

The technique to bring about this sharing comes from the rhythms of the dance itself. By dancing together, the bodies of the serviteurs are attuned, so that their minds may be attuned, so that they may share the same *konesans.* Deren writes: "It is the drumming which fuses the fifty or more individuals into a single body, making them move as one, as if all of these singular bodies had become linked on the thread of a single pulse . . ."[79]

Dunham describes her breakthrough into this consciousness: "The joy of dancing overwhelmed me and I found myself sometimes in front of Doc, at other times in front of Téoline or La place or Georgina in the ruptured movements of the feints, then gasping, stumbling, teetering on the verge of rhythm and fasting-induced hynposis, returning to the sheer joy of motion in concert, of harmony with the self and others and the houngfor and Damballa [Danbala] and with all the other friends and enemies past, present and future."[80]

Vodou means both dance and spirit, a movement of the spirit both calling for and being called by the actions of human beings. The spirit of vodou is thus a dance, and the spirits of vodou are a series of dances, brought alive by the Haitian people. In the dance the spirit is worked into presence, alive to comfort, discipline, and enable its children in their struggle.

3

Candomblé in Brazil

Candomblé is the name given to a variety of African religious traditions established in Brazil during the nineteenth century. It has been continually nourished by contacts with Africa, and its priests and priestesses have been dedicated to maintaining the purity of its African roots. The city of Salvador da Bahia, or simply Bahia, is famous for this disciplined fidelity to the ways of the "old Africans," and it is from Bahia that the models for Afro-Brazilian religions radiate. By word, rhythm, and gesture, candomblé seeks to incarnate the ancestors, forging the link between the royal powers of Africa and their children in Brazil.

Candomblé is at once a space, a dance, and a community.[1] It is a consecrated, privately owned area within the environs of Bahia, often walled or hedged, where ceremonies to the spirits take place. It may be a large compound of many acres containing numerous shrines and sacred sites, or a simple building and yard screened from a city street. A candomblé is also the actions of the community within its sacred precincts. Devotees refer to group actions in honor of the spirits as "making candomblé," especially with reference to dances with drum music. Finally a candomblé is the community of devotees themselves, for the ultimate locus of the spirits is literally inside this community. Like vodou, the spirit of candomblé is shared in the dances carried out in sacred spaces oriented to Africa. What follows is a portrait of the community of candomblé, the service which manifests it, and the spirit to which it is devoted.

COMMUNITY

As the Haitian people were struggling toward freedom at the close of the eighteenth century, other colonies were becoming more firmly locked into economies driven by slave labor. Many more African slaves came to Brazil in the nineteenth century than in the previous three hundred years after the Portuguese landing in 1500.[2] Of the more than three and one-half million Africans who came through the Middle Passage to Brazil, nearly a million and a quarter came through Bahia, making it the largest slave port in the Americas.[3] In the early nineteenth century Bahia received a large number of people from what the Brazilian slavetraders called the "Mina Coast," the present-day countries of western Nigeria, Benin, Togo, and Ghana.[4] This sudden and dramatic presence of Africans from contiguous areas, in a relatively short period of time, created a cultural homogeneity and hegemony which would distinguish Bahia as the preeminent city of the African diaspora of the nineteenth century. A French consul in 1848 wrote of the preponderance of "Nagô" people, an ethnic designation broadly synonymous with the African people termed "Yoruba" by English-speaking ethnographers today:

> . . . the Nagos . . . probably account for nine-tenths of the slaves at Bahia and can be recognized by three deep lateral marks tattooed on each cheek. They are nearly all embarked at Onim [Lagos] or Porto Novo; the Hausa [are] mostly employed at Bahia as palanquin bearers; they nearly all come the Onim route.
>
> The Gege or Dahomeyans, who are a powerful nation, have fairly numerous representatives at Bahia; they used to be embarked at Whydah, but now, for the most part, they come from Porto Novo.[5]

The presence of these African ethnicities struck Bahian slaveholders with particular force. Some eleven rebellions organized by slaves and free people of color challenged their control over the city between 1807 and 1835. The power of the ethnic and religious solidarity displayed by Afro-Brazilians was not lost on the merchants and landowners of Bahia who petitioned the Portuguese Crown in 1814 for a free hand in crushing any signs of black independence. In the wake of a bloody uprising in 1814 they wrote to prince Dom João:

> . . . gatherings of blacks can be seen at night in the streets as before, conversing in their language and saying whatever they like, and with constant whistling and other signals. They are so impertinent that even in our language they blurt out their reasons for putting off the day of their planned revolt. They know about and discuss the disastrous occurrences that took place on the Island of Saint Domingue, and one hears mutinous claims that by St. John's Day there will not be one white or mulatto alive.[6]

It was clear to these citizens that the gatherings of candomblé were important cells of revolutionary activity, and like Haitian vodou, a potentially successful means to organize the overthrow of the slave system. The free citizens petitioned the crown to be able to prohibit gatherings with drums called *batuques* and were frustrated by the restraining hand of the local governor. Remembering the bloodshed of recent events, they presented their fears to the crown with sarcastic anger:

> In payment for the barbarousness with which they treated people in the places they burned, where the houses numbered over 150, and the people killed more than a hundred, it is even suggested in this first order that interference with the *batuques* which might be performed elsewhere should be carried out with great moderation. Perhaps we should ask them on our knees not to dance the *batuque* and not to convert this country into a new Mina Coast, as they have been doing up to this time . . . [7]

The very first ordinance in the slave laws of 1822 authorized Bahian militiamen to reconnoiter slave districts "severely prohibiting their meetings under the pretext of performing *autabaquis*.[8] Both white authorities and the Afro-Brazilian communities found in candomblé a

WORKING THE SPIRIT

linkage of African ethnic identity, religious ceremony, and cultural resistance. From the early nineteenth century until the very recent past, the candomblés were periodically harassed and suppressed. When they did not pose a threat as centers for insurrection, they offered an assertive alternative, a world where, in the words of one nineteenth-century observer: ". . . in dancing and singing, they forget their ills and servitude, and only remember their native country and the time that they were free."

The "memory" of freedom was and continues to be powerfully made present in *candomblé*, and the houses offer an alternative to the values of white society and the racism that so frequently underlies them. American anthropologist Mikelle Omari writes: "Candomblé Nagô offers Afro-Bahians a channel through which they may gain a significant measure of self-esteem, social solidarity, prestige, and social mobility in a system which celebrates African values, behavior and skin color."[10]

Unlike the Afro-Haitians, whose revolution threw off slavery in 1804, Afro-Bahians were never able to overturn the slave system. Their bondage persisted more than eighty years longer, until emancipation in 1888. Yet despite the most virulent attempts to suppress the *autabaque* gatherings, Afro-Bahians were able to create a remarkable realization of a "new Mina Coast" in their candomblés. Their large numbers, the currency of their contacts with Africa, and their dedication to a once and future freedom made for a remarkable continuity with the traditions of their ancestors and nurtured in Afro-Bahians a force for resistance to the brutal system of oppression that they endured. The "*autabaquis*," the drum ceremonies of the Nagôs, the Jejes, and to a lesser extent, the Hausas and various Angolan peoples, were the means by which the Afro-Brazilian identity was maintained amid the horrors of a slave society. These gatherings became the models for the great houses of candomblé that arose in the mid-nineteenth century, which the present candomblés proudly name as their source.

The demographic shifts of early nineteenth-century Brazil ensured the permanent presence of the cultures of several different African ethnicities or *nações*, "nations," in Bahia. Contemporary candomblés identify them-selves with these African *nações*, though the wide variety of African ethnicity in nineteenth-century Bahia has been condensed into three principle *nações*: Nagô, Jeje, and Angola.[11] Within these classifications, which some houses would find too general, can be found Kêtu, Alakêto, Efan, Ijexâ, Ebá, Mina Nagô, Xambá, Tapa, Congo, and Mina Jeje. Add to these the Muslim designations of 'Malê and Muçurumin, and the large numbers of candomblés called *caboclo* that receive Amerindian as well as African spirits, and the rich contributions of specific African peoples are apparent. If the name Nagô may be accepted as referring to a generally homogenous culture, language, and religion, nearly every house in Bahia receives Nagô spirits, if not exclusively. The nineteenth-century observ-ers may have exaggerated when they claimed that nine out of ten Africans in Bahia were Nagô, but there is abundant evidence that the Nagôs were a dominant presence in the cultural life of Afro-Bahians. Not only did thousands of Nagôs come to Bahia as slaves, but free Nagôs became important figures in the trade of the city. In Pierre Verger's terms, there was a continual flux and reflux in the trade between Bahia and Africa, not only *in* Africans but *by* Africans, both in Bahia and on the Mina Coast.[12] Free African and Bahian *emancipado* merchants traded tobacco, fire-arms, sugar, and slaves across the Atlantic. They established multiple contacts between Africa and Bahia so that African goods were readily available in Bahia. African and Afro-Brazilian persons of means were able to travel between the old world and the new, and family and religious ties could be renewed. A number of Africans freely emigrated to Brazil, often at the behest of emancipated members of families and congregations of candomblé. Too, large colonies of Brazilian Nagôs returned to Africa to establish communities that continue to maintain their Brazilian identi-ty.[13]

In this world of brutal slavery, crushed insurrection, constant trade, and cultural renewal, the most prestigious of the Nagô houses of can-domblé was established. Around 1830 a Nagô priestess from the Kêtu region of what is today Benin, a free woman titled Iyá Nassô, came to Bahia to establish a religious community. Her mother had been enslaved and brought to Bahia, but had won her freedom and returned to Africa, where she became initiated as a priestess. She enjoined Iyá Nassô, together with two other priestesses, to return to Brazil in order to bring the foundation power of the spirits (*axé*) to the Nagô community in diaspora in Bahia.[14] Toward the end of her life, Iyá Nassô sent her successor Marcelina back to Africa for a seven-year stay to complete her education with African religious teachers.[15]

The relative frequency with which exceptional individuals traveled to and from Africa to refine their understanding of Nagô theology and ritual raised in candomblé a special interest in the fidelity of the rites to their African sources. The continual renewal of candomblé ideas and practices by African emigrants and visitors created historical layers of African influence in every candomblé house and complex claims to authentic African precedents. Today every large Nagô house of candomblé has sent members to Africa, and the question of the *pureza* or purity of Bahian practice in relation to African standards continues to stimulate the most lively debates among the houses.

Afro-Brazilian life in Bahia offered many advantages for the development of great centers of African religious learning. Compared with the Creole peasantry of mostly rural Haiti, Afro-Bahian urban life allowed for relative freedom of movement, independent patrons who could endow the centers, and sufficient wealth and mobility to sponsor teachers and students to cross the Atlantic.

The history of some candomblés is better known to us than that of specific vodou ounfos partly because Brazilian intellectuals were attracted to the candomblés and wrote about them, but mostly because the candomblés themselves achieved a level of institutionalization and permanence never equaled by vodou ounfos.[16] The house of Iyá Nassô, most commonly called Casa Branca today, became the principle line from which most Nagô houses of candomblé trace their descent. Since the fortunes of a candomblé are tied to the charisma of its leader, it is always a delicate moment when leadership is passed on. The *deixaram o cargo*,[17] or willing of the office of leadership, has been the source of several succession disputes in Bahian candomblé which have led to the formation of sometimes competitive, sometimes cooperative, "branch" houses.

When Iyá Nassô's daughter, Marcelina, died, arguments about her successor led one of Casa Branca's senior priestesses, Maria Julia da Conceição to found the Ilé Iyá Omin Axé Iyamassé, a house best known today as Gantois, after the Bahian neighborhood in which it is located. A similar dispute around 1910 led a charismatic Casa Branca priestess named Aninha to form a new community called Ilé Axé Opô Afonjá. Despite the disagreements that led to this fission into new institutions, the younger candomblés have always recognized their debts to Casa Branca. Aninha of Opô Afonjá was the most eminent priestess in Bahia during the first four decades of the twentieth century and Menininha of Gantois became a national figure before her death in 1986, but each organized their ritual calendars around the cycles of Casa Branca. "Engenio Velho [Casa Branca] is the head and Opô Afonjá is the arm," was how Aninha characterized their relationship.[18] These three communities—Casa Branca, Gantois, and Opô Afonjá,—comprise what is often called the candomblé elite of Bahia. They are the great houses, known for their unbroken link to Iyá Nassô, their fidelity and dialogue with African ceremonial models, and the social prestige of their members.[19]

Most of the Nagô candomblés of Bahia can trace their origins to one of the priestesses of Casa Branca, Gantois, or Opô Afonjá. Yet given the large number of contemporary candomblés, it might be imagined that not all these ties can be verified. In the 1930s a Bahian journalist and ethnographer, Edison Carneiro, sought to organize the candomblé houses into a self-protective union and thereby demonstrate the political power that the numbers of their adherents represented. He argued that a public organization, with a popular writer among its members, might shield the candomblés from the police harassment they were enduring at the time. The union counted some sixty-seven candomblé houses as members, representing seventeen nações. In 1950 Carneiro estimated that there were around a hundred candomblé centers in Bahia, each supported by an average of three hundred people. In a city of four hundred thousand, this would have made candomblé devotees about 7.5 percent of the city's population.[20] By 1980 a census carried out by the Federacão Baiana do Culto Afro-Brasileiro registered fifteen hundred candomblés and estimated innumerable clandestine centers amid greater Bahia's two million inhabitants.[21]

While the elite houses have continually added to their permanence and prestige, the great bulk of the other centers are small, short-lived, and devoted to the *caboclo* Amerindian spirits. The gap between the elite houses and the *caboclo* candomblés, like so much of candomblé self-identity, is measured by the elites' claims to the purity of their African practices. The American anthropologist Donald Pierson quotes an official of an elite house as saying, "Si seja mistura, é bobagem." "If it's mixed, it's nonsense."[22] In the same vein, the priestess Menininha told Ruth Landes that people came to her house of Gantois because of its Nagô purity: They like to watch us because they know we're genuine, they know that everything under my direction comes straight from the old Africans as taught me by my mother Pulcheria."[23]

The candomblé is at once a community and the activities that show it as a community. It is a mutual aid society, a residence, a family, and a dance. One of the formative influences on the establishment of the candomblés was the brotherhoods and sisterhoods of black slaves and *emancipados* organized by the Brazilian Catholic Church. Roger Bastide argues that the Portuguese colonists of Brazil were frustrated in recreating the town life of Portugal because so few of the Portuguese immigrants were members of the artisan classes. African slaves and *emancipados* filled these positions in the trade guilds of Brazil's towns and cities, but they were refused membership in the white Catholic brotherhoods and sisterhoods that organized them.[24] There followed a highly segregated "white Church" and "black Church." On some occasions this ecclesial segregation forced the construction of separate buildings for their separate services. The name of one of the most famous churches in Bahia, the magnificent Nossa Senhora do Rosário dos Pretos [Our Lady of the Rosary of the Blacks] indicates its grounding in a large Catholic religious brotherhood and its segregated status. It was built entirely with money raised by its black parishioners and is located in the square called

Pelorinho, "the Pillory," commemorative of the ordeal of Brazilian slavery.

The black Catholic brotherhoods and sisterhoods in some cases shared the same membership with the candomblés, in other cases they acted as alternatives to the candomblés, and in still others they were the very same organization with different names.[25] Their most visible function was and continues to be the mutual aid of their members. Among the poor in a poor city, the contemporary candomblés provide care for the sick, orphaned, and hungry, and burial for the dead. In slavery times they raised money for the emancipation of slave members, and even now they offer refuge for members who have run afoul of the law.[26] Some candomblés act as day-care centers for children and the elderly, and they may raise funds for their members' tuition, bail, or emigration. Some of the larger candomblés function as residences for their members, either those in need of special care, those undergoing lengthy initiations, or those with special skills needed by the community. In 1991 there were some thirty families living at Opô Afonjá, spread out in numerous small buildings within a large walled compound in the Cabula neighborhood of Bahia. Mikelle Omari lived at Opô Afonjá in the early nineteen-eighties. There she heard the word roça or "country" used to describe the life of the candomblé. She found that: "The frequent use of the term roça when discussing the Candomblé activities and the fact that a special uniform is worn in the sacred space support the interpretation of the Candomblé as a separate reality. There is a sense of leaving urban openness and entering a rural, cloistered space."[27]

The organization of a candomblé is that of a family, related not by blood but by initiation. One is reborn into a candomblé family presided over by a mother or father "of the spirit." The Nagô terms iyalorixá, "mother of the spirit" or the less common babalorixá, "father of the spirit," are used by the community when referring to senior female and male initiates. Their Portuguese equivalents, mãe de santo and pai de santo are known throughout Brazil to refer to priestesses and priests of African-derived traditions. The closer a candomblé community comes to the African standards of purity set by the elite houses, the more women are found in leadership positions. While *babalorixás* or *pais de santo* may preside over newer Nagô and *caboclo* houses and dominate the Angolan ones, the established Nagô and Jeje candomblés have been controlled by women since their founding. Ruth Landes titled her study of black Bahia *The City of Women*, highlighting the dominance and independence of candomblé women in every aspect of their lives.[28] They were loath to marry and accept the legal control of men over them. Even if they were married they were always known by their affiliation with their spirits and never by that with their husbands. One of Landes's friends during her stay in Bahia was always referred to as Zézé de Iansá (roughly, Jo of Iansá, the spirit of wind and force), and never as Mrs. da Silva.[29] Edison Carneiro told Landes: "It is almost as difficult for a man to become great in candomble as it is for him to have a baby. And for the same reason: it is believed to be against his nature."[30]

The candomblé belief is that men have "hot blood." They have neither the patience to submit to the discipline of candomblé, nor the control of their passions necessary to incarnate the spirits. Mãe Menininha told Landes, "The old Africans always said that a priestess should be so old that she could no longer remember the passions of youth."[31] It is these elder, senior women who direct candomblé and pass on the purity of the way of worship to new initiates into their families.

This is not to say that men are absent in candomblé, only that the critical offices of priesthood are only for the very few. Men serve a complementary function in the organization of the elite houses as *ogans*, literally "masters," a small board of advisers and protectors who see to the material welfare of the community. Today these board's include some of the most prominent citizens of Bahia, professionals and municipal and state politicians who, for a variety of motives, wish to be associated with a candomblé. Certain *ogans* also take on ritual roles as directors of the drummers at candomblé ceremonies or presiders over the ritual slaughter of animals at feasts.[32]

Priesthood is essentially the capacity to carry and pass on the presence of the spirit or *orixá* that one has received from another priestess or priest. One has reached the level of spiritual maturity when one can pass on or give birth to the presence of the spirit in a spiritual "daughter" or "son." One's progress in candomblé begins when one is first called by the *orixá* to its service. The call usually takes the form of a crisis in an individual's life which he or she will take to an *iyalorixá* or *babalorixá* for resolution. If the *iyalorixá* or *babalorixá* determines that the problem is caused by an *orixá*, it can be resolved only with some commitment to the service of the spirit. The *orixá* is seen as both the source of the problem and as its solution, the focal point on which the life of the one called can be transformed.

On some occasions a parent will dedicate a child to an *orixá* seeing to its initiation when very young in exchange for the spirit's power to solve a problem. More often a young adult will appeal to an *orixá* for help in meeting a life crisis, such as serious illness, and upon recovery will dedicate herself or himself to the *orixá*'s service. A costly and lengthy ceremony begins one's life in the candomblé as a *iaô*, a bride of the spirit, a new wife with all the menial duties of a junior member of the household. If the spirit desires it, after seven years, a *iaô* may receive *deká*, necklaces, clothing, and altar objects that mark one as an *ebomin*, a senior woman in the candomblé. An *ebomin* is empowered to establish her own fundamental altars and, if the spirits desire it, be an *iyalorixá* in her own right, passing on her spiritual experiences to new initiates. The *iyalorixás* say, "To climb the ladder of the candomblé, a person mounts one rung at a time."[33]

The elite Nagô candomblés of Bahia have always been headed by women who have passed their authority, not always without dispute, to juniors in their houses. Ruth Landes gives us a portrait of the hierarchy at Gantois during the early years of Menininha's long reign. When Landes met Menininha in the late nineteen-thirties, Gantois was a community of some two hundred active participants with some fifty of them initiated priestesses.[34] Menininha had received the charge of leadership from the beloved Pulcheria who had initiated Menininha into the mysteries of the *orixá* Oxun when Menininha was only an infant. Thus while she was forty-six years old in the reckoning of secular and Europeanized Bahia, Menininha was forty-four years "in Oxun," the true mark of maturity and seniority.

In the confines of a *terreiro*, the sacred grounds of a candomblé, or in a conversation about candomblé life, initiates will give their ages according to their initiatory births and recognize the authority of their sisters and brothers on that basis. Each candomblé initiate has a human and an *orixá* parent. As they give their spiritual ages, they will also speak of the proximate human mothers who brought them into the spiritual world and the *orixá* who is their ultimate parent. On formal occasions a member will greet her or his senior in the spirit with a full prostration, indicating the relative importance of each member and the spirit whom the prostrator carries. Thus the candomblé is a family of human and spirit children and parents, with humans acting as mediums for the *orixás* under certain conditions and acting on their own under others.

The head of the candomblé is usually addressed as "mother": *mãe* in Portuguese, *iyá* in Nagô. Beneath her is the *iyá kêkêrê*, the "little mother" who is her assistant and usually understood to be her successor. The *iyá kêkêrê* is largely responsible for discipline in the candomblé. In Menininha's Gantois this role was fulfilled by Laura, who told Landes that she was fifty-five years old "in the world," with thirty-eight years to her Oxun. In candomblé, like vodou, the spirits are not necessarily single entities, but families or constellations of personalities, that can be conceived as having one, or a few, or unlimited identities. Thus candomblé members will distinguish among the *orixás* that have chosen them to be their children. Menininha's Oxun was both the same spirit as Laura's and could be spoken of as the same during certain circumstances, while at other times they would be distinguished in speech and in ritual attention.

Landes reports that during her visit Menininha and Laura were not getting along, and there was a good deal of gossip that Laura was jealous of Menininha's elevation and was using sorcery against her. As mentioned previously, succession disagreements are frequent, and though Menininha became the most famous of all *iyalorixás*, even her prestige could not forestall disputes about the succession of her daughter in the late 1980s.

Assisting the *iyá kêkêrê* is the *iya morô*, filled in Menininha's Gantois by Maria, who was forty years old with thirty-three years to her Omulu, the *orixá* of disease and health. Beneath her stood Eudoxia, the *iya basé*, the "mother who cooks," with twenty-eight years to her Omulu. Knowledge of the proper preparation of the foods of the candomblé is a critical duty. The *orixás* each have their own dishes which must be prepared and arranged at feasts according to certain orders and numbers. The success of the ceremony depends not only on culinary skills, but on a vast repertoire of secret prayers which must accompany the food's preparation. All Bahia loves *acarajé*, the bean-cakes sacred to Iansá, but only the *iya basé* knows the active ingredients which will tempt the *orixás* to the feast.

In addition to the senior women were a number of priestesses who cared for particular sanctuaries in the Gantois compound, others who led the songs of the liturgy, and still others who were in charge of the introductory rites to Exu, the spirit who opens and closes all candomblé undertakings and who merits duties separate from the *orixás*. A priestess, again, has the ability to "give birth" to her own initiatory children. If she wishes, she is free to establish her own *candomblé*, or may choose to remain in service to her original house.

Beneath the *iyalorixá* in the larger Nagô houses are the *ebomins*, the "elder sisters" of the initiatory family, who are primarily responsible for acting out the liturgies and preforming the work of the *terreiro*. An *ebomin* has at least seven years of life in the spirit, has undergone a costly and definitive initiation ceremony, and enjoys many preferments in clothing and ritual accoutrements.[35] She completes the relationship begun by the *iaô*, the junior wife of the *orixá*, who serves the elder sisters and *iyalorixá* on all occasions. These three levels of priesthood, *iyalorixá*, *ebomin*, and *iaô*, mother, elder sister, and junior wife, comprise the primary relationships of the candomblé. They themselves are attended by functionaries who have not been called to priestly service who can act as their personal aids during ceremonies.[36] All are supported by a large number of faithful attendees at ceremonies and still greater numbers of occasional visitors and clients.

The candomblé provides services to the wider community in the form of counseling and therapy. Priestesses charge fees for consultations and

WORKING THE SPIRIT

serve a community that has virtually no access to the services of university-trained medical and legal professionals. They have also, especially in more recent years, enjoyed the patronage of wealthy and celebrated clients who have furthered the success and acceptance of the candomblés by the wider Brazilian society and media. Candomblé offers a thorough system of diagnosis and prescription based on the reading of sixteen cowrie shells.[37] The play of the shells, *jogo de búzios*, constitutes the instrument by which a trained *iyalorixá* or *ebomin* can consult the spirits and treat any infirmity or misfortune which is brought to them. The fall of the shells refers to an archetypal spiritual situation, a difficulty faced by the ancestors in Africa which acts as a paradigm for the diagnosis and treatment of the consultee's problem. The consultee is referred to the spiritual sources of his or her difficulty and offered a prescription for its resolution, usually involving certain ritual steps which will reestablish his or her connection with the *orixá* that has offered the paradigmatic problem and solution. The most frequent treatments involve the use of healing leaves, and priestesses learn a vast pharmacopeia of spiritually and chemically active plants. It can be argued that it is this knowledge above all else that gives the *iyalorixá* her authority and constitutes the principle secret teaching of initiation.[38]

It is in this professional context that the candomblé directly affects the wider society, contributes to its guidance, and receives from it important financial support and cultural prestige. While very few Bahians are initiates of candomblés, and relatively few attend public ceremonies regularly, it is likely that a great many have consulted the *búzios* with an initiate. Still, the most celebrated point of contact between candomblé and Bahia is in the public festivals that draw thousands of Bahians into the streets and have become international tourist attractions. While the *carnaval* in Rio de Janeiro has reached the gigantic status of the "eighth wonder of the world," the Bahian *carnaval* has become famous throughout Brazil as the "roots" *carnaval*, a self-conscious celebration of African authenticity. So many of the troupes have adopted candomblé costume and music into their processions that Bahian *carnaval* has been called "candomblé in the streets."[39] Other calendar feasts bring thousands to the church of Bonfim and the beach at Rio Vermelho, where Catholic and candomblé services are conducted simultaneously. The parallelism or *sincretismo* of these occasions is often decried by purists in both the Catholic Church and the candomblé, but their popularity expresses the nearly universal acceptance of the outer forms of candomblé piety by Bahians and Brazilians in general.[40]

The candomblé has provided occasions for resistance to physical enslavement and cultural repression. It provides its family of initiates financial, legal, and medical assistance, with a variety of support services absent or out of the reach of most Afro-Bahians. It supports itself from the jobs that its members may have and from the counseling and medical services which it provides to the wider community. Together with these economic and social purposes, the candomblé exists to serve the *orixás*, the Nagô spirits. The *orixás* live in activities of the candomblé and, as they are empowered by careful ritual attention, so the community empowers itself. The *orixás* are made present in the service of the community. They are shown in the innumerable gestures of the candomblé, in the foods, speech, and music which communicate their power. But more than anywhere else, the *orixás* are present in the bodies of the devotees themselves. They are placed there in the ceremonies of initiation, and one serves the *orixás* and the community by offering oneself as a medium for their presence. As in the portrait of Haitian vodou, the keys to candomblé services are found in the reception of the spirit in initiation and in its manifestation to the community in dance.

SERVICE

The general word for service in candomblé is *obrigação*, obligation, with the dual implication of duty to the community and to the spirits. One is bound to the community through work for the spirits, and only in the communal context of the *terreiro* can this work be cultivated and shared. There are many ways of service to the spirits, but the one that receives the most ritual atention, that shows the community to itself in the purest form of spiritual presence, is the incorporation of the spirits in human mediums. In human mediums the *orixás* may manifest themselves with all the subtleties of human intention and all the dynamism of human dance. The *orixás* may move and act with the capabilities of the human community, and the community may move and act with the timeless authority of the *orixás*.

Iaô: Bride of the Orixá

To become a medium an individual must be called by the spirit through a direct disturbance in her or his life. The more dramatic and obvious the disturbance, the more likely that one is being called. Often a serious illness, a direct confrontation with the reality of death, will constitute the first evidence of a call. Or it could be a spontaneous manifestation of a spirit at a ceremony where an *orixá* incorporates itself unbidden in the consciousness of an untrained individual. In each case, the cusp of a life-or-death situation is seen as the *orixá*'s demand for the life of an individual. He or she must die to life in the ordinary world and enter a new one in the candomblé. The *búzios* are consulted, and if an *orixá* is determined to be at the source of the disturbance, preparations are made, with more or less urgency, to begin the process of initiation into the life of service to the spirit and the candomblé community which sustains it.[41]

In his 1978 film *Iawo*, Geraldo Sarno gives us a unique opportunity to observe some of the rites of initiation into a Nagô-Jeje *terreiro* in Bahia.[42] We are led through the major steps of transforming three *abians*, young women called by the *orixás*, into *iaôs*, brides of the spirit.

Once it has been determined through the fall of the *búzios* that the women have indeed been called by their respective *orixás*, they are under "obligation" to "seat" or "make" the *orixá*, to bring the presence of the *orixá* into their lives and selves. Through prayers and offerings, the *orixá* of each *abian* must be "seated" or made present in a variety of objects culminating with the head of the individual herself. These *assentamentos* or "seats" are the initiate's altarpieces and are kept in the shrine room of her *terreiro*. They comprise a stone, the central focus of externalized worship of the spirit, which is fed, bathed, and cared for as the "head" of the *orixá* in its most durable of material forms. Surrounding the stone are various tools and emblems of the *orixá* which also carry its presence and receive offerings. These may be swords, staffs, crowns, and other regalia finely worked in iron, copper, or brass depending on the *orixá* involved. Yet the most profound *"seat"* of the *orixá*, the altar receiving the most attention and preparation, is the head of the initiate herself. Initiation into candomblé, in addition to bringing privileged access to the spiritual power of the *orixás* through objects, also initiates the reception of the spirit into the *abian*'s very consciousness when it is "seated" in the *abian*'s head.

When the resources for the long and costly process of initiation have been assembled, the *abians* take up residence in the *terreiro*, the sacred precincts of the candomblé. They are housed in a special small room called *runkô*, itself set off from the ceremonial and living quarters of the community. They are said to be members of the same "boat," fellow passengers on a great journey.[43]

They will remain in the *runkô*, except for daily ablutions and select public appearances, for at least six months.[44] Though they are constantly together, each *abian* is being prepared to "make" a different *orixá*, and so subtle but important variants enter into each *abian*'s experience. At each stage of the long process, confirmations are sought about the *orixá* to be made. Great cautions are taken to ensure that the *abian* is being prepared for her proper *orixá*. Should a mistake be made, disaster would follow. In fact at the beginning of Sarno's film, the initiation of a fourth *abian* is shown to be postponed. She was separated from the others when it could not be confirmed which *orixá* was calling her. The three *abians* who proceed to undergo the initiation are making the *orixás* Iansá, Iemanjá, and Omulu, *orixás* associated with stormy winds, maternal seas, and transformative diseases, respectively.

The first rite shown is the *catulagem* or cutting of the *abian*'s hair. The women, who look to be in their early twenties, are seated on mats on the ground, each within the spread knees of the woman behind, as if in a small canoe. They are dressed in pure white dresses, shoulderless and elasticized at the bust. A senior priestess holds a lighted white candle while another cuts the hair of each *abian* in turn. The priestesses chant soft songs for the appropriate *orixá* as they carefully clip the hair as closely as possible to the scalp. A white metal bell with a long handle, called *adja*, is rung hard and loud over each *abian*'s head as the *orixá* is invoked. Each head is bathed in an herbal infusion called *amaci*, carrying the candomblé's *axé*, the spiritual power residing in the residue of all the *terreiro*'s sacrifices of old. Each abian is given bracelets, armlets, anklets, and a necklace bathed in the herbal liquid. The anklets contain a small bell, a sign of submission to the *iyalorixá* and the *terreiro*, while the armlets and bracelets are particularized for her *orixá*.[45] Around her neck is placed the *kele*, a heavy necklace of beads coded to the colors and numbers associated with her *orixá*.

During the long months of isolation the *abians* are being molded to better receive and manifest the presence of their *orixá*. The consciousness of each *abian* is made more permeable by the world of the spirits and, as they become dependent upon the senior priestesses who are preparing them, they manifest a child-spirit called *erê*. The *erês* are intermediate spiritual beings between the personal consciousness of the *abian* and that of the *orixá*. They are explained in a variety of ways: as children of the *orixás*; or the *orixás* themselves as children; or a special childish dimension in the personality of each *orixá*.[46] They are transitional manifestations of the *orixás* and often appear before and after the adult spirits themselves arrive. The *erês* of Sarno's film laugh and giggle, blow toy whistles, and act like silly three-year-olds. They have been known to run about the *terreiro*, playing tricks and making all kinds of messes. But they are also quiescent and may render the *abian* motionless at the verge of consciousness for prolonged periods.

As the reception and manifestation of the *orixá* is a reorganization of the consciousness of the initiate, the focus of the initiation process rests on the *abian*'s head. The presiding priestesses set out candles and drape the *abians* in white cloth in honor of the foundation *orixá*, Oxala. Washed in the herbal infusions of the *axé* of the *terreiro*, each *abian* undergoes the *raspagem*, the shaving of her head by her sponsoring priestess. The *adja* bell is again rung virogously and, with her head's preparation of exposure and herbal and sonic intensification, the *orixás* speak through the *abians* and whisper their names to the priestesses.

With the identities of the manifesting *orixás* confirmed at this level, the *abians* are ready to be presented to the community of the candomblé. They proceed from the *runkô* into the public dance pavilion to the accompaniment of drums and the admiring eyes of the community of initiates, who sing songs in praise of the new initiates. Their heads are made luminous and cool by being painted with *efun*, a white chalky paste. The reference to the color white intensifies the presence of Oxala, the most senior *orixá*, and the foundation of all the others. All work with the *orixá* is built upon Oxala, and so as each *abian* is prepared to receive Iansá, Iemanjá, or Omulu, their heads are cleansed and consecrated by Oxala. The *abians* prostrate themselves before the drums, and then, bent over in the posture of supplicants, they dance before the community to the rhythms of their *orixás*.

The *abians* are ready to have the first offering made to the spirit inside them. Each head has become an important medium for the presence of its *orixá*, and the presiding priestess offers food to the spirits through this altar. Each *abian* holds a small white bird in her hand while the priestesses invoke the *orixá* within. The center point of the abian's head, the point of intersection between the spirit and the human, is marked with *efun*. The bird is throttled, its blood poured over the consecrated head and its feathers plucked and stuck to the drying blood. The *abians* sit quietly while their *orixás* are strengthened by the infusion of lifeblood.[47]

After a second appearance before the drums and the community, the *abians* receive their final intensification of the head in the form of an incision. A cross is lightly cut in the center of the scalp, literally opening a point of intersection between inner and outer worlds. A thick poultice of the herbs of their *orixás* is rubbed into the spot, again literally placing the *orixá* inside them, inoculating them with the *axé* of their spirit. Their arms and shoulders are also incised with the marks of their *nação*, in this case the Nagô-Jeje nation maintained by the *terreiro*.[48]

With the presence of the *orixás* now firmly in place in the heads of the *abians*, they are now considered true *iaôs*, brides of their *orixás*. They are ready for their final presentation to the community, this time a large public feast which includes dignitaries from related *terreiros*. During the festive evening the newly made *iaôs* come out three times before the community, each time in different costume and to different rhythms of the drums. On the first emergence from the *runkô*, they are dressed in white skirts with fine long cloths tied around their chests and in bows behind. The first appearance is in honor of Oxala, the foundation *orixá* whose creative color is white. Their heads are again painted with white *efun*, crowned by a small mound of ingredients called *oxu* at the point of their incision.[49] Placed in a band around each forehead is a single red parrot feather, reminding the *iaô* that the white creativity of the male *orixá* Oxala is complemented by the red of the female spirit Oxun.[50] They are bent well forward, from the waist, arms dangling as the drums announce them and their *orixás* to the large and happy congregation. Perhaps as many as three hundred people crowd the dance pavilion and many of the attending priestesses wear the full petticoats of the traditional Bahiana costume which constitutes the formal wear for the women of the candomblé. The priestesses guide them in their steps before the drums, ringing the *adja* to summon and direct the *orixá* in their heads.

On their second excursion they are dressed in the colors of their *orixás*, in the petticoated skirts reminiscent of the Bahiana style but with only the long *pano da costa* tied around their chests. Iansá, the warrior woman like the wind, wears pink skirts with a white tie. Iemanjá, the mother of the waters, wears blue and white like the waves. And Omulu, the earthly father of disease and death, wears multi-colored prints. At this stage the *orixás* within the *iaôs* will repeat the earlier, private disclosure of their names for the public at large. The drums play the rhythms of each of the *orixás* and pause in expectant silence. Each *iaô*, cradled by a visiting dignitary or sponsor who will witness the presence of the *orixá*, in turn whispers her *orixá* name. The dignitary relays the name to the congregation, and amid their applause and delight, the drums sound the *orixá*'s rhythms while the spirit in flesh dances joyfully to the songs of the community.

On their final appearance the *iaôs* are dressed in the full regalia of their *orixás*. Iansá dances in pink taffeta, her head surmounted by a high-peaked, studded pink crown with short lines of beads covering her face. She carries a bouquet of long lilies in her right hand and a short, ornamental copper sword in her left. Iemanjá wears white. Her crown is smaller and clear beads shield her face. Her bouquet of lilies is tied with a blue ribbon, and she holds the *abébé*, the white metal mirror and fan of a great lady. Omulu's costume is the most dramatic of all. His head is covered in the *iko*, a great cone of dried raffia, golden palm straw from Africa. His skirt is also of raffia. In his hand he carries the *xaxará*, a short ornamental broom which sweeps the *terreiro* free of disease and death. Each *orixá* dances before the drums while the community opens itself to the reinvigorated *axé* that the newborn spirits bring to the *terreiro*.[51]

Sarno's film concludes with the public presentations of the fully "made" *iaôs* incorporating their *orixás* in full regalia. The strict seclusion of the *runkô* has come to an end, and only a few rites remain to reintroduce the *iaôs* to the world that they left behind. Notable among them is the *paná*, a necessary but informal rite among candomblé initiates that brings the *iaôs* from their long seclusion back into the world of everyday exchanges. The *iaôs* are made to pantomime ordinary activities like cooking, cleaning, and selling, while great sport is made of their efforts.[52] At one point the *iaôs* are "sold" at auction to the highest bidder, an opportunity for sarcastic humor, but also a serious way to raise money for the expenses of the initiation, and to set what will be longstanding relationships of patronage and mentoring.[53]

In many candomblé houses the process of making a *iaô* is brought to a conclusion with attendance at Mass at the Church of Bonfim, thus fully integrating the *iaô* into the official life of the city. Yet the process of initiation is never complete, and the outward ceremonies are only markers of a deepening inner relationship with one's *orixá*. After seven years a *iaô* may be called to make the *obrigação* to receive *deká*, and become a senior initiate, an *ebomin*. Now the *assentamentos*, the altarpiece "seats" of the *orixás* that the *iaô* received at her initiation and which were kept in the shrine room of the *terreiro* will be given over to her own care. As an *ebomin* she is empowered to make her own shrine, and she may transfer the *axé* of the mother *terreiro* to found her own candomblé. Yet she always must remain loyal to the mother house and greet her superiors with the prostrations required of her. The mother *terreiro* still retains some of the *axé* of her initiation in its shrine room. This symbolic control is far-reaching although, in fact, the loyalty of daughter houses is perhaps challenged as much as it is honored.[54]

Sarno's film shows a continual intensification of the presence of the *orixá* in the heads of the initiates. The *orixás* first manifest themselves in disturbances to the heads of their children. They call human beings through life-transforming, perhaps life-threatening, events such as disease and accident. By clearing the head of its outward coverings and inner distractions, the presence of the *orixá* is recognized within the individual. The confirmation of this presence is found in the altered state of trance, when the spirit incorporates itself in the body of the human medium. The public presentation of the *orixá* in the body of the devotee is the most direct experience of the spirit that might be shared within the community. It is the desideratum of the candomblé gathering. As the individual is under "obligation" to manifest the spirit in her own person if called, the community performs its *obrigaçâo* in manifesting the spirit in dance. The *orixás* are available to the community of the candomblé by the preparation of the *iaô* through her initiation. They are shared through the controlled construction of ritual time and space by means of festal offerings, drum and vocal music, and dance. The original meaning of the word candomblé is a kind of drum rhythm, a rhythm that activates the spirits to manifest themselves in dance.

Festa dos Orixás

We have seen that the distinctions among the various African ethnic groups in nineteenth-century Brazil were expressed in the different *nações* or nations of the candomblé. What made a *nação* a *nação* was the community's fidelity to a complex of gestures of service known to be, for example, Kêtu or Jesha or Jeje. The complex is made public and shared in the drum rhythms, songs, and dances of the *obrigição*. A candomblé is a house united by its rhythms and distinguished from others by its patterns of rhythmic actions. A priestess in Sarno's, *Iawo* uses the phrase, "when the candomblé is playing" to describe the ceremonies of the *obrigação*.

Each candomblé house has determined a liturgical calendar in which each of the major *orixás* is given an annual public *obrigação*. The cycle of the ceremonies may once have depended on the Catholic calendar since the feast days of saints provided some of the few opportunities for Afro-Brazilian gatherings and expression.[55] Though some elements of the Catholic correspondences remain in the festivals, the cycle is determined today by an annual divination among the senior houses, and the calendars of the houses are aligned with each other.

Though each *orixá* takes its turn as the *dono da festa*, the owner of the feast, all the *orixás* of each *terreiro* are honored at the *dono*'s ceremony. The structure of these ceremonies is generally the same. One of the most important *orixás* honored in Bahia is Oxossi, the hunter-king. Oxossi, in ancient times, was the king of Kêtu, one of the most prestigious of the Nagô homelands in Africa. In the ritual time of the *obrigação* he lives on as a regal warrior, hunter, and herbalist. All the *terreiros* of Bahia hold an annual *obrigação* for Oxossi, remembering his past glory and his present power to defend, feed, and heal his community.

On a clear afternoon in the warm Bahian winter of 1991, a festival for Oxossi is being prepared at Casa Branca, the oldest Nagô house in the city. On this site, once well beyond the city of Salvador, was an old sugarmill which gave shelter to the *iyalorixás* who had repaired there in the nineteenth century to escape frequent police persecutions. Now the city has engulfed Casa Branca, a few acres of steep hillside ringed by crowded, busy neighborhoods. Cut high into the terraced slope is a long, one-story building, gleaming with fresh whitewash. It dominates several small, equally bright outbuildings, large herb and vegetable gardens, a well, and a number of sculptures. The trunk of a huge ficus tree is tied with a large white cloth bow, a shrine to *irôkô*, the cosmic tree which grounds the *terreiro* to the holy mother earth.[56] The outbuildings are shrines to some of the *orixás*, Exu and Xangô in particular. The white house is reached from the street below by a long twisting staircase which ends at an entrance located well to the left of the building. Inside is the *barracão*, a large dance pavilion with a high ceiling and tiled floor. To the right are the private rooms of the *terreiro*: the *runkō* seclusion room for the novices; altars for the *orixás*; vesting and storage rooms; work space and kitchens.

Preparations for the *obrigação* for Oxossi have begun many days before the public service this evening. The *barracão* has been decorated with Oxossi's colors and emblems. Oxossi's herbs have been freshly picked from the forest and now carpet the floor of the *barracão*, giving it the look of the forest and the pungent smells of fresh greenery. An ensemble of foods sacred to Oxossi has been prepared according to the strictest rules of slaughter, cooking, seasoning, and presentation. Guinea fowl have been purchased in the market and prayerfully slaughtered by the *axôgún*, the *ogan* charged with Ogun's knife. On the day of the feast the dressed meat has been cooked and seasoned in the forest plants of Oxossi's domain. The fowl together with the *orixá*'s dish of *axoxô*, corn cooked with coconut, have been arranged before Oxossi's fundamental symbols in the *pegi*, the inner shrine room of the *terreiro*. The light liquor *alua* has been prepared. Tonight these foods will be shared with all the candomblé that they may join in communion with the *orixá* and each other.

At sundown the festival is officially opened with an offering to Exu, the liminal spirit who "clears the way" for the others. Like Haiti's Legba, Exu lives alone at the borders of the human world, forever "on the road." Water, rum, and manioc flour fried in *dende* oil are presented with songs to the dangerous spirit at his house on at the edges of the *terreiro*. Then they are literally thrown into the street, to "send Exu away," so that he will cross over to the world of the spirits and guide them to the human community, and so that he will not linger to disrupt the ceremony with his restless energy.[57] A song calls upon Exu in his elemental manifestation as *iná*, fire:

> Iná, I present you with my humble respects
> Iná, Iná, I present you with the respects of the world

Iná, don't come with cruel thoughts
Iná, Iná, don't come with cruel thoughts for the world
Iná, Iná, come and protect the world.[58]

Once Exu has accepted the offering, the conditions have been established so that the *orixás* might manifest themselves among their children in the *barracão*. Drummers arrive and tune their instruments. Dignitaries from other communities are greeted and seated in places of honor. The seniority and spiritual accomplishments of each member and visitor are marked through the formal courtesies of prostrations, handshakes, and embraces. Everyone presents himself or herself to the drums. Friends and neighbors of the *terreiro* arrive and find seats along low backless benches toward the main door. Even some tourists come to sample the pageantry of a candomblé festival. Many are armed with cameras and likely frustrated by the signs on the *barracão* walls forbidding photography.

The room is a large one, some forty feet square, its stucco walls and tile roof painted bright white. Radiating from the top of a central column are strings of sky-blue streamers which shimmer with the movements of the people gathering below. This bright pale blue is Oxossi's color, and it appears in decorations throughout the room. The walls are hung with shields of Oxossi, decorated with his hunting symbols of bow and arrow and powder horn. A small shrine to one side of the room features statuettes of Catholic saints festooned with fresh-cut flowers and herbs. Near a small, balustraded enclosure for the drummers at the back of the room stands a larger statue of Oxossi, dressed in his characteristic soft leather hat. The eye is taken back, though, to the center of the room. Surrounding the top of the central column is an ornate baldaquin, a fabric canopy in gold and blue.

The column is called "the staff of Oranmiyan," a reference to the ancient pole at the center of the world in Africa.[59] At its base, in a small recess beneath the tiles is the *entoto*, the most powerful concentration of the presence of the spirits, the *axé* of the entire community. The *entoto* is the residue of all the works of the *terreiro*, the foundation symbols of the community patinated with a portion of every sacrifice conducted within its precincts. It is the *terriero*'s link with Africa and the earth itself. Surrounding the column and the *entoto* are ten or twelve formal wooden chairs. These are placed facing outward, in the four compass directions. Senior *iyalorixás* and *ogans* from different candomblé houses are seated in them.

At last three of the white-clad *ogans* who have gathered in the corner of the *barracão* take their seats behind the three drums. These are handmade, conical, staved drums of the "conga" type.[60] The largest, called the *rum*, directs the rhythms of the other two smaller ones, the *rumpi* and the *lê*. All three are grounded in the metal bell, *agôgô*, which keeps the basic time. The heads of the drums, like those of the human initiates, have been consecrated into the spirit, and so they, too, are mediums of the spirit's voice.

As the gathering of some two hundred people settles, the drummers begin a series of preliminary rhythms in honor of the spirits. Ten *iaôs*, the junior initiates of the house, begin to file into the *barracão*. They are attended by *ekedis*, older women who support and direct them. They are dressed in their finest Bahiana clothes: brilliant pink and lime floral skirts flaring out over stiff petticoats; starched white lace blouses; and tied around their breasts or waists, shimmering wraps in gold, silver, and white. Their heads are covered with clear white headties. They dance fairly rapidly in a circle around the center column and the enthroned dignitaries. Backs are slightly bent, shoulders loosely hunched, elbows crooked sharply and extended a little from the body. At times their hands clench, at others they open and turn in swimming motions. Their feet are bare and step slowly and deliberately, crushing the leaves on the floor and perfuming the air.[61]

The chief *ogan* begins the first of three or seven songs to each *orixá* to be honored tonight. This is the *xiré*, the "play" or "entertainment" for the *orixás*, calling them to manifest themselves in the bodies of the dancers. "*A xiré Ogun o*" . . . ("We play for Ogun") calls the *ogan*, and the congregation responds in kind.[62]

> Ogun Onire O
> Welcome Ogun of Onire

From across the ocean
  Captain, you have heard our summons.
When we behold your bloody robes,
  Durable father of iron,
We shall step back to let you by.
  Welcome Ogun of Onire
Open the way through the bush
  Put by your wrath, warrior,
Ogun, come and dance with us.[63]

After perhaps as many as seven songs for Ogun, the congregation takes up sometimes three, sometimes seven songs for each the *orixás* to be honored tonight. Oxossi follows Ogun, then Omulu, Iemanjá, Xangô, Iansá, and Oxun. Each song contains a series of phrases, sometimes intensifying into a single phrase which may be repeated for several minutes at a time. Each sung phrase is given expression and force by loud, hard, and ever-shifting drum rhythms and by vigorous cooperative movement and gestures of the *iaôs*. Each rhythm phrase and dance posture is related to the others. At some point during the rhythms for her own *orixá*, a *iaô*, will leave the circle to dance before the drums. Here she honors her *orixá*, displays her virtuosity, and opens herself for the manifestation of the spirit within her.

For Oxossi the congregation sings again and again in Nagô: "Oxossi shoots his arrow quickly!" Edison Carneiro described an appropriate dance for Ruth Landes:

Suppose that you are dancing for Oxóssi, the hunter. Touch your right forefinger to your left thumb and, besides these, let only your left little finger be extended. Shimmy your shoulders. Shake your arms, but keep your shoulders still. Keep your buttocks turned out. Your feet dance in the same tramp-tramp, but the upper parts of your body move in different rhythms, depending upon the drums. Now, flop your body down from the waist, and sweep it languorously from one side to another. Twist your pelvis around.[64]

Rhythms, dances, and songs follow for each of the other *orixás*, and it is some two hours before the cycle is completed. As the master of the feast, Oxossi has been the first to manifest himself in the body of the *iaô*, and he now calls each of the other *orixás* to come to the celebration. Each of the *iaôs* has come forward before the drums and either immediately or shortly thereafter has received her *orixá*. It is clear that it is this manifestation of the presence of the *orixás* that the congregation has been waiting for. All eyes watch expectantly as each of the *iaôs* begins the movements which indicate the incorporation of her *orixás*. As she dances before the drums, the drummers switch into the concentrated *adarun* rhythm, "the voice that you have to say yes to."[65] Supported by the *ekedis*, the *iaôs'* bodies bend rapidly from the waist, thrusting forward, then well backward. Their shoulders shift as rapidly, back and forth, in a shuddering motion. An *ekedi* will often place her hand gently behind the head or under the chin of the rocking *iaô* should the movements become too sharp. Eyeglasses are removed, necklaces readjusted, and the shawl adjusted to bind the body of the *iaô* to its *orixá* head, like a horse is bridled for its rider. They will often give a shout in Nagô to show that the *orixá* is now in place.

In the film *Iawo*, a senior priestess describes her feelings as the *orixá* begins to manifest itself in her body:

> I feel this way when the candomblé is playing . . . that the Orisha wants to get me, my legs tremble, something reaches up that takes over my heart, my head grows, I see that blue light, I look for someone to grab but can't find anyone and then I don't see anything anymore. Then everything happens and I don't see. Then I think that the Orisha must be something like a wind, it comes toward you like a wind and embraces you. Like a shock in my heart, my heart beats as fast as the lead drum plays, my head grows, and it seems like I see a blue light ahead of me and a hole appears in the middle of the room. Then I want to run, to grab someone, but people seem far away, out of reach. Then I don't see anything anymore.[66]

The spirit-filled dancers come, one by one, to dance alone a final time before the drums. Then, escorted by the *ekedis*, they retire to the dressing rooms beyond the *barracão*. When the last *iaô* leaves the room, the drums stop, people stretch and chat, and await the return of the spirits in glory.

Roger Bastide calls the long first phase of the *obrigação* the "danse d'appel," the dance of appeal to the *orixás*, invoking them to manifest themselves amid the community within their *iaôs*. After a short time, the spirits will return in a "danse de dieux," "dance of the gods," a royal procession of the *orixás* enthroned in their mediums.[67] The drummers return to their places and take up the processional rhythms. The congregation comes to attention and stands. Expectant smiles are on all faces as a pair of *ekedis* emerge from the vestuary and flank the door to the *barracão*. In single file, the *orixás* emerge into the hall enthroned in the heads of their mediums, mounted on their human horses. The *iaôs*' faces are serene, their eyes downcast. Each wears gleaming regalia and their dances are stately and aloof.

First to emerge are two Oguns, the hard *orixá* of iron and blood. They wear chromed helmets, winged like those of ancient charioteers. Silver chains clank on their bright metal breastplates, armlets, and wristlets. They are armed with short straight swords. Following the Oguns come two Oxossis, dressed as the royal hunter of Kêtu. They wear soft leather hats and jerkins of untanned buckskin over their flaring Bahiana skirts. Each holds the *ode*, the bow and arrow of Oxossi. These are cast in one piece in gleaming silver metal. One of the Oxossis holds a small ornamental blunderbuss intricately worked in shining brass. Both have powder horns in silver draped around their shoulders. Omulu follows, trembling beneath his raffia *iko*, the golden palm straw crown that hides his face and upper torso. It is wrapped at the top in an elaborate cincture of black cloth and beads. He dances vigorously with the *xaxará*, the leather, shell-and-bead-wrapped broom with which he sweeps away disease and misfortune. Next is Iemanjá, the mother of the *orixás* and owner of the seas. She is dressed in white and blue and wears a silver crown that dangles clear beads before her impassive face. In one hand she carries a curved silver sword hugged tightly to her breast, in the other hand she delicately turns the *abébé*, her mirrored fan. Two manifestations of her son Xangô follow, crowned, both with an *oxé*, or doubled-headed axe, in each hand. Xangô's senior wife Iansá is next, crowned in shining copper and carrying a copper sword and an *iruke*, a black, horsetail flywhisk, symbols of her fiery military strength and her royal power. Last is Oxun in bright yellow with a brass crown and *abébé*. All the clothes and instruments are kept secure in Casa Branca's vestuary, bright clean and ready for these moments.

The appearance of the *orixás* into the *barracão* is like a burst of light, dazzling and multifaceted. The polished crowns and instruments, and bright silk and satins of the garments, augmented by the rhythmic propulsions of the drums startle the senses to appreciate the epiphany of the *orixás* among the congregation. The atmosphere during the royal progress is one of reverence and joy. Bowls of rice and flower petals have been passed around the congregation and handfuls are tossed over the *orixás* as they pass. Nearly every face is smiling; happy whispers are exchanged. As each spirit files by, the congregants hold up their hands before their chests, palms out. It is a gesture of supplication, of openness to receiving the spirit's blessing, and perhaps it also protects the congregant from the power of the *orixá*. At times an *orixá* will leave the line to embrace someone, but these are only brief interruptions of the stately promenade. After several circuits around the *barracão*, each *orixá* comes to dance alone before the drums. The steps are complex and vigorous, and the community watches carefully to evaluate them and learn. Each dance highlights some feature of the personality and history of the *orixá*. Ogun dances with hard thrusts of his sword alluding to his battles. Oxossi picks healing leaves from the forest floor and draws his bow on his quarry. Omulu sweeps away disease and purifies the earth with his *xaxará* broom. Iemanjá brings the rolling ocean waves from her breasts. Xangô brings down lighting and justice. Iansá whirls in the storm winds. Oxun dances in luxury and refinement. With each dance the community participates in another phase of its history. Each dancer recalls the great dances of the past and the royal ancestors of Africa who now can emerge in this sacred space and time.

Perhaps another two hours pass. The *orixás* begin their final circuit of the *barracão*, turn one last time to the congregation, and back into the vestuaries. The drums come to a hard stop and the formal ceremony ends. Intimates of the *terreiro* and invited guests may now partake of Oxossi's feast. His foods are presented once again before his shrine in the sanctuary and then shared by those present. People sit casually around tables and benches and talk of the music and dancing. The *iaôs* will spend the night in the *terreiro*, attended by the *ekedis*, and gradually their *orixás* will leave them. There is often a lengthy transitional period when the *orixá* is replaced by its *erê*, the child spirit who manifests itself at the threshold of *orixá* consciousness. The night has been a good one. Oxossi is pleased with his ceremony, and the terriero is renewed with the power of the hunter king of Kêtu.

SPIRIT

The spirit of candomblé is the royal power of the *orixás* made present in the dances of their courts in Brazil. The candomblé rejoices at the public reinfusion of divine power. The members reaffirm their identity as Brazilian descendants and participants in African nations, they recognize the presence of the ancestors within and among them, and they share and show that power to serve the spirits and each other.

If the Haitian *ounfo* shows a world of revolutionary power and the easy familiarity of men and women of the land, the candomblé looks to the royal courts of Africa. While it may borrow elements of protocol from the Portuguese and Brazilian courts of Brazil's past, or from the still older ceremonials of Roman Catholicism, the candomblé *terreiro* faithfully carries on the royal traditions of Kêtu, Oyo, Ijesha, Oshogbo, and many others. In the services of the *ounfo*, the *lwa* enter into the drama of the ordinary lives of their Haitian serviteurs. They speak, joke, curse, prophesy. They are outsized images of and for the Haitian social environment: precarious military strength; lust of refinement; cousin farmers; and mocking death. The Brazilian *orixás*, by contrast, seem aloof, incarnate in the pageantry of the royal progress and dances of the *barracão*. They are dressed in extraordinary finery, wielding the most elaborate regalia. And amid this formal, hieratic display, they don't speak. The faces of their horses are without affect, eyes are nearly closed, masks to reveal the *orixá* manifesting itself through them.

The candomblés of Bahia were unique among the communities of the African diaspora in the degree to which they were able to maintain continuous and reciprocal contacts with Africa. Yet, while the elite can-domblés can all boast members who have visited Africa, the great major-ity of Bahians experience the mother continent in the dances of the *barracão*.

Roger Bastide notes how the architecture of the candomblé repro-duces Africa in reduced form. Drawing a parallel with the Christian church's reduction of pilgrimage to Jerusalem into the stations of the cross in a Catholic cathedral, Bastide writes:

> The *candomblés*, with the temples, the *pegi*, the groves of sacred trees, the houses of the dead, the spring of Oxalá, represent a reconstruction of the lost Africa. Moreover the first sacred stones were actually brought over from Africa, still impregnated with the supernatural force of the *orixás*—a force that, through mystic participation, was transmitted to the whole of the surrounding space.[68]

To enter the candomblé is to make Africa present, either by returning to Africa or bringing Africa to Brazil.

At Casa Branca the center pillar, the "staff of Oranmiyan," orients the community to Africa, the origins of the candomblé and of the earth itself. The staff is planted in the earth, connecting the community of Brazil with the earth of Africa. It brings the sky, the realm of the *orixás*, together with Onilé, the earth and ground of all life. By its reference to Oranmiyan, an ancient king of the Nagô people, the pillar has been likened to a phallus impregnating the cavity of the earth, engendering *axé*, the creative power of the universe.[69] At the pillar's base is secreted the *entoto*, containing the foundational symbols of the community, originally brought from Africa by Iyá Nassô a century and a half ago. The rhythms, songs, and dances call the *orixás* out of the earth, separating them out of the *axé* of the *entoto* into the personalities that will manifest themselves in the dancers. The invocation to each *orixá* is accompanied with bows "with eyes on the earth," a sign of respect in averting the direct gaze from the *orixá* and of recognition of the ground upon which all life stands. Sky and earth form twin halves of the calabash of the universe. Offerings to the *entoto* are accompanied with songs to Onilé:

> Onilé mojuba O
> Iba orixá—iba Onilé
> Ee Onilé mojuba
> Iba orixá, iba Onilé
>
> Onilé, we salute you
> The calabash orixá, Onilé is a calabash
> Onilé, we salute you
> The calabash orixá, Onilé is a calabash[70]

As the dancers orient themselves to the earth, they position themselves and the community in Africa. The staff of Oranmiyan stands in the earth of Ilé Ifé, the holy city and center of the earth's creation. By means of the ritual actions of rhythms, song and dance, human beings and *orixás* are brought into increasingly more intimate contact. On the one hand, the *orixás* are brought from Africa to Brazil. In the *xiré* we heard the *ogan* sing: "We play for Ogun, Welcome Ogun of Onire from across the ocean."[71] Members of the candomblé told Donald Pierson that each *orixá* has a home in Africa and that "they are summoned and they come at once."[72] Yet, just as the *orixás* are drawn to Brazil, so too, the community is carried to Africa. By orienting themselves to the earth of Ilé Ifé, they become contemporaries of the *orixás*, abolishing the ocean of space and time that separates them from the spirits.

The intimacy of the relationships between the *orixás* and their human children is shown in the *obrigaçãos* of candomblé: the private services of initiation and the public ones of the dance. As in vodou, the initiates of *candomblé* are brought into structures of ever-deepening relationships with the spirits. While the relationships, especially in the beginning, can be formal, even harsh, they often develop into a profound identification between human being and *orixá*.

In Ruth Landes's study of candomblé women, many of the human-spirit encounters were stormy.[73] The *orixás* were quick to punish their children when they neglected their *obrigaçãos*. She relates a story told by Edison Carneiro which he had learned from Mãe Germina, an *iyalorixá* in Angolan candomblé:

Once a pregnant lady vowed to Iemanjá, Queen of the Sea, that if a daughter were born, it would be consecrated to her. The great goddess of the depths granted the wish. A little girl was born who grew big and strong, but the mother forgot her vow. The family lived here in Itapagipe, by the sea, but the child was never allowed to enter the water.

One lovely morning a boat race was held in the bay of Pôrto dos Tainheiros, and the whole family went to it by canoe. The moment the child arrived at the water she became very restless. She screamed, and pulling the dresses of her mother and aunt, she called, "Mamma, see that pretty lady looking at me! Look Auntie, how the lady is speaking to me!" In a flash, then, she threw herself into the water.

The mother and aunt cried frantically, and someone sent for Pai Cache-Col—the same one who now practices in the south of the state. This Negro, Cache Col, came as fast as he could, bringing African drums and a golden tray. He told the orchestra to play, and he sang sacred songs, and he showed the tray to the Queen of the Sea. "Take this O Iemanjá," he called, "and return the girl." Iemanjá bargained obstinately with him, and tantalized the people by tossing the girl up and then dropping her into the water. The mother was in despair. The big drums roared, never ceasing, beating out songs of the mãe d'agua, the Senhora Iemanjá, from whose womb came all the orixás. Unable to lure the goddess out with the tray, Cache-Col finally threw it to the bottom of the bay, and only after it had sunk into the waves was the child returned. Then Cache-Col saw to it that the child was consecrated as a priestess of Iemanjá.[74]

The story draws together the themes of vows and calls, and of birth, death, and rebirth with initiation into the service of the *orixá*. The drums and offerings bring the initiate back from the depths of death, substituting unaware, natural life for life in the *orixá*. One dies and is reborn in Iemanjá, through the *obrigação* of drums and sacrifice.

In the film *Iawo* we see that throughout the six months of isolation, instruction, and presentation, the initiates are brought to deepening and more fluid relationships with their individual *orixás*. The spirits are ever more firmly "fixed" in their "heads." The actions of cutting and shaving, bathing, incising, and "feeding" the head, all "fix" the *orixá* within the very center of a person's consciousness. The *orixá* is recognized as a part of the person, "seated" or "mounted" upon their *ori*, the "soul" that precedes the birth of the body and survives its death.[75] Fixed within the container of the head, the *orixá* can manifest itself through the body, "incorporate" itself, just as the *ori* incorporates itself at the time of biological conception. Assisted by rhythms, songs, and dance, the *orixá* is delivered to the community by the mother, who gives birth to the spirit in her own body and the body of the human children in her care.

If metaphors of birth and rebirth describe the manifestation of the *orixás* in human initiates, images of horses and riders are employed to describe the relationship of service and control. As in Haiti, where the spirits instruct the congregation to "tell my horse" some information, so too in Brazil, the *orixá* is said to "mount" its human initiate and direct it as a rider directs a horse. When the spirit mounts the *ori* to take command of the body of the initiate, her garments are readjusted and tightened, to cinch her saddle and position her bridle for the *orixá* rider.

In describing her experience of manifesting the *orixá*, the priestess in Sarno's *Iawo* declared that the *orixá* was like the wind that embraces her, like a "shock in my heart." Her "head grows," people seem far away, "then I don't see anything anymore." The spirit is sudden, invisible, electric. The experience is disorienting, then invisible itself. As the external spirit mounts the internal person, the internal person becomes transparent to the spirit. And the spirit becomes manifest to the community. This is the service of community.

The *orixás* are thus understood as both external forces to and interior dimensions of human beings. As external agents they are vastly senior to humans beings, seen either as ancestors, charged with uncounted generations of applied spiritual force, or as the very forces of nature themselves, immensely older than humans and beyond their control. As interior dimensions of the human person, the *orixás* are a component of the human soul, an agency within every human that is recognized, "fixed," by rites of intensification.[76] The initiate is brought to "see" that the *orixá*, once external and responsive only to exchanges and inducements, is now part of her very self.

We see in rites of initiation and manifestation the same reciprocity of human and spirit that we found in the orientations of the *barracão*. Just as the *orixás* are "summoned" from Africa and manifested in Brazil by means of the work of the congregation, so too the spirits are placed inside the heads of the *iaôs*. Yet, as the community was brought to Africa, so the *orixás* are brought out of the bodies of the *iaôs*. The rites "fix" the presence of the *orixás*, give them location. This is as much to say that the *orixás* are everywhere and that the rites locate them "here," as it is to say that the *orixás* are everywhere and the rites allow them to be recognized, for those with eyes to see, "here."

Edison Carniero told Ruth Landes another of Mãe Germina's stories about Iemanjá:

People were gathered in the suburb of Tojuca at the end of the railroad line. Their candomblé was going strong, and a priestess was dancing, possessed of Iemanjá. Suddenly she began to run, and no one could stop her. Madly she raced into the river Catú with her clothes on. She disappeared, and her body did not rise again to the surface. Back on the bank the drums roared sacred songs, calling upon the goddess to return her. After a long time the priestess came out of the water, looking like Iemanjá herself. She was dressed in new garments delightful to behold. She returned to the temple, dancing as never before, and at dawn danced back to the river. She stepped into the water, then stepped out again. And everyone was still with astonishment, for her wonderful clothes were gone and she wore again her old ones. So people say that the Queen of the Sea actually came to earth that night to play with her favorite children in the suburb of Tojuca.[77]

Here, again the themes of service in the ceremonies of candomblé are played out. The natural element of the *orixá*, water, is paralleled by the rhythmic actions of the drums and dance. Both act as a medium to transform the human into the divine, or better, to reveal the human as divine. This is the service of the *candomblé*, it makes present the spirit of the ancestors. It gives its initiates eyes to see the past and present glory of the community within the harsh and oppressive world of Brazil. If the liberating force of Haitian vodou is found in the incarnation of the spirit of the successful revolution, so Afro-Bahians are liberated by reaffirming and reexperiencing their participation in the nations of Africa. As long as the rhythms are touched, the songs sung, and the congregation dances, the spirit that has sustained and enlightened the people cannot die. Service in candomblé is sharing that spirit through the rhythmic channels of power called *orixás*. The participants in candomblé manifest the spirit through their work, their service to the spirit, and to each other.

Cuban and Cuban
American Santería

Like the candomblé of Bahia, Cuban santería has its origins among the Yoruba priests and priestesses of the *orishas* who were enslaved at the close of the eighteenth and the first decades of the nineteenth centuries. Both in slavery and later when free, the Yoruba in Cuba and their descendants maintained a number of African religious practices by developing complex parallelisms among their experiences with their Yoruba ancestry, the other African traditions that had been brought to Cuba, and the Roman Catholicism that was the official religion of the island. The name *santería* reflects correspondence that they forged between the Catholicism enjoined upon them by Spanish law and their religious devotions remembered from Africa. They developed multiple levels of discourse to organize their heterogenous religious experience, referring, in more public and secular contexts, to the Yoruba *orishas* by the Spanish word *santos*. Alerted to the energetic devotions to these *santos* practiced by Afro-Cubans, outsiders labeled their religion *santería*, "the way of the saints."[1]

Since the Cuban revolution of 1959 over one million Cubans have come to the United States, among them many priestesses and priests of santería. This second diaspora of Yoruba religion may prove to be as significant as the first. With increasingly public postures and well-articulated presentations of the religion, devotees of the *orishas* living in the United States are challenging and reinvigorating all the African-derived traditions of the Americas. Devotion to the *orishas* is fast becoming one of the preeminent models for the revival of African consciousness in the United States. As more and more people of African descent throughout the Americas look to find what is African in the designation African American, they are finding the traditions of the *orishas* to be their inspiration and guide.[2]

This pan-diaspora tradition of the *orishas* has its origins in Cuba but has taken on a life of its own beyond the island and its *exilados*. In the major cities of the United States, particularly New York and Miami, priests and priestesses of santería number in the tens of thousands, and it is likely that they outnumber their brothers and sisters in Cuba. Beyond the priesthood, there are hundreds of thousands of Americans who participate in the tradition, ranging from relatively fewer committed "godchildren" of a particular line of *orisha* initiation, to numberless "clients" seeking consultations with priestesses and priests for help with critical problems. Nearly everyone of Caribbean background living in North American cities is touched by santería in some way.

Santería is a way of interaction with the *orishas*, the elemental powers of life. By speaking, feasting, and dancing with the *orishas*, human beings are brought to worldly success and heavenly wisdom. Santería is the spiritual road the Yoruba developed in Cuba. It sustained them through slavery and freedom and continues to sustain them in the harsh world of urban America. To understand santería we will again explore the community that developed and maintains it, the service that expresses it, and the spirit that gives it life and power.

COMMUNITY

With the successful revolution of Haitian slaves at the close of the eighteenth century, European investors were forced to look elsewhere for the profitable returns that they had realized from the plantation of Haitian sugar. The trade of the Spanish West Indies, once closed to all but

Spanish ships, had been forcibly opened by the British navy toward the close of the Seven Years War in 1762.[3] And so to Cuba came the massive apparatus of plantation culture, now made yet more efficient by refinements of technology and capital. Between 1774 and 1865 nearly 700,000 slaves were brought from Africa to work and die in this new industrial machine.[4] Yet the efficiency of this developed system of labor exploitation also made for conditions capable of maintaining African communities in exile. For with the massive importation of slaves from concentrated areas of the Western coast of Africa, large numbers of people were brought to Cuba in a relatively short period of time who spoke the same language, shared the same values, and venerated the same spirits.

African peoples reestablished, and in some cases reinvented their ethnic identities in Cuba. In many of the island's cities and towns they were able to form chartered assemblies of *cabildos* where people from the same African *nacion* or "nation" could gather for mutual support, entertainment, and worship. Among the nearly one hundred different African peoples who lost members to the Cuban slaves trade, at least sixteen *naciones* maintained registered *cabildos* in Havana by the time of emancipation in the 1880s.[5] Some *cabildos* identified themselves with a particular city of origin in Africa such as Ijesha or Kêtu in present-day Nigeria. In the cities of Havana and Santiago de Cuba, Yoruba and kiKongo were widely spoken and understood well into the twentieth century.

Cubans today still trace family trees back to African regions and cities, but, as in Haiti and Brazil, the prominent ethnic designations in Cuba, such as Lucumi (Yoruba), Carabali (Efik), Arara (Fon), and Congo (baKongo and others), have become liturgical rather than ethnic descriptions. Though many people are proud of their Yoruba or Kongo blood, their participation in these traditions is marked by initiation rather than descent. One chooses or is chosen to awaken one's African identity by being initiated into *la regla lucumi* or *la regla congo*, and many people receive initiations into different traditions. Nor were initiates limited to people of African descent. Folklorist Lydia Cabrera has documented the presence of white Cuban initiates into Carabali societies in the early nineteenth century.[6] Today Cubans across the racial and ethnic spectrum are devotees of African rites.

With the disintegration of the ethnic *cabildos* toward the end of the nineteenth century, Yoruba institutions increasingly took on the liturgical forms of the rites of private "houses" rather than the civil or "national" assemblies of African ethnicity.[7] The "house" of santería is a community related purely by the kinship of initiation into Yoruba rites. *Ilé* means literally "house" in Yoruba, and the Spanish equivalent is frequently *casa*. It has the more important extended meaning of "community" and "family." An *ilé* may be a "house" in the sense of a physical place: a building, court, or room where ceremonies are performed. In a particularly affluent or institutionally minded community, the *ilé* might be a separate building reserved for ceremonies, but in the great majority of communities, the *ilé* is a residence of a senior priest or priestess. He, or more often, she, is the head of the *ilé* in the deeper sense of "family." She or he is "godmother" or "godfather" to a family of sisters and brothers *en santo*, in the spirit. The family is ordered by seniority of initiation, the members' birth order in the spirit. The godmother (*madrina*), or godfather (*padrino*), as the head of the *ilé*, presides over these ceremonies of rebirth. They become the parents of the spirit reborn in their godchildren by directing the ceremonial delivery of the initiates' new spiritual selves. This new birth constitutes entrance into the family of the *ilé*. Members owe to each other the respect and responsibilities of brothers and sisters, and the deference and guidance appropriate between juniors and seniors. They owe filial devotion to their spiritual parents, who in turn guide and strengthen their growth *en santo*.

An *ilé* may be a small group of godchildren gathered around a single godparent, or a large hierarchy of priestesses and priests organized into a spectrum of initiated offices by a presiding *madrina* or *padrino*. Each initiation received by an *ilé* member sanctions certain kinds of spiritual work. While each *ilé* is fully autonomous in its organization and decisionmaking, a small *ilé* will have to join with others in order to be able to perform certain ceremonies requiring the special competences of higher or more esoteric initiations. Yet each *ilé* divines its own destiny, and the *madrina* or *padrino* is responsible for its membership, economy, calendar, and style of ritual observance.

A priestess in santería is called an *iyalorisha* (*iyalocha*) in Lucumi, meaning mother or wife in the *orisha* or spirit. The widely used Spanish equivalent is *santera*, one who "has," "makes," or "works" the spirit. A male priest is called *babalorisha* (babalocha), "father in the spirit" and *santero*. *Santeras* and *santeros* serve a variety of spirits called *orishas* and are dedicated to one particular *orishas* who has called them to its service. The *orishas* are independent, personal spiritual beings who empower all life. Santería is the development of the relationships between human beings and *orishas*.

Priesthood in santería is the capacity to pass on initiations, to create one's own family of godchildren. Thus priestesses and priests can establish more or less independent *ilés* of their own or join existing houses to form large extended families of initiates under a particularly powerful godparent. There is a certain amount of fission and fusion among *ilés* as different personalities seek their own spiritual visions. Thus the *ilé* is structured by the variety of initiations held by its members and capabilities of the members to pass them on to others.

Because of the necessity for discretion in professing a non-Christian religion in public life, it has been very difficult to determine the number of people who practice santería. Periodic suppressions from colonial times to the present, coupled with the tradition's emphasis on esoteric knowledge, have made most *santeras* and *santeros* loath to discuss their religious convictions with outsiders. One can participate in santería in a variety of ways, and so it will be useful to distinguish levels of participation in the tradition.

Knowledge of the existence and alleged practices of santería is general among the Cuban population and the Caribbean-American communities of the United States. Everyone "knows about" santería and knows "others" who practice it.[8] This general interest is in the instrumentality of santería to effect healings and cures. It is likely that most Cubans at some critical time in their lives have had some consultation with a *santera* or *santero*. But this casual contact, through hearsay or extraordinary consultation, does not constitute membership in the *ilé*. One must accept the godparenthood of a particular *santera* or *santero* and fulfill minimum responsibilities of service to her or him. This would entail attendance at and contribution to the feasts of the godparent's patron *orisha* sponsored by her or his *ilé*. People in this category would number in the hundreds of thousands, both in Cuba and the Cuban diaspora. Along this continuum would be those godchildren of the *ilé* who attend greater numbers of feasts, who are friends of a number of the *ilé*'s priestesses and priests and who are available for a variety of small services required by the *ilé*. They might be involved in all manner of ceremonial preparations such as accumulating the ingredients and cooking for the feast, running errands, sewing ceremonial clothes, and cleaning and maintaining the *ilé*. This constant presence at the ceremonies of the *ilé* provides one with the elementary language of the tradition, its exoteric songs and dances, and access to the personalities who might serve as one's godparent in the tradition.

The most important distinction to be made among the participants of the *ilé* is that between these faithful attendees and the true *santera* or *santero* who has "made the saint." This is a ceremonial passage into a lifelong commitment to a particular *orisha* wherein the initiate is reborn *en santo*, in the spirit. The discipline and expense necessary to be qualified for the ceremony, together with the seriousness of the pact of service to a patron *orisha* ensure that only a fraction of *ilé* members will be *santeras* or *santeros*. Where a medium-sized *ilé* may have twenty or thirty active attendees, it is likely that seven or eight would be initiated *santeras or santeros*.

Women comprise about 80 percent of the membership of the *ilé*. This number includes both *santera and nonsantera*[9] The plurality of women members and initiates may stem from the increased opportunities for leadership which santería offers when it is compared with European-derived Christian institutions. Both in Cuba and in the Cuban diaspora, women often have fewer opportunities for gathering outside the home than do men, and the *ilé* may be seen to provide an alternative and wider sisterhood than that of the home. *Santeras* will frequently say that women are "naturally" more sensitive to the spirit, that their experience with ambiguous emotions that characterize spiritual work is more extensive than that of men, and that their very bodies are more "open" to spiritual communion.[10] Yet despite women's relatively unrestricted paths for leadership, the largest *ilés*, and the leaders with the widest repute, seem to be men. Again this may have something to do with pressures against women rising as the scale and public nature of the *ilé* grows, or it may be their preference, or even natural ability to form smaller and more intimate communities.

Membership in an *ilé* is never considered to be a matter of personal choice, but rather a directive or call from an *orisha*. A few members, responding to a special call, might have been initiated as children, but most were chosen by their *orishas* for initiation in early adulthood. Many testify that it was their experience of a life-threatening illness which first prompted their devotion to an *orisha*. Illness, they say, is a call from the *orisha*, a crisis to a waken one to one's destiny as a servant of the *orisha*. Their subsequent pact with the spirit reflects both their respect for the power of the *orisha* to claim their lives and their gratitude for the *orisha*'s agency in effecting a cure.

Though each ceremony has a predetermined fee or *derecho* owed to the officiants, these are too low to constitute a living for the santería priesthood. Most *santeras* and *santeros* have jobs, often as domestics and laborers. These jobs are rarely very secure, and frequently members of an *ilé* turn to the spirits for help in meeting the very practical problems brought on by racism, poverty, and unemployment. The *ilé* is a mutual aid society, and, true to its origins in the *cabildo*, will often act as an institution to raise money for the emergency needs of its members. The *ilé* provides a great deal of support for people thinly served by government or charitable institutions. Perhaps the most important service offered by the *ilé* is health care. *Santeras* and *santeros* are justly famous for their diagnostic skill and herbal treatments. As in Haitian vodou and Brazilian candomblé priestesses and priests are expert in a vast pharmacopeia, and believers are quick to offer testimonies to the miraculous intervention of the *orishas* in effecting cures prescribed by *santeras* and *santeros*.

Since the Cuban diaspora of 1959, *santeras* and *santeros* in the United States have found themselves enmeshed in a new system of social organization and stratification. While the category of "lower class" is not absent from North American ways of organization, Cubans have found questions of color and ethnicity to be much more significant in the United States. North Americans see Cubans as "Hispanic" or "Latino" if they are light or medium complected and as "black" if they are dark. The *ilé* provides a place to leave behind these external, if not oppressive, markers of identity and reaffirm one family, one house in the spirit.

The *ilé* has provided a fraternal and sororal support system for some of the most oppressed people on earth. It has acted as a family in a society where no family life was possible and as a lodge to ease the burdens of the cultural dissociations that its members have been forced to undergo. What gives meaning to these medical, social, and cultural functions of the *ilé* is the service rendered to the *orishas*. In the minds of its members, the core function of the *ilé* is to honor the spirits and receive from them in turn guidance and assistance in all of life's endeavors. The *orishas* offer their children spiritual experience and heavenly wisdom which is marked by progress in the initiatory hierarchy of the *ilé*. The *ilé* sets out a path of spiritual growth, a road *en santo*.

There are essentially two complementary "roads" or paths (*caminos*) of initiation into santería: the *camino de Orula*, the path of knowledge; and the *camino de santo*, the path of the spirit. The former develops the intelligence to be able to read the activity of the spirit in ordinary life. The latter develops the spiritual faculties of the "head" to receive and manifest the spirit directly into the community. Each path brings its initiates toward the knowledge of their destinies and the ability to fulfill them with grace and power.

The *camino de Orula* is the road of the spirit of knowledge, known as Orula or Orunmila. It is said that Orula was present at the creation of the world and at the beginning of every life, and so sees into the destinies of things. Orula developed an art for human beings to interpret destiny, a method of divination called Ifa. Sometimes Orula is himself called Ifa recognizing that he is both a personality and a process. The master of the Ifa process is called *babalawo*, or "father of the mystery." Although there seem to be some instances of women *babalawos* in Nigeria, in the New World the office is to be held solely by men.[11] At some time during a man's participation in santería, the Ifa oracle may show that his *camino de Orula* is open and that he is called by Orula to be a *babalawo*. He receives a mark of entry on to this path in a ceremony called the "hand of Orula," and he begins what will be years of training in order to learn the techniques of Ifa from his *padrino de Orula*, a *babalawo* who is called to be his tutor and godfather. The training, which requires many years of study, culminates in a lengthy, costly, and elaborate initiation ceremony known only to other *babalawos*[12] Their ability to "read" Ifa for others, to divine the past, present, and future of the people who consult them, places them at the center of santería. They are considered by all to be the tradition's most senior priests.

Ifa is only one of several forms of divination practiced by santería priests and priestesses. While Ifa is reserved for the *babalawo* priesthood, a more common form of divination involves the mastery of verses associated with the patterns in the fall of sixteen cowrie shells. This *dilogun*, or "sixteen" divination is the prerogative of all priestesses and priests in the path of *santo*. It is said that Orula kept the art to himself until his wife Yemaya tricked him into revealing its secrets. The master of *dilogun* is the *italero*, who reads the shells for initiates on their great days of entry into *santo*.

Nearly all santería ceremonies begin with individuals seeking to know the spiritual source of their problems or the spiritual powers necessary to be invoked to achieve some end. Often as not these issues are the perennial ones of health, wealth, and love. Why has a person become sick and what spiritual power might be brought to bear to heal her? How might a person find a job or win the lottery? How can an errant spouse be brought home? An individual takes these problems to the *babalawo* who reads Ifa, or to another priestess or priest who reads *dilogun*. She or he determines the spiritual causes of the problem, and prescribes a certain path of behavior, an *ebo*, a "work." This might be an herbal bath, or fumigation of the house, a sacrifice to a patron spirit or a feast to honor the spirit and the other members of the *ilé*. At every step of the process, the knowledge of the *babalawo* is necessary to aid the person in communicating with the spiritual world.

The *babalawo* is also preeminent for his knowledge of the details of the tradition. In order to master Ifa, he must memorize in Lucumi thousands of verses of Ifa's poetry. These verses provide the texts of the essential information about the spirits, their histories, their characters, their songs and dances. The knowledge of these texts makes the presence of the *babalawo* essential for the conduct of many santería ceremonies, particularly the initiations into higher and more esoteric priesthoods. The path of the *babalawo*, *el camino de Orula*, is a path of knowledge, the acquired knowledge of precedents and prescriptions, and the accumulated wisdom to apply them to the lives of his godchildren.

Because of their knowledge of the herbalism, choristery, and ritual theology of the tradition, *babalawo* are often the *padrinos* of their own *ilés*. They have a large network of godchildren whom they have initiated into a variety of offices. They may act independently by visiting a number of different *ilés* as professional ritual consultants, but the path of knowledge cannot exist on its own. It must be accompanied by the path of the spirit. This other great path of santería, *camino de santo*, works with a different kind of spiritual wisdom, by developing the "heads" of the members of the *ilé*.[13]

The "head" or *ori* in santería is a spiritual faculty within the physical head of every individual. It preexists the physical body, choosing the destiny of an earthly life.[14] At death *ori* is disengaged from the body and moves on to other destinies. The *camino de santo* is a path of the development of an individual's *ori*, bringing the capacities of this spiritual dimension of the human psyche to guide and empower the whole person. Along the *camino de santo*, the *ori* is cleansed and strengthened to meet the challenges of life and reveal to the person the spiritual influences at work in the visible world. Most misfortune in life is attributed to a failure of people to listen to their *oris*. They do not keep their heads clear and cool, and so lose touch with the fundamental insight that is there to guide them.

The particular direction of the *camino de santo* is revealed to the person through divination, either by a *babalawo* or another priest or priestess. An oracle determines that her or his *ori* is on the path of a particular kind of spiritual power. This path takes the form of a relationship with the spiritual force and personality called *orisha*. The relationship with the *orisha* will become the primary focus of the individual's life. The *orisha* will provide all the directions for the development of the individual's *ori* and draw the individual ever deeper into the invisible meaning and power of the visible world. The *camino de santo* is the spiritual path of *ori*, the head, to work out its destiny *en santo*, in the way of the individual's patron *orisha*.

The seal of this personal relationship with an *orisha*, the "pact" with the *orisha* which confirms the initiate *en santo* is a formal initiation called *kariocha* or, in Spanish, *asiento*. This ceremony "seats" or "enthrones" the spirit on the head of the individual and marks the initiate as carrying the spirit within her or his person. Once the *orisha* is seated on a person's head, he or she becomes a true *santera* or *santero*, one who "has" the saint, and one who can "make" the saint for others. For once the *orisha* is enthroned on the head of an initiate, he or she can transfer that spirit, "give birth" to that spirit, in the heads of new initiates and, so, become a *madrina* or *padrino* in her or his own right. This capacity to "make" the *orisha* in others constitutes the priesthood of santería, the institutional line that separates the ordinary believer from the leadership of the *ilé*.

Santería is a path of growth *en santo*, growth in the service of the spirit and the family of the *ilé*. One learns to serve the spirit by serving one's sisters and brothers, godparents and godchildren in the spirit. This path begins with a call from an *orisha*, usually first perceived as a disturbance in life. This can be a problem which might prompt a visit to a priestess or priest; persistent headaches, difficulties with finding work, bad luck in love. To the trained eye these problems indicate the activity of an *orisha* seeking to arrest the attention of a spiritually naive person. The oracle will reveal the spiritual source of the problem, the *orisha* who is behind it, and the kind of service that the *orisha* is demanding. For those chosen, however, the *orisha* is sometimes demanding their very life. Many devotees remember that their call to the *orisha*'s service came through a life-threatening illness. In the throes of the experience, an *orisha* reveals itself as both the cause of the crisis and the hope for its resolution. The face of death opens up the devotees to the spiritual realities of life, and he or she begins a lifelong commitment to their patron spirit. Acquiescence to the demands of the spirit brings new life and a path of guidance forevermore. Individuals may postpone their obligations to the *orisha* and the spirit may be mollified by promises and increasing involvement in the life of the *ilé*. One may begin to respond to the call to service by simple gestures of care, assistance at ceremonies, small duties, favors, and gifts. Eventually the fulfillment of the pack with the *orisha* can no longer be delayed and a person will undertake the rigors and expenses of the *kariocha* initiation, the initiation into priesthood in santería.

SERVICE

Initiation is a commitment of service, both to the spirits to whom the initiate is bound as well as to the community. Without a community there would be no spirits, and without spirits no community is possible. The spirits call to serve them is the same call to serve the community of santería, for though the spirits offer spiritual wisdom and worldly power to the individual, it can be achieved only by humility before elders and generosity to juniors in the tradition. As with vodou and candomblé, the spirit is served in santería by actions which make the spirit present to a group of people. The more fully, powerfully, and gracefully one acts to make the spirit alive to others, the more one grows in the tradition.

Growth in santería begins with tiny acts of piety, humility, and generosity. One begins to be able to recognize the presence of the spirit in the actions and objects that the community has placed it in. One receives elementary objects which hold the power of the spirit and learns the basics of their care. If the community, in the person of an *iyalorisha* or *babalorisha*, sees that the novice has grown sufficiently so that a particular spirit is calling her or him to his service, a more intense cycle of ceremonies to show that presence may be put into motion. A *babalawo* or other priestess or priest will be consulted to determine the *orisha* who is "behind" the novice and if her or his path is open to priesthood. If the answer is yes, the novice undergoes a one-year process of transformation that is called in Lucumi, *kariocha*.

Kariocha

Santeros employ a variety of interrelated terms for the same process of initiation into the priesthood of the tradition. One may hear initiation referred to as *hacer santo* ("making the saint"), *coronación* ("crowning"), *asiento* ("seating"), or the most technical and so the most reserved term from Lucumi, *kariocha* ("to place the *orisha* on the head"). Each word reveals a good deal about the central values of santería and the relationship between humans and *orishas*.

To "make the saint" (*hacer santo*) is probably the most common term used to describe the process of initiation into the priesthood of santería. In describing their spiritual age, an initiate might say that she "made the saint in 1975." Or, when assisting at an initiation ceremony, one might say that "we made the saint last night." The usage emphasizes the role of human action in constructing the presence of the spirit out of symbolic ingredients. The *orisha* is "made" by the consecration of herbs, animals, foods, songs, and gestures. These are organized by the actions of sanctioned priestesses and priests to place, or perhaps reveal, the presence of the *orisha* in a variety of media, culminating in the body and personality of the novice.

Coronación likens initiation into the mysteries of the *orishas* to the crowning of African kings and their counterparts in Lucumi *cabildos*.[15] "To make a saint is to make a king," says Cuban *babalorisha* Oddedei, one of folklorist Lydia Cabrera's most accomplished teachers.[16] In Yoruba coronation ceremonies the king's head is covered with a crown that indicates that his head, *ori*, his personality center, is no longer his own, but carries the direct presence of his royal ancestors.[17] There is usually an image of a face on the front of the crown, which is likened both to this transpersonal royal presence and to Obatala, the primordial king of Yorubaland. When the king is crowned he is at once all his ancestors and his archetypal royal predecessor Obatala, the "owner of all heads." *Santeros* speak of priestly initiation into santería as being "crowned with the orishas." Their heads now carry and can be identified with the *orishas* that have been placed there at initiation.

Asiento has a double meaning in Spanish, connoting both "seat" and "seating" and "agreement" or "pact." Following the royal imagery outlined above, a throne is constructed for the novice and she or he is "seated" on it to receive the crown of the *orishas*. Thus the initiation is at once a "crowning" and an "enthronement." But the image of seating conveys another meaning that reinforces the relationship between humans and spirits. Just as the novice is seated on a throne before the community during the sacred time of initiation, so too the *orisha* is seated on a kind of throne, the head of the novice. The novice becomes a seat for the orishas as they take their place "upon" the novice's head. The central ceremony of initiation into santería is at once a "seating" of the human individual within and before the community and a "seating" of the *orisha* within and upon the human novice.[18]

The idea of *asiento* as "pact" comes forth in the recognition of initiation as a commitment between the *orisha* and the human being. The newly made initiate, regardless of her or his gender, is called *iyawo*, literally "bride" or "junior wife" in Lucumi. To be a *iyawo* is to be married to the spirit, with all the mutual rights and obligations of marriage. Throughout the temporary one-year novitiate that constitutes *iyawoage*, the junior "bride" is beholden to the spirit husband, a subordinate but reciprocal relationship of mutual service.

Kariocha is the Lucumi term for initiation and as much is reserved for the most serious and private discussions of the entry into the priesthood. *Ka ori ocha* means to place the *orishas* over one's head and recapitulates the metaphors of making, crowning, and seating that we have discussed above. The most fundamental and puissant symbols of the *orishas*' presence that are "made" during the initiation ceremony are stones (*otanes*).

WORKING THE SPIRIT

These *otanes* are found in the natural environment most dear to each *orisha*: Yemaya's ocean; Oshun's river; Eleggua's crossroads. They will be placed in the care of the novice for the remainder of her or his life and will be the principal altar through which she or he will interact with the *orishas*. At a key point in the middle of the ceremony of initiation into santería, the *otanes*, carrying the most concentrated presence of the *orishas*, are literally suspended over the novice's head. This "placing" of the *orishas* generates all the metaphors of entry into the religion. The head of the individual, the seat of his or her personality and destiny, is placed in a special relationship with the stone "heads" of the *orishas*. By being placed above the head of the novice, the orishas "crown" her or him, and so the orishas are "seated" on the throne of the head, established in a hierarchical relationship of above and below. The head provides the platform, the locus, the "seat," for the activity of the *orishas* in the world, the point out of which they can manifest themselves in all the complexity of the human body and intelligence. The head is a throne which the royal spirit can ascend, a "horse" which the spirit can "mount" and direct.

The metaphors do not end with the hierarchical relationships of above and below or the juxtapositions of upon and beneath. The *orisha* is not just "on" the initiate, but also "in" her or him. By a variety of symbolic actions the *orisha* is placed both "upon" the individual as the seat of the spirit, and "within" the individual as the spirit's vessel. By ingestion, anointing, and incision, the sacred ingredients which "make" the *orisha* are literally placed inside the body of the initiate. She or he eats and drinks *orisha*-consecrated foods, is soaked in *orisha*-valent poultices, is infused with *orisha*-active herbs and preparations. The spirit, now dwelling "in" the initiate, can be shown or manifested through her or his actions in public ceremony and in ordinary acts of generosity and power.

These metaphors of construction, seat, pact, throne, head, crown, "in" and "on," are documented in a remarkable ethnographic film by Judith Gleason and Elise Mereghetti, *The King Does Not Lie*.[19] Shot in Santurce, Puerto Rico, in 1991, the film chronicles the sequence of actions undertaken by an *ilé* that will initiate a young man into the priesthood of Shango. The meanings of the actions are illuminated by interviews with *santeros* and *santeras* and enriched by voiced-over English recitations of Lucumi texts.

We are told that Shango has "claimed the head" of one of the uninitiated members of the *ilé* and the women of the community are mobilized to make a throne for the coronation of a new king.[20] A section of a room is designated to be the *igbodu*, the sacred precinct where humans and *orishas* may interact. It is cordoned off from ordinary space by white cloth curtains, and its walls are draped with sumptuous cloth hangings of brilliant satin chevrons in Shango's colors of vital red and cool white.[21] As *santeras* carefully prepare the throne room, others are sewing the coronation garments that the new initiate, the *iyawo*, will wear when he is presented to the community at large. These are of red and white satin as well, hung with gold braid and beaded with pearls, and fashioned into Shango's characteristic costume of blouse, vest, paneled apron, and short trousers.

Outdoors, male members of the community prepare to gather the stones and plants which will embody and activate the *orishas* that are "made" through the ceremony. At least a hundred smooth stones are found in the riverbed and carried back to the *ilé*. The *orishas* are questioned by means of *obi*, the fall of four coconut shells, which determines whether the stones "vibrate in accordance with the *iyawo*'s head," and thus will be suitable vehicles for the *orishas* presence. The selected stones will become part of the permanent altar of the *iyawo*, the primary symbolic medium for presence of the *orishas* in his home and life.

The presence of the *orishas* in the mineral medium of stone is complemented by the preparation of certain plants. A *santero* obtains permission of Osanyin, the spirit of forest leaves, to enter *el monte*, the wilderness, and gather samples of the twelve leaves necessary to make Shango.[22] The leaves are bundled and brought back to the *ilé* where they are crushed with the stones to liberate their healing essences. An infusion of cool herbal water, laced with palm oil and other sacred substances, will provide an energizing bath for the stones, together with cowrie shells and other emblems of the *iyawo*'s alterpieces.

Two nights before the coronation day we are shown a uniquely Puerto

Rican element of the *ilé*'s ritual sequence that serves to frame the Lucumi core. A *misa blanca*, a spiritist service, is held to consult the ancestors of those present on their moral preparedness for undertaking the actions to come. Manifesting his spirit guide, one of the senior *santeros* tells the young men present to get their minds off their girlfriends and onto their departed mothers.

The next day the *iyawo* is taken to a clear mountain stream to be bathed in the life-giving waters of the *orisha* Oshun. A small offering of honey, palm oil, shrimps, and cornmeal is given to the river, asking the lovely *orisha* to "sweeten the passage." The *iyawo*'s old clothes are torn from his body as he is washed of the impurities of his old life. Before the camera an older *santera* reflects on her initiation:

> The experience in the river was beautiful . . . it was a beautiful place . . . I've never been able to find it again. And the water was nice and warm. I wasn't afraid, but I felt so different from that moment on. And going in silence and coming back in silence made me feel like I was another person already.

The *iyawo* is brought back to the house for the preliminary sacrifice of the *kariocha* cycle. He is seated before his ritual sponsors while a dove is offered to his *ori*, his inner spiritual self, which must sanction the seating of the *orisha*. In this calming ceremony the head and cardinal points of the body are "fed" with a poultice of ingredients sacred to Obatala, the *orisha* of clarity and serenity. The *iyawo* sits draped with a white shawl over his shoulders. He wears the great beaded necklace of Obatala across his chest hung from his right shoulder. All work with the *orishas* begins with this clarification of confusion. The *iyawo*'s head is anointed and tightly wrapped with a white kerchief, and he is left to sit in contemplation with this first purification of the "inner head." As the dove is immolated and its blood dripped on the *iyawo*, the congregation sings in Lucumi to the head and to Obatala who underlies all heads:

> *Eiyele tun* . . .
> The dove is full of devotion
> May we not see death upon our horizon

> Blood is falling drop by drop like rain
> And the dove flies toward heaven . . .

While the *iyawo* rests in isolation elsewhere in the house, certain priests and priestesses meet in the *igbodu* to prepare the cooling leafy water of Osanyin, the *omiero*. While they shred the "leaves of life," they sing in affirmation of their nature and history:

> *Kama ya iya* . . .
> Let us not tear ourselves from mother
> Let us never abandon our mother tongue
> Let us never forsake our way of worship
> Let us never sever the bond with our people
> Leaves of life
> Leaves of river and sea will save us
> Come with me to the hill of joy
> Where all leaves pull off easily . . .

Beginning with Eleggua, the opener of all ways in the spirit, they pray to each *orisha* and invoke its power to manifest itself through the stones, cowrie shells, and herbs that are bathing in the *omiero*. The *iyawo* is led to the entryway of the *igbodu* dressed in white and draped with a large white sheet. "Ago, Ago," he says, "open up." From within comes the question, "Who is knocking?" He answers, "Iyawo." "What are you seeking?" "Santo." "Which santo?" "Shango." These ritual questions constitute the initiate's verbal assent to the irrevocable transformations to come. Still covered in the white cloth, he is led into the *igbodu* and helped to step into a large steel tub. His necklace and head wrap are removed and, as his head is washed, the *santeros* and *santeras* sing:

> *Aidiji dide Eshu odara* . . .
> Fearless Elegba, stand up
> It is good [for you to] stand up, fearless one
> Everyone make way for the owner of the road
> Bathe the head with leafy water
> That it may flourish forever and ever . . .

After the women leave the room the *iyawo*'s clothes are ripped from him again. He stands upon them in the tub, and naked, with eyes closed, he is bathed in the *omiero*. Cleansed in the power-filled water, he is wrapped in white cloth and led out of the area. The *igbodu* is then prepared for Shango's coronation. The floor is painted with red and white pastes, ready, "to receive the imprint of Shango's cloud mortar." The *iyawo* now dressed in white shirt and pants and with his head still wet from the *omiero* bath, is seated on the *apotí*, Shango's mortar-throne. *Santeras*, in turn, cut his hair and then shave his head.

> *Awa ni ibo leri* . . .
> We have a need to clear the headland
> Impinging on its owner
> Elegba permits us to grasp the knife
> And cut away the cover.

The *santeras* shave the head in a clockwise direction, the cycle of release and death. Completely shaved, the exposed head is now open to the full presence of the *orisha*. A white poultice of herbs is placed upon it, then the red blood of a quail. The *santeras* then paint the head of the *iyawo* in a counterclockwise pattern, the motion of growth and birth. Pure white *efun* chalk and red crushed camwood form concentric circles atop the initiate's head. His face is painted with the royal marks of the leopard.[23] At this point certain elements of the ceremony were considered by the *ilé* to be too secret and sacred to be filmed. Out of deference of these wishes, the filmmakers edited out the reception of the "deeper engravings" of the "leopard": very small cuts in the skin of the cheeks, nape, forehead, and center of the scalp. These cuts are made as openings through which the herbal presence of the *orisha* is injected into the *iyawo*'s body.

The moment has come for the *kariocha* proper, the crowning of the initiate with the stones and emblems of the *orishas*. Four cloths are suspended directly over the head of the *iyawo*: white, blue, yellow, and red. These represent the four directions of the canopy of heaven, and the four elements, air, earth, water, and—crowning the others—Shango's fire. Each of the tureens carrying *orisha*'s stones and emblems is placed on the cloths, resting against the nape of the *iyawo*'s neck.[24] These he carries and may pass on. The final container, the wooden *batea* of Shango, is placed on the cloths on the *iyawo*'s head. Drums sound, songs ring out to the owner of the crown. The *iyawo* buckles as he receives Shango to the shouts of "Kawo, Kabiesile!" "Welcome home your majesty!"

Again out of deference to the wishes of the community, the filmmakers do not show us the ensuing spirit manifestation. Though manifestation does not always happen at this time—and for some *santeras* and *santero* it never occurs—an *orisha* will often choose this moment to take her or his "seat." The personality of the *iyawo* becomes transparent to the personality of the central *orisha*, and the *orisha* speaks and acts through the body of the *iyawo*. The *orisha* Shango, placed within and on the novice in herbal and mineral forms, now acts through him, in his form as a personality, the exuberant king of Oyo.

In this holy state the *orisha* through the *iyawo*'s is usually fed with the blood of freshly-killed animals. The *iyawo*'s tongue is sometimes cut with small incisions to insure the novice with the gift of the *orisha*'s speech. The blood of the sacrifice with the blood of the *iyawo* strengthens the *orisha* and completes the cycle of herbal, mineral, and animal applications of his power. The *orisha* though the *iyawo* will address the community, making all the proper salutations and thanking them for the ceremony.[25]

As Shango is fed through the *iyawo* manifesting him, other *orishas* are fed through their newly consecrated altar mediums, the stones. A series of animals sacred to Shango are killed and their fresh blood poured over the stones. The congregation sings in Lucumi:

> *Agbo fi roro fi roro bale* . . .
> Shango's ram is swinging his mane upon the earth
> The ram is suddenly still . . .
>
> *Eran popo fun mi; eran popo fun mi eje* . . .

Fresh blood combined for my well-being
Breath of life, blood is falling on ancestral ground . . .

The feast is not only for the *orishas*; the humans attending them must also join in the feast. "*La sangre para el Santo, la carne para el Santero.*" "Blood for the saint, meat for the priest."[26] The animals are dressed and cooked in old recipes sacred to Shango. They will be served at the great feast on the following day, the *dia de media*, or second of the great three days of *kariocha*.

In *The King Does Not Lie* the middle day opens with the *iyawo* on the floor of the *trono*, eating consecrated food and shaving with an electric razor on a long cord. He is then repainted in his leopard markings, dressed in the sumptuous coronation clothes, and wrapped with a belt of *mariwo* palm fronds.

> *Fin fin okan*
> With my heart I spot the royal animal.
> And behold, today, Shango is becoming a royal leopard!
> And palm fronds will render him impervious to danger.

In full royal dress, complete with crown and *oshé* axe-scepter, the *iyawo* holds court before the wider community: priestesses and priests from other *ilés*, friends, and family. A percussion ensemble, consisting of a bead-netted gourd called a *chekere*, an iron bell, conga drum, and two rasped gourds called *guiros*, has already completed the traditional cycle of rhythms, the *oro de igbodu*, in the privacy of the sanctuary. The percussionists, having stood before the enthroned *iyawo* and the fed stones of the *orishas*, saluted each in turn through its special rhythms. In Cuba or New York the rhythms might have been provided by sacred two-headed *bata* drums, but these are relatively rare and the "*guiro*" ensemble has been substituted here.

The film takes up the ritual sequence with the movement of the *guiro* orchestra from the *igbodu* to the patio outdoors, where the wider community has assembled. This second, public cycle of rhythms is called a *bembé*, and, as opposed to the "dry" rhythms of the *igbodu*, it calls for singing and dancing. An *apón* songmaster sings a sequence of *orisha* songs accompanied by the percussionists. He is skillful in getting everyone present to enjoy themselves. They respond to his vocal calls and come forward to dance to the songs for their own *orishas*. The songs and rhythms invite the *orishas* to manifest themselves among their initiates and dance and feast with the congregation.

Perhaps because of the presence of the cameras, or the community's desire not to have the spirit manifestations filmed, the *orishas* do not choose to "mount" their human children at this particular *bembé*. The congregation is content to praise Shango, the patron of drumming and dancing.

> Kabiesi [Majesty]
> Lively king
> You make your dance a thing of joy
> Look at us from hands to feet to hips
> Resemble you in generosity and precision
> Elegant, leisurely king
> In whose company everyone can enjoy life fully
> *Kawo-e, Kawo-e, Kabiesile!*
> Welcome, Welcome, Welcome home your majesty!

At the conclusion of the *bembé*, a bucket of water holding all the lingering doubts and negativity of the community is danced to the outside of the house. With prayers to the threshold guardian Eleggua and to Olokun, ruler of the ocean's depths, the water is tossed into the street.

In the morning of the third day the community gathers for *nangaré*, the only part of the initiation cycle that honors the Creator, God Almighty, Olodumare. A simple porridge is made in memory of Shango's rescuing the people of Tapa from drought. With Olodumare's help Shango transformed a handful of cornmeal and a little water into a feast for many. In this way the community, spent with the luxury of yesterday's feast, remembers their dependence on the creator through good times and bad. Each person sips from the common calabash and thanks God almighty for the gift of life. Greeting the rising sun they sing:

Ina tutu kwel aiye . . .
O Great Fire
Please cool the earth
That we may have crops again . . .

The focus then returns to the *iyawo* for the third day of his initiation, the day of *itá*. *Itá* is a thorough divination with sixteen cowrie shells, the oracle called *dilogun* taught to all priestesses and priests. On this day the reading is deep indeed for it will determine the basic orientations of the *iyawo*'s life *en santo*. He will learn his own particular roads in the spirit, the ethics and styles appropriate to the spiritual life that he has just undertaken, and the spirits that he will receive in the future. *Itá* will reveal the *iyawo*'s own character dispositions and the life restrictions or *ewo* that will maximize his resources in dealing with problems. The fall of the cowries may reveal the events of the future, the challenges that the future offers the *iyawo*, and the means to meet them. At a special moment the cowries reveal the *iyawo*'s new name, "*Oba ko puro*," "The king does not lie." This name is drawn from the *dilogun* verses known as *Obara*:

> There are those who will say that you are lying
> When in fact you are telling the truth
> Much suffering to endure
> Before the inevitable blessings . . .

A final rite brings the *iyawo* out into the world after his isolation of the *ilé*. He is taken by his initiation sponsor to greet the "owner of the market," the *orisha* Oya, in a large produce market in town. He leaves an offering of coins in the four corners of the store, purchases fruit for his *orishas*, and steals some fruit for Eleggua. It is said that market owners are familiar with the small ritual thefts of white-clad *iyawos* and look the other way.

The next day the *iyawo* will return to his ordinary life in urban Puerto Rico, but it is a new life *en santo*. A novitiate year awaits the *iyawo* once he returns to his own home. Each *orisha* may demand different *ewo*, or restrictions, for the course of the year, but the basic pattern is set by the *orisha* Obatala, "the owner of all heads." The *iyawo* must wear white and keep his head covered at all times. He must refrain from any adornment. He may only eat certain foods, and he must avoid a variety of places where spiritual influence may be so powerful as to destabilize his vulnerable state. The most conservative houses demand a full year of sexual continence. All these measures are to protect the "new head" of the *iyawo* to rebuild his relationship with the outside world through the lens of his *orisha* and his duties toward the spirit.

Gradually, in three-month intervals, the restrictions are lifted and the *iyawo* is considered mature enough to wear ordinary clothing and jewelry, associate with friends and travel as he likes, and live an ordinary life within the bounds of the lifelong guidelines revealed in the *itá*. The *iyawo* now becomes a *santero* himself, the servant of all his seniors in the *ilé*, yet capable of giving birth to the *orishas* that he carries within himself into the heads of his own godchildren. As the servant of the *ilé* he will be expected to attend all the important functions of the house, to cook and clean, as well as sing and dance, to manifest the spirit in the variety of ways that *santería* recognizes it. The most puissant manifestation of the *orisha*, as we have seen, is in the heads of its devotees, using their bodies for the service of the house as living personalities. As *kariocha* places the *orisha* "on" and "in" the heads of its devotees, the dance ceremonies of *santería* release this spirit to be fully present among the assembled congregation. We may look now at this most concentrated service to the spirit and the community, the drum dance called *bembé*.

Bembé

The central public ceremony of santería, where the spirit is most widely recognized to be shown to the community, is a drum dance that goes by a variety of names depending on the kind of drums to be used. In the Cuban-derived communities of the United States, the most general term is simply *tambor* in Spanish or *bembé* in Lucumi. A variety of drums might be used in a *tambor* or *bembé*, and there is considerable dispute among *santeros* about what kind of drums are appropriate in what contexts. The most prestigious drums are called *bata* and, depending on the care given to their preparation, the *bata* are considered to be the most universal method of calling down the *orishas*.

Bata are hourglass-shaped wooden drums with different-sized heads at each end. The heads are often banded by a ring of small bells, while the body of the drum might be draped in elegant cloth robes. The drums are held across the knees of a sitting drummer who plays a head with each hand. *Bata* are grouped in threes: the largest being the *iyá* mother drum whose larger head might be eighteen inches in diameter. The *iyá* is the leader of the rhythms and directs the other two. The middle-sized *bata* is the *itotele*, and the smallest is the *okonkolo*. At a *bembé* the three *bata* might be accompanied by another musician with a bell or a calabash with a bead net called a *chekere*.

To fulfill the call to the *orisha* that makes a *bembé*, the drums must be complemented by singing and dancing. We turn to Migene González-Wippler for her description of a *bembé* that she attended in New York sometime in the 1970s.

Bembés might be called for a variety of reasons, and almost all take place in the homes of *santeras* and *santeros*.[27] A *bembé* might be held to celebrate the anniversary of an initiate's *kariocha*, to appeal to or thank an *orisha* for a special favor, or to celebrate the calendar feast of an *orisha*. Like the Nagô of Brazil, the Cuban Lucumi adapted their annual festivals to the liturgical calendar of the Roman Catholic Church. The *bembés* for the *orisha* Babaluaiye are celebrated on the Catholic feast of St. Lazarus, a popular saint in the Latin world whose tradition developed out of a parable told by Jesus (Luke 16:19–31). Babaluaiye is the same *orisha* as the Brazilian Omulu, and his name reflects his dreadful and miraculous power. Babaluaiye is the spirit of sickness and health and the transformed vision of the world that disease affords. His worship is a plea and commitment to transform the pain of suffering into wisdom. Both the names "Babaluaiye" ("Father of the World") and "Omulu" ("Child of the Lord") are euphemistic avoidances of a name so powerful that it should not be spoken lest it visit disease on those who speak it. Many *santeras* and *santero* will not even say "Babaluaiye" and prefer the Catholic parallel term "San Lazaro."

On the feast of San Lazaro, 17 December, Migene González-Whippler attended a *bembé* for Babaluaiye held by a well-known *santero* named Manolito. "Several hundred" people attended the ceremony. Manolito had created an elegant throne of silks, fruits, and flowers in order to display the fundamental symbols of Babaluaiye, and all the guests prostrated themselves before the symbolic presence of the spirit.

> In one corner, in the center of an exquisite altar, stood a large and ornate statue of Saint Lazarus, flanked by two heavy golden candlesticks upon which burned two tall white candles. On both sides of the altar, two large porcelain urns, laboriously embossed in gold and purple, over-flowed with masses of flowers. Directly over the altar, and extending to the sides, was a pallium formed of intertwined flowers and masses of *cundiamore* (an herb used to cure diabetes, and sacred to Babalú).[28]

Seated before this display and facing the shrine are the drummers who begin with the *oro de igbodu*, a litany of unaccompanied rhythms for each of the *orishas* of the house in strict sequence, culminating with those of Babaluaiye. The congregation, which had been chatting and enjoying a variety of foods beloved by Babaluaiye, moves to stand behind the drummers and hear their rhythmic praises to the *orishas*. After some time when the *oro* is complete, the drummers move to face the congregation, opening up a space on the floor for dancing. This second, longer sequence is called *eya aranla*. Again the appropriate rhythms are played for the *orishas* of the house, this time accompanied by the singing of the songmaster *apón* and the responses of the congregation.

First is Eleggua, the opener of the paths, familiar to so many societies of the African diaspora.

> O great one, I salute you.
> O great one, I salute you.
> O great one, I salute Eleggua, Eshu on the road.
> Open up, Open up.
> Open up, Open up.
> Open up, *Ilé*, Open up.[29]

Songs for each of the *orishas* follow in turn and with each new spirit being praised, members of the congregation who were crowned with that spirit come forward to dance in its honor. Children of Obatala dance with slow, stooped movements of the old king. Initiates of Yemaya roll and turn with the turbulent motions of the sea. Children of Oya whirl with the warrior power of the wind, and children of Oshun move with the hauteur of the beautiful young queen.

After a short intermission, the drumming and dancing take a different turn, a deliberate call to the *orishas* to mount their human horses and speak directly with their devotees. As the drumming resumes a dancer comes forward whose authority and precision of movement impresses González-Wippler. He dances with a limping movement, stamping on one foot, trembling yet still moving elegantly to the rhythms. The *apón* recognizes that Babaluaiye has descended on this dancer and, exchanging places with the *chekere* player, moves up to the dancing Babaluaiye. The *apón* speaks to the *orisha*, spurring him by the rhythm of the instrument and verbal barbs to speak to the congregation. González-Wippler asked her *madrina* who had brought her to the feast about the dancer for Babaluaiye and received this answer:

When someone wants to give a tambor to an orisha for whatever reason, he must first find a santero or santera who's a child of that orisha, and who knows how to dance to the batáa. If the omo-orisha [child of the orisha] agrees to dance in the tambor, then the person offering the tambor must pay him a derecho [fee] for the service and have a beautiful costume made, in the colors and style worn by the orisha, for the omo-orisha to wear. But he's not allowed to wear it until after he's danced to the orisha and been possessed by the saint. Then some other santeros take him to another room and dress him in the orisha's costume. When he returns to the main room, the orisha occupying his body blesses those present at the tambor.[30]

As the special Babaluaiye dancer settled into his manifestation, he was indeed brought into another room to be outfitted in his ceremonial clothes. During his absence others in the congregation began to receive their *orishas* as well. González-Wippler notes that another Babaluaiye descended on one of his children, followed by an Obatala, an Agayu, Yemaya, Ogun, and Oya. Each roved the room with characteristic movements and demeanor. Yemaya smiled and embraced her congregation with maternal acceptance. Ogun scowled and played roughly with the children in attendance. The second Babaluaiye performed healings for supplicants with cigar smoke and strong gestures with his hands. González-Wippler describes an encounter with Oya the stormy warrior queen *orisha*.

> An elderly iyalocha, her gray hair streaming wildly around her face, came in from the back of the room, possessed of Oyá. In her hands she carried a large basket full of popcorn which she gave by the handful to a chosen few. Standing at the outer edge of the circle, I saw her approach. I saw her bright restless eyes single me out among the rest of the people. Soon she was by my side offering me a fistful of popcorn. I lowered my eyes, unable to withstand the orisha's persistent, unwavering glance, and extended my hands. I felt the soft light touch of the popcorn, then the hands of the orisha closed around mine. The feeling of unearthly power exuding from those glacial iron hands was so extraordinary I felt my arms tingle all the way up to the elbow. Her touch terrified me, but I made an effort to control my fear—and looked up to find her smiling cagily.
>
> "Don't be afraid, my daughter," the orisha said. "Take of Oyá's strength. Don't fear her. She'll be good to you always."[31]
>
> Amid these manifestations the premier Babaluaiye returns, dressed in the orisha's traditional costume—knee breeches and a close-fitting tunic reaching just to his hips. Both garments were of sackcloth, trimmed in purple braid with gold designs along the sleeves and legs. A wide purple band circled the omo-orisha's forehead and two purple alforjas [shoulder bags] were crisscrossed over his chest; in one shoulder bag he carried toasted corn and in the other the kept his beggar's alms. Bare-legged and barefoot, he carried a large sheaf of herbs tied with a purple ribbon in his right hand and a long staff in is left. The people offered him alms as he went by, and he humbly accepted them.[32]

Babaluaiye proceeds through the crowd toward the drums, receiving prostrations and greetings from all nearby. When he reaches the drums his special rhythms are struck up and the entire congregation, orishas and human beings, sing his praises. Babaluaiye holds the power of death over all houses, and his songs reflect the necessity of submission to this power:

> All people sleep and never wake up.
> Babalu, please wake me up in my room.
> Babalu, spare me my house.
> I will follow the ancestors,
> Follow the ancestors home.
> Happy, happy, happy home.[33]

Babaluaiye proceeds to organize a healing for the feast's patron, Manolito. Together with the other Babaluaiye and Obatala, and premier Babalyaiye passes fruits and live doves over Manolito. They lick his exposed skin, like the dogs in Jesus's story of Lazarus. Babaluaiye then throttles the doves and shares their blood with the other *orishas*. He daubs some blood and feathers on Manolito's head, feeding his Babaluaiye within.

The *orishas* continue to dance performing healings for supplicants and offering advice and blessings to those who approach them. González-Wippler does not tell us how the *bembé* ends, but a usual practice is for the drummers to play rhythms to induce each of the manifested orishas to "dismount" their human children. This is not always easy to accomplish as the *orishas* are strong-willed and delight in their participation at the feast. But, once, achieved, the drummers play a short series of unaccompanied praises to each of the house's *orishas*. A pail of water is danced before all the company, taken outside, and emptied into the street. This cleanses all present. The pail is returned empty before the drums. With a flourish the music stops and the *bembé* is concluded.

The spirit of santería, like that of vodou and candomblé, grows out of the community in action. The *orishas* are made present *by* the actions of the community and *in* the actions of the community. There are no *orishas* without human beings. The human beings who "make" the *orishas* have grown out of a particular historical experience of urbanism, enslavement, and transculturation. In the second diaspora of Cubans in the United States, *santero* have once again adapted elements of the religion to translate into the new communities of urban America. They have struggled to bring together, under the harshest and direst of circumstances, the many disparate elements of their multiple heritages into a "mosaic" of religious actions.[34]

Like vodou and candomblé, santería has built its mosaic from the outside in. While freely adapting externals to styles and forms of their environments, the *santero* have constructed an inner core that is consonant with the community's Lucumi roots. These "inner" African actions correspond to the inner core within the devotees, their "heads" which they have inherited from their ancestors. Vodou frames its services with the Catholic prayers of official Haiti, before moving to Dahomey. Candomblé sheds its Brazilian identity as it moves within the sacred precincts of the *terreiro* and the courts of the *orisha* kings. For santería the externals are the names and images of the saints which give the tradition its "external" name, *santería*. While the entire display of the *igbodu* is a collage of allusions to all levels of the community's experience, the *orishas* are only "made" by the herbs, blood, rhythms, and songs brought from Africa. The spirit of santería is thus to be found in its orientation to Africa, the reciprocal relationship between spirit and human beings, and the shared manifestation of the spirit in communal dance.

The innermost space of santería is the *igbodu*, the sanctuary room of the *ilé*. Igbodu means literally "sacred grove" in Lucumi and recalls its African usage as the place of encounter between the spirits in the unknown "beyond" the town and the known human community within. In his study of the symbolic architecture of the *ilé*, David Brown extends an insight of Roger Bastide. Bastide saw that candomblé "reduced" the sacred geography of Yorubaland into the precincts of the *terreiro*.[35] Brown sees the same process brought still further in the Cuban and Cuban-American context. He writes: "Where the Candombles could offer discrete little houses (*casas*) or rooms (*cuartos) to each orixá*, La Regla de Ocha installed all of the *orichas* in a single room, the *igbodún* or *cuarto sagrado* ("sacred room"), or even in a multi-shelved cabinet called the *canastillero*."[36]

This process of "condensation and miniaturization" begins with the reconstruction of the African grove in the open air plaza of the Cuban residence and is brought farther yet into the apartments and houses of urban North America. In each case the African sacred space must be reconstructed within already existing domestic architecture which was built for very different purposes.

The reconstruction of the *igbodu* in urban America reminds us of the primacy of Africa in the spirituality of santería. The transportation of herbs, stones, and animals with Lucumi identities to the *igbodu*, both for initiation in Puerto Rico and for the *bembé* in New York, shows the recreation of African vegetable, mineral, and animal worlds. As these are energized with songs, rhythms, and dances, they become African as do the human beings who make the spirits present. The *orishas* "live" in Africa and by means of the actions, the "work" of the community, they can live in Cuba or Puerto Rico or New York.

The *orishas* "live" through the "work" of the community. The *orishas* need the "work" of the community to live. The generalized term for any "work" for the *orishas* is *ebo*, which is usually translated as "sacrifice." While the preparation of food for the spirits and the letting of blood is an important kind of *ebo*, any activity in honor and praise of the *orishas* is *ebo*. Any action from the simple respectful touching of the ground to the *kariocha* or *bembé* is an *ebo* for the *orishas*. The purpose of *ebo* is, first, to bind the individual in a series of exchanges with the spirits and, second, to awaken the individual to the subtle presence of the spirits within herself or himself.

In *kariocha* the *iyawo* makes a pack with the spirit—"life for life"—that she or he will give his life to the spirit in exchange for a life of power and grace. Often this pact is made as a release from the physical death of the individual; the novice offers her or his life to the *orisha* in order not to die. The spirit will thwart death in exchange for the initiation of the individual. The novice makes a *promesa* to the *orisha* that she or he will give her or his new life to the spirit. This involves an ever more fluid series of exchanges between human being and spirit. The human gives *ebo*: food, praise, fidelity, obedience. The individual becomes a *iyawo*, a bride to the spirit, bound by the complex reciprocity of marriage. Humans and spirits "give that the other may give," growing stronger and more confident in the reliance that one might place in the support of the other. This understanding of *ebo*, the relationship of human and spirit, is based on respectful exchange, a dialogue between unequals: Queen and subject, parent and child, spouse and "bride."

But the dynamism of the initiatory system suggests a mysticism of identity as well as the dialogic relationship of human being and *orisha*. In *kariocha* the *iyawo* not only makes a pact with the *orisha* but has the spirit placed "upon" and "inside" her or him. Even though the spirit may prevent the physical death of the *iyawo*, she or he must still give her or his "life" in the ceremonial death and rebirth of the *kariocha*. One dies to the old life and is reborn *en santo*, in the spirit. The innermost identity of the *iyawo*, the *ori*, becomes the "throne" or "seat" for the *orisha*, the head's "master." Santería shares this Yoruba psychology with candomblé where the *orisha* becomes an alternate personality, a more powerful and authentic dimension of the self. The dominant *orisha* is both the *iyawo*'s "parent" and herself or himself, for the spirit is within her or him. In the dynamic progress of santería initiation, the *iyawo* becomes her or his *orisha*, through the development of small and large exchanges and in the manifestations of the *bembé*.

The transformation of *kariocha* gives *santeros* new eyes to "see" the presence of the *orishas* in objects and people. The *orishas* are manifested through a variety of symbolic media. The *orishas* are both "in" herbs and "are" herbs; "in" natural forces and "are" natural forces; "in" drum rhythms and "are" drum rhythms; "in" human beings and "are" human beings. It is through the work the *ebo* of the community that these complex dialogues and identities can be experienced. In initiation they can be seen with new eyes and in the *bembé* they can be shared, in movement to "work" the spirit for all the community to see and feel.

The *ebo*, the "work," binds the community to the spirit, and reveals the spirit within the community. The spirit is shown and shared through the bodies of its "horses," "children," and "brides." At the *bembé* for Babaluaiye the atmosphere was festive, joyous, and dramatic. González-Wippler says of her experience greeting an *orisha*: "Obatalá turned his dark luminous eyes upon me, opened his arms, and gently, with infinite tenderness, pressed me against his chest. Suddenly I was flooded with love. I leaned my head on his shoulder and his touch was bliss. I never before knew or felt such softness and warmth. I wanted to remain in his embrace forever."[37]

From the harsh world of plantation Cuba to the mean streets of New York, the *orishas* allow the community to show this love that can only "descend" or emerge from the hard work of the dance. The *orishas* and the community depend on this work to live. From all the notions of *orisha* that we have considered—parent, spouse, liege, self—it is perhaps most purely expressed in the *bembé* as rhythm. The *orishas* are "called" by their drumbeats, but they also "are" these rhythms, vibrations of the experience of the community. The rhythms are echoed, redoubled, and textured by the counterpoint of the *bata* orchestra, the sounds of the bell and *chekere* gourd, the songs of the *apón* and the responses of the congregation, and finally, in the dances of the *orishas* and human beings. The spirit lives in Ilé Ifé, and Ilé Ifé is where the community works to make the spirit present.

Revival Zion in Jamaica

Revival Zion is a religious tradition of Jamaica which offers an African way of entry into the spiritual world of the Christian scripture. Its name is taken from the Christian revivals which ignited Jamaica in the 1860s, but its roots go back to the many different African religious traditions brought to the island in the eighteenth century. From these roots Jamaicans of African descent developed new traditions in slavery and in freedom. As they came to explore the world of the Christian Bible, they found that the African experience of the ancestors could be remembered and celebrated. In the Bible, the desperate trials of enslavement, impoverishment, and exploitation could be met with power. The Bible offered a vision of a new heaven and new earth. This is the world of Revival Zion, and this portrait, like those of vodou, candomblé, and santería, will bring us toward the religious experience of Jamaica's revivalists by describing the community which developed and continues to maintain the tradition, the services they perform to embody it, and the spirit which inspires it.

COMMUNITY

Between 1655 and 1807 nearly 750,000 African men, women, and children representing scores of different cultures were brought to Jamaica as slaves to labor in the cultivation, production, and export of sugar.[1] Yet a census of 1807 reveals a slave population of some 320,000, indicating something of the dreadful mortality of slave life.[2] To these survivors fell the task of reconstructing a coherent society out of the remaining fragments of African social institutions that had been handed down over generations of people enduring the unremitting coercions and constraints of plantation life. Afro-Jamaicans found their equilibrium in a variety of neo-African religious institutions, elements of which have come down to the present day. Our first records of the religious life of Afro-Jamaicans come to us from planters and colonial officials, who by the end of the eighteenth century began to recognize, if not understand, two related religious institutions among the slaves, *obeah* and *myal*.

In a 1789 report answering queries from London about the treatment of slaves, the legislator and historian Edward Long wrote of a kind of "witchcraft or sorcery," a "science" brought from Africa to Jamaica called *obeah*. On the authority of *obeah*-men among the slaves, he writes:

> The Negroes in general, whether Africans or Creoles, revere, consult, and abhor them; to these oracles they resort, and with the most implicit faith, upon all occasions, whether for the cure of disorders, the obtaining of revenge for injuries or insults, the conciliating of favour, the discovery and punishment of the thief or the adulterer, and the prediction of future events.[3]

Long attributes the efficacy of *obeah* to two factors, the credulity of the slaves and the natural effects of poison. He continues:

> A veil of mystery is studiously thrown over their incantations, to which the midnight hours are allotted, and every precaution is taken to conceal them from the knowledge and discovery of the white people. The deluded Negroes, who thoroughly believe in their supernatural power, become the willing accomplices in this concealment, and the stoutest among them tremble at the very sight of the ragged bundle, the bottle or the eggshells, which are stuck to the thatch or hung over the door of the hut, or upon the branch of a plantain tree, to deter

marauders. In the case of poison, the natural effects of it are by the ignorant Negroes ascribed entirely to the potent workings of Obi.[4]

In addition to the preparation of symbolic, therapeutic, and toxic medicines, *obeah* is also associated by later writers with the control of the spirits of the living and the dead. Writing in 1828, Alexander Barclay recounted a fragment of slave belief learned at a public trial:

> I was present some years ago, at a trial of a notorious Obeah man, driver on an estate in the parish of St. David, who, by the overwhelming influence he had acquired over the minds of his deluded victims, and the more potent means he had at command to accomplish his ends, had done great injury among the slaves on the property before it was discovered. One of the witnesses, a negro belonging to the same estate, was asked—"Do you know the prisoner to be an Obeah man?" "Ess, massa, shadow-catcher true." "What do you mean by shadow-catcher?" "Him ha coffin (a little coffin produced), him set for catch dem shadow." "What shadow do you mean?" "When him set obeah for summary (somebody), him catch dem shadow, and dem go dead.[5]

The shadow being discussed is an aspect of a widespread Jamaican spiritual and psychological concept. A shadow is seen as the outer form of an invisible dimension of the human person which is separable from the whole, vulnerable to spiritual attack, and survives the body after death. After the death of an individual, his or her shadow is called a *duppy* and is considered a potent, if volatile, spiritual force. For the good of the community a *duppy* can be neutralized by a series of complex funeral ceremonies carried out by the deceased family, or it can be harnessed by *obeah* practitioners to perform protective or aggressive tasks.[6]

Together with his description of *obeah*, Long refers to another practice among the slaves called *myal*, which he categorizes as a subset of *obeah*. While *obeah* practitioners work in secret at the behest of clients, *myal*, for Long, is "a kind of society." He writes:

> Not long since, some of these execrable wretches in Jamaica introduced what they called a myal dance, and established a kind of society, into which they invited all they could. The lure hung out was, that

every Negro, initiated into the myal society, would be invulnerable by the white man; and, although they might in appearance be slain, the obeah-man could, at his pleasure, restore the body to life.[7]

Long speaks of an elaborate initiation into *myal* involving the ingestion of an extract of the herb colalue, which would produce a trance mimicking death. Another herbal preparation resurrected the initiate from this state, and he or she became a member of the *myal* society, immune to the invisible coercions of Africans and European alike. The Baptist missionary James Phillippo writing in 1843 confirms Long's ideas of slave religion:

> Myalism, as well as Fetishism, were constituent parts of Obeism, and included a mystery of iniquity which perhaps was never fully revealed to the uninitiated. The votaries of this art existed as a fraternity composed of individuals from the surrounding neighbourhood, who were regularly inducted into it in accordance with certain demoniacal forms. They adopted every possible means to increase their numbers, and proposed, as the advantages of membership, exemption from pain and premature death; from death, especially as designed by white men; or certain recovery from its influence when life was actually extinct. It was understood to counteract the effect of Obeism, but was often much more demoralizing and fatal in its results.[8]

These accounts point toward a communal religious tradition, a "dance" with an initiatory structure, a mechanism of social responsibility and control, and an independence and militancy in the face of white power. While Long emphasizes the initiatory nature of myal, later observers give us a picture of *myal* as a ritual dance. An eyewitness to a *myal* ceremony in the 1840s, the Presbyterian missionary Hope Masterson Waddell wrote:

> There we found them in full force and employment, forming a ring, around which were a multitude of onlookers. Inside the circle some females performed a mystic dance, sailing round and round, and wheeling in the centre with outspread arms, and wild looks and gestures. Others hummed, or whistled a low monotonous tone, to

which the performers kept time, as did the people around also, by hands and feet and the swaying of their bodies. A man, who seemed to direct the performance, stood at one side, with folded arms, quietly watching their evolutions.[9]

While the tone of this description is aloof and condescending, Waddell's observations of a "wheeling" dance in the form of a ring, the distinctions between the ring dancers and others, the importance of keeping time, and the direction by a leader are all borne out by subsequent observers and in contemporary Revival religion. Waddell tells us that he interrupted the meeting and attempted to quiet the "mad" dancers. He was told, "They are not mad." "They have the spirit." "You must be mad yourself, and had best go away."[10]

The Moravian pastor J. H. Buchner writing in 1854 described a *myal* dance from the same period.

As soon as the darkness of evening set in, they assembled in crowds in open pastures, most frequently under large cotton trees, which they worshipped, and counted holy; after sacrificing some fowls, the leader began an extempore song, in a wild strain, which was answered in chorus; the dance followed, grew wilder and wilder, until they were in a state of excitement bordering on madness.

Some would perform incredible evolutions while in this state, until, nearly exhausted, they fell senseless to the ground, when every word they uttered was received as a divine revelation. At other times, Obeah was to be discovered, or a "shadow" was to be caught; a little coffin being prepared in which it was to be enclosed and buried.[11]

This often-cited account, if it, too, may be freed of its ethnocentrism, centers on many of the elements of early Afro-Jamaican spirituality. We have a community meeting at a prearranged and holy place around a sacred tree. Animals are offered. The liturgy develops in the call-response music between leader and chorus and in the ensuing dance of "some." The ceremony is constructed (by getting "wilder") to culminate in altered states of consciousness ("madness," "senseless"). Buchner rightly sees that the purpose of this dance is to produce revelations as the dancers are filled with the spirit of prophecy or perhaps act as mediums to spirits. To these elements is added the detection of *obeah*.[12]

Writing many years after these events of the 1840s, the Reverend Thomas Banbury records a *myal* song:

> Lord have mercy, oh!
> Christ have mercy, oh!
> Obeah pain hot, oh!
> Lord, we come fe pull he, oh!
> A no we come fe pull he, oh!
> You fada want you, oh!
> Boy, you fada want you, oh!

Banbury continues:

This last song was sung on a shadow catching occasion. Many songs were used when taking up obeahs, which they did openly in the day time, in the presence of a large concourse of people who flocked from all parts to see it. The overseers and bookkeepers on the sugar estates all were present. There were present an attorney and a proprietor. An Englishmen and member of the House of Assembly, who took them in on his estate, gave them room and encouraged them in every way. They publicly dug out of his yard a lot of obeahs for him.

Another of the obeah-pulling songs was:

> Dandy obeah da ya, oh!
> Me wi' pull he, oh!
> Any way him run, oh!
> Me wi' pull he oh.[13]

The connection between *myal* and the neutralization or "pulling" of *obeah* is maintained by contemporary Jamaicans. Today, *myal* is used to refer to the altered state of consciousness achieved at the dance. The Jamaican-American scholar of religion Leonard Barrett asked a *kumina* initiate, "Do all persons dancing at Cumina receive possession?" She answered, "Not all persons dancing in a Cumina meeting receive myal."[14] Barrett goes on to say that in a state of *myal* the *kumina* initiate is able to detect evil and good spirits, and the workings of *obeah*. Another *kumina* initiate quoted by Monica Schuler drew a similar connection between *obeah* and *myal*: "When we got myal, we can find a thing bury, but when we normal, we can't do these things."[15]

From these observations we can see *obeah* and *myal* achieving interrelated roles in nineteenth-century and contemporary Jamaican society. *Obeah* is the art of sorcery, practiced in private, if not secret, and reflecting the disintegrative forces of a society under stress. By contrast *myal* might be seen as a force for social integration, bent on the exposure of *obeah*, and defusing it with the power of communal values expressed in public ceremonies.[16] Yet from the descriptions above we can find important social functions met by both the practitioners of *obeah* and *myal*. All accounts testify to the ubiquity and universal resort of *obeah* among the slaves. The *obeah* practitioner provided medical and jural aid for the plantation workers in a society devoid of these institutions in any other form. If the *obeah* specialist was fearful, he or she was also the source of comfort, healing, and justice.

Myal, too, represents a reassertion by the community of its authority over the legitimate and illegitimate uses of invisible power. *Myal* dancers and seers are exposing what the community has determined to be the illegitimate uses of *obeah*, rather than a condemnation of the private use of spiritual force. Long may be confused by reporting that the *myal* initiation was directed by the *obeah* man, but if he is correct, it indicates that the private uses of spiritual force are sanctioned in public ceremonies. To find justice in the unjust world of slavery and emancipation, Jamaicans could turn to *obeah* practitioners, whose work was brought under scrutiny by the communal consciousness of *myal*.[17]

What must be remembered in evaluating these planters' and missionaries' opinions of *obeah* and *myal* is that these practices were not only a source of disruption among their workers and flocks, they were also a direct threat to these white authorities. Long notes how carefully the identities and workings of *obeah* practitioners were concealed from whites. In Banbury's account of the *myal* dances of the 1840s, a proprietor commissioned the *myal* people to dig up numerous *obeah* medicines from his own yard. In addition to the cultivation of the psychic powers of aggression and protection, *obeah* practitioners were skilled in the preparation of poisons, and the planters and overseers were very much afraid of this weapon of the slaves. Long connects the uses of *myal* herbs, and the communities formed to administer them, with the great slave rebellion of 1760. Not the least of the powers the *myal* initiation was invulnerability to death, as Phillippo puts it, "especially as designed by white men." Beginning in 1760 a series of laws prohibiting the practice of *obeah* were enacted by the Jamaican legislature and continue to be enforced today. Thus *obeah* and *myal* are complementary uses of spiritual power, wielded independently by the slaves and their descendants, to secure justice among themselves and from the whites who sought to control them.

Yet *obeah* and *myal* are concerned not only with social control, but also with the development of a spiritual sensitivity and empowerment. The *obeah* practitioner is a "scientist," a student of the workings of the visible and invisible world. He or she undergoes long apprenticeship in the development of this knowledge. The pharmacopeia of Jamaican "balm work" is vast, and the ability to manufacture and activate medicines takes many years to master. The invocation of *duppies*, as well, requires great strength and insight. The "scientist" is "four-eyed," having developed the gift to see both the visible and invisible world.

The extraordinary insight of the "scientist" is complemented by the spiritual vision of *myal* attained in communal dance. *Myal* brings revelation of the invisible world. This state of mind allows the dancers to see the invisible workings of *obeah* as well as to transmit messages from the other world. It is these institutions for the cultivation of spiritual sight which the slaves and their descendants brought to the Christianity available to them in nineteenth-century Jamaica. The community of Revival Zion, the Jamaican "children of Zion," grew out of this meeting of Afro-Jamaican and Christian traditions.

In Banbury's description of the *myal* movement of the 1840s he notes that they were called "angel men" as well as "Mial people," and that they preached that Christ was coming and that the world was coming to an end. In the *myal* song cited above we find the connection made between the mercy of Christ and the release from the heat of *obeah*. Thus by mid-nineteenth century the newly emancipated estate workers of Jamaica were perceiving themselves in Christian terms if not as Christians.[18] But it is a Christianity independent of European leadership and rooted in the cosmology and ceremonial activity of the African past. While a small group of Moravian missionaries established a permanent mission to the slaves as early as 1754, it was not until the 1820s that other denominations began similar work, and these missions were never staffed in significant numbers. Alongside the reports of great "progress" among the slaves and freedmen, the English missionaries were ever mindful of the problems in assessing what they called the "sincerity" of conversions. An Anglican pastor, writing of his parish in 1816, put it this way:

> The fact is, in respect to slaves in general, that their knowledge of the English language is so very limited that they can derive little or no advantage from their attendance at church. They are so conscious of this defect, that when I go to church for the express purpose of catechizing them, very few will attend, and not one of these will utter a word but what has been put into his mouth. How then, it may be said are twenty-six thousand slaves [in St. Thomas's in the East in 1816] to be instructed? The subject has frequently engaged my thoughts, and I cannot conceive any other mode than this: let the young creole slaves be taught to speak and read, and at the same time be instructed in the first principles of the Christian religion, in public schools established in different parts of the parish; and let them communicate what instruction they have received in their own way to their African brethren, to whom it is impossible for white people to make themselves understood.[19]

It was one thing for the missionaries to recognize the necessity for black leadership and another to accept it. In 1783 a freedman from Georgia came to Kingston, George Lisle, whose preaching "took very good effect with the poorer sort, especially the slaves."[20] He was twice imprisoned, once for inciting insurrection and once for debt, but he and a group of followers persisted in establishing a large number of Baptist congregations throughout the island. Lisle emphasized both the biblical and African foundations of his movement and called his congregation the Ethiopian Baptist Church. The movement came to be known as the Native Baptists, recalling their struggles for independence from English authority. By 1860, they accounted for 50 percent of the church-going population of Kingston.[21] Their success did not go unchallenged by white missionaries, who were quick to find evidences of heathenism in the unsupervised embrace of Christianity by black flocks. James Phillippo, the English Baptist missionary writing in 1843, exempts Lisle and his immediate circle from scorn, but writes of others: "Many of them, from motives of ambition and pecuniary advantage, soon acquired a knowledge of the formularies of the English Church; and, at the conclusion of the war with America, some who had been imported from that continent, mysteriously blending together important truths and extravagant puerilities, assumed the office of teachers and preachers, disseminating far and wide their pernicious follies." Phillippo goes on to outline these follies: "Dreams and visions constituted fundamental articles of their creed. Some supernatural revelations were regarded as indispensable to qualify for admission to the full privileges of their community. Candidates were required, indeed, to dream a certain number of dreams before they were received to membership, the subjects of which were given them by their teachers."[22]

Although his opinion of the ways of the Native Baptists was identical to that of Phillippo, the missionary historian of Jamaica, William Gardner, saw the connection between "extravagances" and Africanity. He wrote in 1873: "With few exceptions, native Baptist churches became associations of men and women who, in too many cases, mingled the belief and even the practice of Mialism with religious observances, and who perverted and corrupted what they retained of these: among them sensuality was almost entirely unrestrained."[23]

This "mingling" of belief and practice, pioneered by independent black Christians among the Native Baptists, would become general among the black population of the island in a great Christian revival which occurred from 1860 to 1862.

The fervor that ignited the mass movement of the Great Revival originally came to Jamaica from England and Ireland, where since 1859 multitudes had been gathering as often as twice a day to sing, fast, pray, and reach the conviction of sin and personal salvation in the blood of Christ. For Jamaica, reeling from an economic depression, frustrated hopes of social change, and shortages caused by the war in the United States, the millenarian message of the revival took on a special urgency.[24] Yet once again, English missionaries were disappointed to see the reviving effects of European Christianity swept away by the "extravagances" of their black flocks. Gardner, who witnessed the revival, wrote this assessment:

> In 1861, there had been a very remarkable religious movement, known as "the revival." It commenced among the Moravians, and gradually extended to all parts of the island. Like a mountain stream, clear and transparent as it springs from the rock, but which becomes foul and repulsive as impurities are mingled with it in its onward course, so with this most extraordinary movement. In many of the central districts of the island the hearts of thoughtful and good men were gladdened by what they witnessed in the changed lives and characters of people for whom they long seemed to have laboured in vain; but in too many districts there was much of wild extravagance and almost blasphemous fanaticism. This was especially the case where the native Baptists had any considerable influence. Among these, the manifestations occasioned by the influence of the Myalmen, as described previously, were very common.[25]

Though the intensity of the Great Revival was to subside, the experience of the mass of Jamaicans in a Christian spirituality expressed in African ritual forms became a permanent part of the Afro-Jamaican religious world. "Revival" and "revivalism" came to be the name given to and largely accepted by the congregations dedicated to the experiences of the 1860–62 period. When the revival prophet Alexander Bedward excited the religious fervor of thousands of Jamaicans in the first decades of the twentieth century, an elderly man told folklorist Martha Beckwith, "I remember the St. Thomas rebellion and the revival in 1860. It was taken up by the whole world. Now today there is Bedward."[26]

Though Bedward's Jamaican National Baptist Church is no longer an incorporated entity today, his influence is still strong in the revival churches, particularly around Kingston.[27] His emphasis on the healing properties of the water from sacred springs, especially those of the Hope River outside Kingston, continues to be a major feature of the revival churches of the area.

Today the problem of nomenclature in tracing the heritage of revival churches is complicated by issues of public perception and self-definition. The word "revivalism" has become associated in middle-class Jamaican discourse with lower-class and "primitive" religious expression, and thus with a pervasive ambivalence toward the island's African heritage. A word still more commonly used and with generally negative connotations for middle-class Jamaicans is *pocomania*, which seems to have come into general usage in the early decades of the twentieth century. The origins of the word are obscure. Edward Seaga argues that *pocomania* may be a corruption of the name for the Central African tradition in Jamaica called *kumina*, and ought to be rendered *pukkumina*.[28] For Jamaicans alienated from the revival tradition, *pocomania* is often ridiculed as "a little madness," an amusing brand of overenthusiastic Christianity. For those more fully committed to mainstream churches, *pocomania* is usually characterized as immoral, debased Christianity superstitiously concerned with *obeah*. Members of Revival Zion churches, the children of Zion, distinguish themselves from *pocomania* by pointing out the biblical foundations of all their activities and citing the failures of *pocomania* churches to do the same.[29]

The distinctions between the institutions created by the heritors of the Afro-Christian tradition in Jamaica seem to be fluid and dependent on the standpoint of the observer. To outsiders, all revival Christianity is *pocomania*. For those within the tradition, distinctions are made in different ways.[30] Some members of the tradition say that one may recognize *pocomania* by its ritual architecture, for "poco carries a pole." Here the importance of a central pole, found in the yard or meeting house, as a focus for ceremonial power is considered to be distinctive of *pocomania*. Another frequently heard distinction among the revival traditions refers to a difference in the style of the spiritual dancing of each group. A church leader makes this distinction between "revival" and "Revival Zion" by distinguishing between their different ways of "trumping," the rhythmic breathing that characterizes the spiritual dance of Jamaican revival. He says: "Zionist claim that they are directly from Mt. Zion. That is their church. But all God's children are from Zion because Zion is the Holy City of God. But only two differences among Revival and Zion—one group trump upward, taking groan down; one groans up and trumps down. One coming down Revival; one coming up Zion."[31]

These ritual distinctions indicate that whether a tradition is "pocomania" or "revival" or "Revival Zion" is resolved in the eyes of the beholder. There are no institutional structures connecting *pocomania* or revival churches: leaders are free to improvise upon the instruction and ceremonial patterns handed down to them by their elders in the tradition. There is often informal "fellowshipping" or mutual attendance at rites between likeminded churches, and leaders will often cooperate on these special and often spontaneous occasions, but there is no authority beyond the leader of the immediate congregation.

Most Revival Zion congregations are small, with no more than fifty members who might be expected to attend rites regularly, but there is usually a much larger extramural population. This includes people who attend rites for special intentions, or who gather outside the churches during ceremonies simply to enjoy the music, gossip, and occasionally assist the dancers if called upon. Most regular members are women, who work for low wages cooking, cleaning, sewing, or laundering. Perhaps one in ten of the regular attenders are men who are often unemployed and work as "scufflers," finding odd jobs to make ends meet. Many more men will gather outside the churches, particularly on Sunday evenings to socialize and meet the women. Men seem more likely to enjoy the services for their aesthetic value and will offer appreciative comments when the service becomes lively and the spirit hot. Men also offer their services as drummers for the congregation though they may not be members of the church nor pious in their Christianity.

The leadership of each Revival Zion church is structured differently: some are headed by men; others by women; some by a male/female team. Some churches employ an austere structure of offices, recognizing only a pastor, deacon or deaconess, and confirmed "saints." Others are staffed by an elaborate hierarchy of shepherds and shepherdesses, captains and mothers, armor bearers and governesses.[32] In each case the authority of the leader or pair of leaders is very strong with few if any institutional checks. Most churches are the creations of individual leaders, and succession to leadership is usually understood as a reconstitution of a new community rather than new leadership in a continuous one. Though the charisms of the congregation may be widely and finely distributed, the church is almost completely dependent on the charisma of the leader.

Revival Zion is thus a tradition of charisma, a set of shared ways of working the spirit in the tradition of the Great Revival and the African traditions which underlie it. Entry into Revival Zion is a process of growth into these ways of the spirit. The individual is called to service through the reception of spiritual gifts which are sealed in baptism by the spirit. These gifts are made available to the community in the services of the Revival Zion church, where the power of the spirit is made present through the songs, dances, and praise of the congregation. We can move now from the history of this community to the services which express it and link the children of Zion to the spirit that inspires them.

SERVICE

The occasions for religious service are many in Revival Zion. There are prayer services in the church nearly every evening of the week and often three distinct services on Sundays. There are frequent calls to bring the spirit into the "streets and lanes of the city," and the congregation will process through the streets, stopping to testify, sing, and draw converts back to the church. There are also a variety of "tables," feasts "laid under the scripture" in intricate symbolic displays in the church.[33] While the Sunday services are a matter of calendar observance, most of the other services are directed by revelations from the spirits and answer to the special intentions of individuals or the needs of the community at large.

Call in the Spirit

Receptivity to the messages of the spirits is the first sign of entry into Revival Zion. And the foremost medium of spiritual communication is dreams. In dreams people have the sight to see the reality of the spiritual world that is ordinarily closed to them when awake. Most children of Zion are first called to service through a dream. A revivalist named Margaret Williston told Beckwith in 1929:

> I was not a great student. I left school in the first book. And after that I got spiritual at twenty-five. The Mammy was from Westmoreland. When there was shouting, I felt that I was almost shut out of the gate of heaven and I closed my eyes and I said, "Lord, if it is they wish that I be separated, let it be thy will." And I dreamt that I saw an angel, and he bids me get a Bible and a Sankey and a rod with a double fold and a lantern which I'm to light on my journey.
>
> I didn't know to pray until I got the Spirit, and the Spirit teaches me to pray and sends me on the highways and the hedges to bid others to come and to tell what a sweet Savior I found. Jesus is Savior in need and Savior indeed. There is not a friend like the loving Savior.[34]

Mrs. Williston draws the connection between the state of mind achieved in the shouting of the church service and that of her dream. Both are privileged states of awareness in which the self is no longer identified with the ordinary self of waking life, but with another faculty of the personality, a personal spirit which is capable of "journeying" beyond the confines of the body and seeing what ordinary eyes cannot. When one is "in the spirit," one can see the angels and hear their messages.[35]

This first experience of the presence of the spirit can transform the individual, opening forever access to the spirit for the benefit of the individual and the community. If an individual has the call and the gift, he or she will be able to make contact with the spirit with more and more frequency and rapport. Usually contact first occurs in dreams, but if one has the gift of discernment one might see the presence and activity of spirits in waking life. The spirits inhabit a different dimension of ordinary time and space, and participation in Revival Zion allows the individual to discern their presence more clearly. Reading scripture under the guidance of elders, praying, fasting and praising the Lord in ceremony, all cut through the confusion of "temporal" life and show the world as it is, alive with the power of God.

A more dramatic way that a spirit may "convert" a person is by means of a trance, known as being "put on the ground" by the spirit or "slain in the spirit." Here an initiating spirit takes full control of the individual's consciousness and leads him or her on a spiritual journey. Each of the stations of the journey becomes a symbolic key for the traveler to understand his or her journey in waking life. The people met and the obstacles overcome "on the ground" are spiritual prefigurations for events in "temporal" life, and the eventual success of the spiritual journey inspires hope for the temporal one.

Most journeys on the ground last for a few hours, but some people have been seized by the spirit for weeks or even months. When a convert is put on the ground by the spirit, all the congregation can do is to attempt to feed and bathe the body of the traveler and stand vigil with prayers. As the traveler begins to return to the temporal world, the congregation will gather at a special feast, a "rising" or "coming up" tabled. The details of the experience will be related, and important messages from the spirits will be relayed.[36]

Through transformative dreams, visions, and trances, children of Zion are "converted," brought to a connection between the ordinary temporal sight of waking life and the special spiritual sight which will allow them to draw the power of the spirit into their lives. A revival leader speaks of this transformative power:

> A great change always comes to the individual when the Holy Spirit chooses him or her, and some people never change back again, but others sometimes spoil it. What I mean is, that it isn't necessarily permanent if you don't keep working at it. By working and trumping and laboring and study, you discern, you grow, because you have an inner teacher, the Holy Spirit, and the apostles and the saints, which works in the inner man and teaches you.[37]

Most children of Zion are visited in their dreams and visions by angels or biblical prophets who become their lifelong guides.[38] An angel or prophet reveals itself as the special guardian and tutor of an individual and one dedicates one's life to working with this spirit, to trusting its special path in spiritual discernment and growth. Children of Zion readily identify themselves as "working with Jeremiah," "working with Isaiah," or "working with Michael," indicating that they have entered into a mutual pact with one of these spirits and that the particular wisdom of this spirit's path in Zion will be their's. As one grows in Zion, one might begin to work with more than one spirit, but it is the path of the first which is remembered as the one which brought one over from temporal life to the spiritual life of Zion.

"The spirit" in Revival Zion is both the particular spirit who guides the individual in his or her work and also the more general power and breath of God, the Holy Spirit, the third person of the Christian trinity. The Holy Spirit underlies and empowers all the work of the particular spirits and is understood to be present in each of the particular powers of the angels and prophets. All work "in the spirit" is understood to be both an ongoing relationship with a particular spirit among many and a deepening connection with the Holy Spirit of God which is one.

A spiritual relationship has only limited value unless it is grounded in the community. A revival leader told Joseph Moore, "You don't get no teachment and that is why you need be with the band . . . you get teachment when you move with the band."[39] One works with these spirits not only for the personal fulfillment brought by the power of the spiritual life, but also to develop the gifts of healing and prophecy for the service of the community. "Having the spirit" means that one must offer this faculty for the benefit of the congregation. Not all church members "have the spirit," but everyone benefits from an individual's particular relationship with an angel or prophet. In the songs and dances of the church, one may bring in the powers of his or her spirit for all the congregation.

Mrs. Williston speaks of "getting the spirit," as her first experience in praying properly. She continues: "When you are in the spirit, you feel that the world is going around and you turn without you want to turn. When the Spirit overflows within you, you have to shout and shout and shout. You have to shout with joy. When you feel that you can't shout with your voice any more—feel as if it were shut down and locked—then you cease shouting."[40]

This experience of being "in the spirit" is the individual's entry into the world of Revival Zion. It is the way to pray, the way to praise God, and the way to heal the community. The experience of having the spirit and the ability to get in the spirit for the benefit of the community seals individuals in the service of God and their brothers and sisters in Zion.

The spirits dictate a variety of services to honor God and to deepen their relationship with human beings. In their devotee's second sight of dreams, visions, and trances, the spirits communicate the details of the services. The arrangement of the tables, the choice of songs to be sung, and which scripture is to be read are all made by spirits. What the spirits and the spirit most desire, however, is praise. On all occasions children of Zion cite Psalm 150 as the motive behind all service:

> Praise ye the Lord,
> Praise God in his sanctuary:
> Praise him in the firmament of his power.
> Praise him for his mighty acts;
> Praise him according to his excellent greatness.
> Praise him with the sound of the trumpet;
> Praise him with the psaltery and harp.

Praise him with the timbrel and dance:
Praise him with stringed instruments and organs.
Praise him upon the loud cymbals:
Praise him upon the high-sounding cymbals.
Let every thing that hath breath praise the Lord.
Praise ye the Lord.

Although the variety of services in Revival Zion is too great to call any one service typical, the major themes of the work of the spirit can be found in one such service of praise, a joyful noise before the Lord enacted each Sunday evening in a small town outside of Kingston.[41]

Journey in the Spirit

The Mount Zion Tabernacle of God is a small, active congregation in a settlement on the outskirts of Kingston. The church is built of plywood, painted in patriotic colors of green, yellow, and black, and roofed in corrugated tin. Large double doors open the church on three sides, and the walls are pierced by several glassless windows. It measures some thirty by fifty feet and might accommodate fifty or sixty people on the low benches divided by a center aisle. A banked altar, draped in white and topped by a plain cross, is set against the far wall. It holds fresh flowers, luxurious Jeremiah leaves, candles, and bottles of spring water and soft drinks.

But the focus of the church, the seal, is placed at its center. The seal is the center point of the building which directly connects the congregation to the invisible world of the spirits. Here, a white pole runs from the floor to the ceiling, branching out at the top into three sections, each of which holds a flag in one of the Ethiopian colors: red, green, or gold. At the very top of the pole, a white flag surmounts the others. The pastor explains that the red flag symbolizes the blood of Christ; the green, health and happiness; the gold, the lost treasures of Africa; and the white, the purity and peace which must stand at the center. At the base of the pole is placed a rock which bears two biblical inscriptions: the self-identification of God to Moses, "I am that I am" (Exodus 3:14); and Jesus' investiture of Peter, "Upon this rock I will build my church (Matthew 16:18). The rock, says the pastor, is Christ, who is the foundation of the church and who is what he is.

The most vital element at the seal, however, is a large urn of water placed on a small table touching the pole. It is the water of life, says the pastor, drawn from a holy spring some six miles away and carried in procession back to the church by three elder women. There it is reconsecrated by a chain prayer and transformed from water into medicine. It becomes the principle medium of the spirits in filling the church. When the water of life is drunk, the spirit actually enters the body. Aspirated over the congregation, the spirit fills the air. It is contained in bottles and jars placed around the church where it acts as an instrument to detect the activity of both holy and malign spirits invisible to ordinary sight. The pastor and those "in the spirit" can discern the presence of *obeah* in the prism of the waters of life and can use the water to trap, neutralize, and expel it. The water acts as a means to second sight, so that the pastor and those in the spirit can "read" something of the character of individuals, the invisible motivations which might lead them to participate in the service.

The water must be protected against malign forces, and so containers of it are covered with white cloths, tied like the cloths which are wound like turbans around the heads of the congregation. Inside the urn is a smith's coal to absorb any *obeah* with which jealous people might try to poison the water. Only certain sisters in Zion are allowed to dispense the water so that all may be assured that this most powerful medium of healing is not made a vehicle for destruction.

The core congregation of the Mount Zion Tabernacle of God, those who attend nearly every service, is almost entirely women, some twenty strong, although fifty or sixty people might be considered regular members. On Sunday evenings, a much larger population attends, and many men and young people put in an appearance, even if they do not actively worship. The church is organized by a single, founding pastor, and recognizes a deacon and a deaconness, a community of converted "saints," and congregation of who do not "have the spirit." Many of the women wear white dresses, especially those "saints" who have the spirit.

Everyone else is dressed in good street clothes, and all wear the distinctive wrap or turban around their heads. Most head wraps are white although some are other colors specified by initiating spirits to the wearers in their dreams. The wraps "show unity" the pastor says and identify the community as children of Zion, the flock of David and Jesus Christ

On a hot Sunday evening in June, the drums of the Mt. Zion Tabernacle of God call out to the neighborhood that the evening service will soon begin. This is the third service of the day, and stalwart members have already been to the church in the morning and at midday. Now the largest crowd of the day is slowly gathering, chatting easily in small groups while the drummers warm up and practice the rhythms of the evening. A variety of men and boys will take up the two drums over the course of the evening service. Most drummers are not members of the congregation, but friends and lovers who enjoy the services and the chance to display their skills. The drums consist of a large shallow bass drum, some twenty-four inches in diameter, and a smaller "kettle" drum about twelve inches across. Each is played with a single stick. Many congregants have also brought tambourines, and as they begin to fall in with the early rhythms, the music is loud and carries far.

The deacon detaches himself from a conversation and begins to bring order to the congregation. The percussion is silenced, those who will come into the church enter, and those who will stay outside begin to arrange themselves for the evening, continuing their chatter in lower tones. The congregation begins to sing well-known "Sankey" hymns from the Methodist Sankey and Moody hymnal. The deacon "traces" the first line, and the congregation repeats it without accompaniment in a nasal falsetto. The tempo is slow, deliberate, and perfunctory.

> God is here, and that to bless us
> With the Spirit's quickening power:
> See, the cloud already bending,
> Waits to drop the grateful shower.
> Let it come, O Lord, we pray Thee,

Let the shower of blessing fall;
We are waiting, we are waiting,
Oh revive the hearts of all.[42]

The deacon often stumbles over the opening lines of the hymns, and after three or four songs the congregation has become impatient and is openly prompting him through his "tracing." The pastor arrives, stern in a tight wrap, and he throws more energy and discipline into the singing.

Revive Thy work O Lord!
Exalt Thy precious name:
And by the Holy Ghost, our love
For Thee and Thine inflame.

As the hymn ends the pastor takes immediate control of the service. With throaty authority he recites from memory Psalm 92.

It is a good thing to give thanks unto the Lord
And to sing praises to thy name O most High:
To show forth thy lovingkindness in the morning,
And thy faithfulness every night.
Upon an instrument of ten strings,
And upon the psaltery;
Upon the harp with a solemn sound.
For thou, Lord, hast made me glad through thy work:
I will triumph in the works of thy hands.

The congregation begins to join him in the recitation and, at its conclusion, calls out hearty amens and praises to the Lord. "Amen," the pastor calls: "Amen," come the responses, enthusiastic but scattered. "Amen," the pastor reaches again, pulling everyone into one voice. "Amen," comes the concerted reply. Not enough. The pastor calls "Amen!" with yet more force, the congregation calls back a thunderous answer. The pastor smiles for the first time, and the congregation relaxes in this new level of harmony. He exhorts them to worship God in the way that they please, to stand up for themselves, "look any John Brown in the eye," "be yourself."

The pastor recites "Make a joyful noise unto God, all ye lands: Serve the Lord with gladness: come before his presence with singing" (Psalm 100:1–2). This is a call for a "lively chorus," which is a Sankey hymn, but this time in faster tempo with percussive accompaniment. The drums fall in, tambourines shimmer, hands clap in counterpoint, and the building is filled with sound. The congregation stands and, moves to the music before the benches, and the crowd outside comes to press at the doors and windows, joining in the singing and movement.

The chorus comes to a close, the drums and tambourines stop, and, as the building still reverberates, the pastor calls on the congregation to praise the Lord. "Praise him again." "Praise him again," he demands, as each volley of "Praise the Lord" bursts from the congregation. "We are going to have Sister Arlene come up and witness for us today."

A diminutive woman in a plain white dress and peaked wrap comes before the congregation and speaks in a high clear voice. She speaks with conviction, and the congregation punctuates her sentences with amens and yeses. She says that everyone in the congregation knows her and sometimes they wish she wouldn't speak so much. But it is because she cares about Mt. Zion and the children of Zion that she must speak her mind. "There is hypocrisy in the church," she says. People appear to be walking in righteousness, but are secretly practicing science against each other. From some parts of the church, enthusiastic amens greet this accusation, from others there is a resigned silence. Sister Arlene continues to say that there are other churches where science is practiced and those who care to can go to them on their road to perdition, but at Mt. Zion we practice only godliness. The full congregation is behind this declaration. As she calls for renewed testimony and amens, Sister Arlene brings the congregation through self-examination to a new level of unity. She calls for another lively chorus, the drums sound, and the congregation's energy and enthusiasm is very high.

> O get together, get together
> Get together in the Lord

Let us all get together in the Lord
O let us love one another
Like sister and brother
Let us all get together in the Lord

"Amen," calls the pastor and the congregation answers with strength. As the joyful noise subsides he tells them of a "coming up table" at a nearby church where they often share services or fellowship. A woman there has been put on the ground by a spirit for four months, and a feast for her return to the temporal world is going to be hosted by this other church on the next night. "She has been on a journey through the blood of Christ," says the pastor. "I'm going because I don't want to hear from anyone else what it is she's going to say."

"We work Revival 60 Zion and they're a Revival 61 hall," he says in reference to the kindred spiritual lineages of the churches.[43] But he warns his congregation that he is suspicious. "There is some kind of science in that church, some kind of de Laurence business. They've got something to hide at all times." He speaks of looking into the waters at the other church and discerning a sword and a knife, signs of science. He saw three upturned plates with triangles on them. His congregation knows this to be evidence of *obeah*, inspired by infamous books of magic published by the de Laurence company. Children of Zion work only with biblical spirits and shun the attractions of science. "Put on your cloak of righteousness and behold," declares the pastor, "Christ is our savior."

"What I want to say will just take two minutes. Just one word from Psalm one thirty and three . . . 'Behold!'" "Behold!" answers the congregation. "Amen!" "*Amen!*"

"Behold."

"*Behold.*"

"How good and pleasant it is."

"*How good and pleasant it is.*"

"For brethren to dwell together in unity."

"*For brethren to dwell together in unity.*"

"Amen!"

"*Amen!*"

"And there was a time in the prophesy," the pastor begins as each of his pauses is filled with amens of greater enthusiasm. "When the Lord declared . . . 'Behold! . . . I send my messenger!' And there was another passage of scripture . . . when the Lord said . . . 'Woman . . . Behold thy son.' And there was another passage of scripture . . . when the Lord said . . . 'Son . . . Behold thy mother.'" The congregation is not only fortifying the pastor and completing the message with responses, but anticipating him, calling to him to respond to their infusion of the spirit. "But you know . . . there's another 'Behold' I want to talk about . . . in Revelation . . ." As one, the congregation and pastor proclaim (Revelation 22:12),

> Behold, I come quickly:
> And my reward is with me,
> To give to every man
> According as his work shall be.

"Amen! "Amen!" The spirit is moving freely among the congregation now, nearly everyone is giving smaller or greater shouts of praise: "Wo!" "Oh yeh!" "Yes, yes, yes!" The pastor calls for another lively chorus, and the drums, tambourines, and voices fill the night air. All attention is focused into the church as the white-clad saints come out into the aisle and circle the seal, moving lightly, in time to the music. They draw others into the parade, even going outside the doors to draw in part of the large crowd there. They uncover the seal jar and ladle water into glasses, giving them to all who ask. The deaconess picks up vases of Jeremiah leaves and parades them about the church. The movement around the seal is serene and solemn, but as the music intensifies the dancers become more angular, bending deeply from the waist. Some fifteen congregants draw tighter around the seal, and while their circle continues to move counterclockwise, their bodies turn increasingly toward the center. Now the tempo is very fast. Three elder women remove the flags from the center branched pole and snap them smartly around the church to welcome the angelic presence. Finally, they come to stand at the doors, guarding the entrances.

After nearly forty minutes of strenuous spiritual dancing, the music stops almost abruptly. The dancers stagger, some are helped onto the benches, others find their way to seats, and four remain including the pastor and the deaconess. In the echoing silence all attention is riveted on the four as they form a tighter circle among themselves. This group is called the "band" or "bands" (always treated as a singular noun), and it gathers to lead the congregation into the heart of Zion.

The deaconess begins a ringing call in a spiritual language that fills the air like a fanfare. At the end of the phrase she calls, "How di do?" in a vigorous greeting to the gathering angels. "How di do?" answers the congregation. "All right, all right, all right," she sings in the same fanfare melody. She begins to punctuate this melody with a hard stomping of her feet as she leads the other three around the seal. Again she stops, trumpets the spiritual melody, reaching higher and sharper notes, and picks up the hard march. The congregation moves feet in time, though not with the same force. With each pause in their march, the four members of the "bands" turn toward the seal. Each extends the right foot, leans back onto the left, and then shifts forward sharply onto the right, bending the back and waist. As they come forward, they expel air forcefully and inhale deeply as they straighten up and shift weight back to the left foot.

This is called "travailing" or working the spirit, laboring in bringing the spirit into consciousness. It is also known as "trumping," either for the musical effect of the loud intake of breath or the pounding of the feet on the floor. Both acts as rhythmic instruments to facilitate and sustain the presence of the spirit. The rhythm of the breathing begins with a simple "hey" at expulsion and a slight whistling effect with intake. But it soon gives way to yet faster cadences. The breathing doubles, the sounds intensify: "Hey . . . hee-hay." "Hey . . . hee-hay!" With each pause the group moves a quarter revolution around the seal. They stagger back to catch some breath, cry in spiritual languages, greet the angels. "How di do?" The congregation returns the welcome, "How di do?" "Greetings messengers!" "Journey us angels." The pastor exclaims a fragment of revelation coming to him, "Numbers and letters to be played!" "The church is filled with numbers and letters!" The deaconess shouts, "Use me Lord. Use me for thy service." Again the trumping is begun, the time still quickened, the four members of the "bands" now clap as well as stamp and shout, "Hey . . . hee-hay, HO!"

Though the deaconess began the sequence of trumping, it seems to be the pastor who calls the rhythmic changes. Revival leaders say that each rhythm has a specific purpose in bringing the community into spiritual consciousness. Each rhythm is called to check negativity and reach unity as well as to honor the particular spiritual presences in attendance. The very number of stamps has meaning in that different communities distinguish themselves and cite their lineage in the revival tradition by the dance numbers. The leader "calls sixty" indicating certain rhythms and number of breaths and steps. As the numbers of steps increase, the congregation is brought to ever higher states of consciousness and unity with themselves and their spiritual ancestors in the sixty tradition.

The trumping on this Sunday evening at the Mt. Zion Tabernacle has been going on for nearly an hour, and the service for almost five. The principals are exhausted. They have worked the spirit and the angels have journeyed them. The congregation as a whole has been brought to the spiritual world of the angels through the "bands," and through the "bands" trumping and travailing, the revelatory message of the angels has been delivered. The message is untranslatable into ordinary language, only those in the spirit can understand. But biblical prophecy will be fulfilled at Mt. Zion church, and the congregation has been duly warned and fully uplifted. As the pastor and the others pause for the last time, he calls for a hymn to close the service. A staid Sankey is sung, the pastor gives his blessing to all, and people file out into the warm night.

SPIRIT

The spirit of Revival Zion is like a wind blowing, a wind channeled and directed by the congregation as they work the spirit to heal, empower, and witness. The spirit is understood in the terms of the Bible, the Holy

Spirit of God, and is seen to be the inspiration of the host of angels, prophets, and saints of the Christian tradition. Yet the Holy Spirit is recognized as not only an abstract theological entity, and the angels and saints are not only venerable figures from the remote past. They are living presences brought into the temporal world by "work," the liturgical forms of the Afro-Jamaican religious heritage. The spirit reveals itself to the individual through dreams, visions, and trances and is manifested among the community through the praise, hymns, and dance of the congregation.

Revival Zion opens the biblical path to the spiritual world by orienting the individual and the community to Zion. We can understand the spirit of Revival Zion by seeing its spatialization of the spiritual world in word and act, its development of a reciprocal spirituality within the human person, and by the sharing of these spiritual faculties in the ritual journey of church service.

The world of the spirit of Revival Zion is related to the temporal world through a combination of spatial, aural, and kinetic cues. The focus of the church is the seal, that center point constructed by rock, pole, table, and water arranged in the center of the building. Activated by the music and movement of the congregation, the angels manifest themselves through the seal. It is said that when the force of the congregation's hymnody is right, the angels come down the center pole into the waters of life at its base. From there they can enter the bodies of the congregation when the water is drunk. Another explanation is that the angels come down the center pole into the ground and enter the dancers through their feet, up their spine, and into their heads.[44] The spiritual world is thus represented as "on high," and the angels travel to the temporal world through the arrangement of scripture, song, percussion, vertical pole, and most important, water. The music and dance "call" the spirits, the pole and water provide the path to enter the temporal world.

The name of the spiritual world is Zion, and its immagery derives from the Zion of the Psalms, the city upon the hill dear to the shepherd-king, David. "Beautiful for situation, the joy of the whole earth, is mount Zion" (Psalms 48:2). "Out of Zion, the perfection of beauty, God hath shineth"

(Psalms 50:2). God dwells in Zion, singers and musicians play in Zion, the source of the waters of life is there. "All my springs are in thee" (Psalms 87:7). Zion is the "place" of the spirits, the spring from which they pour into the church when drawn by the praises of song, dance, and righteousness.

As the dwelling of the spirits, Zion is the land of the ancestors, the golden past of Africa, lost by sin and oppression.[45] But Zion can be recovered, temporarily in the ceremonies of the church, individually in the conduct of the spiritual life, and fully in the great time to come. "All they that despised thee shall bow themselves down at the soles of thy feet; and they shall call thee, the city of the Lord, the Zion of the Holy One of Israel." (Isaiah 60:14). The Lord will "roar out of Zion," and her enemies and oppressors will be destroyed. Thus Zion is at once a place, a locality of past greatness, a source of inspiration channeled and made present in the church, a future hope for the redemption of this world. In Zion the temporal and spiritual were brought together in the past, are brought together under ritual conditions in the present, and will be brought together in the apocalypse to come. The children of Zion are brought to "behold" Zion amongst them.

Revival Zion thus conceives the spiritual world as at once distinct and at the same time engulfing the temporal one. The spiritual world saturates the temporal world, yet it is only apparent to those who have eyes to see. The spiritual sight or consciousness of Revival Zion is imaged as a kind of geography, the terrain of which is Zion. As the spirits "travel" to the temporal world "from" Zion, so too the children of Zion "journey" from the temporal world "to" Zion. This journey is a shift in consciouness made possible by the elements of ceremony. The music and hyperventilated dance of the "bands" open the eyes to the presence of spirits and the ears to their message. It is the liturgical repetition of praise that opens up the world of Zion. The separation in space and time between congregation and Zion is overcome "in the spirit," in the altered state of awareness offered by the spirit in response to the music and dance of praise. The "bands" journeys to the glorious Zion of the past, the invisible Zion of the present, and the mighty Zion yet to come. The language of geography—journeys, cities, mountains, rivers—is employed to speak of a spiritual understanding, a view of the temporal world with spiritual eyes.

For most children of Zion these spiritual eyes are first opened in the most ordinary altered state of consciousness, dreams. A guardian angel calls the human being to its service, a call which the human can resist only at peril. It is often in the liminal state of a serious illness that the call of the spirit can first be heard. "Dissociated" from ordinary ways of seeing the world, the reality of the spiritual world becomes apparent and the survivor emerges transformed with new knowledge and vision. The spirit offers a pact: for human praise and devotion, the spirit grants guidance and protection. Once accepted this relationship grows as the spirit leads the human being to ever deeper levels of understanding, ever clearer discernment of the hidden activity of the spirit in the temporal world. The devotee "works with Jeremiah" or "works with Gabriel" in a reciprocal relationship of teaching and learning, revealing and "seeing."

When the chidren of Zion speak of "my spirit," they may be referring to the guardian angel who guides them, or to a particular faculty of the human person. In Afro-Jamaican psychology, the human person is often seen to be composed of two invisible dimensions, sometimes called "shadows," or "spirits."[46] There is a "soul" or "good shadow" or "good *duppy*," which survives the body and goes to God after death. There is also an "evil shadow," a "trickify *duppy*," which, after the death of the body, lingers around the gravesite and its former home, restless and impatient for appeasement. It is this *duppy* which must be dispatched by a nine-night funeral vigil to join its counterpart in heaven. Uncontrolled by community ritual sanctions, this *duppy* can disrupt human lives by its own willfulness or it can be captured by *obeah* workers to carry out aggressive commissions.

When one is "in the spirit," in the special consciousness of spiritual awareness attained by the "bands" in the church, the guardian angel subsumes the "soul." "My spirit," in the sense of the guardian angel with whom the individual has a pact, becomes "my spirit," that dimension of the individual that transcends the temporal world. When this identification is completed in a public, ritual context, the individual is "converted," and his or her soul has now joined the community of saints, the community of the spirits of the Bible. The spirits of the Bible are thus converted souls, brought over to Zion by senior angels through the ceremonies of their communities. And so, Zion is literally the world of the ancestors: the ancestors of the past in Africa, the ancestors of the present in ceremony, and the ancestors to come in the eschaton.

Zion is a community of spirits, some visible and some invisible, differentiated only by those who lack the eyes to see. It is the community which offers salvation, deliverance from evil, and life everlasting. The "bad" *duppies* are those who lack community, who have no one to pray over them and no one to guide them into the everlasting life of Zion. The evil of the world is detected, neutralized, and even converted by the community of Zion. *Obeah* is detected by *myal*, the consciousness developed in community ceremony. *Duppies* "set" and shadows "caught" by *obeah* practitioners are liberated by the community of Zion.[47] What is buried is made visible in the waters of life, and the *myal* consciousness of the church service.

The directives of the spirits in dreams and visions can be carried out only in the ceremonial journey of church service, and an individual can be converted only with the "bands." The purpose of spiritual gifts is to share them with others. One develops "my spirit" to share it with the others, to offer its particular wisdom and power for the journey of the "bands." This is the meaning of service in Zion, to offer up oneself for the uses of the spirit. A revivalist told Joseph Moore, "First the Holy spirit comes then little by little you trump and labor and the evangelists come down and use you."[48] In the midst of her journey at Mt. Zion Tabernacle the deaconess exclaimed, "Use me Lord. Use me for thy service."

Revival Zion takes the "bands" on a journey from the ancestral Zion of Africa to the second coming of the Zion of Revelation. The great time of the eschaton is apparent to those in the spirit, one must only "behold." Zion is comfort to the afflicted, hope to the poor, and power to the oppressed. The children of Zion have found the hand of God in every assertion of African power in Jamaican history. The Lord roars from Zion, and the sinners and oppressors do not hear until it is too late. Revival Zion journeys its children into the power of the ancestors, and works that power into the harsh world of Jamaica.

The Black Church
in the United States

"The Black Church" is a general term for many diverse ways of expressing the religious experience of African Americans in the United States.[1] "The Black Church" may be defined strictly as the shared institutions among Protestant Christian denominations that have been developed and administrated by African Americans. Methodist and Baptist churches in particular have been founded by African Americans, and it is their ways of organization and worship that usually form the model for the idea of "the Black Church."[2] "The Black Church" may be extended to encompass other institutions as well: smaller, independent Christian churches, such as Holiness, Pentecostal, and Spiritual churches. From these denominations we may turn to the numberless "storefront" congregations that rise and fall with the charisma of their leaders. "The Black Church" may also include significant black initiatives within denominations largely administered by white Americans, such as the Roman Catholic or Episcopal churches. At its furthest, "the Black Church" could include non-Christian religious bodies developed by African Americans such as Islam or the Yoruba traditions that have been brought to the United States from the Caribbean and Africa.[3]

Amid the diversity of class, color, and sensibility that characterize these different institutions, it is impossible to abstract an "essential" set of characteristics that can be applied to all of them. Urban professionals in Philadelphia have created very different institutions and ways of worship than farmers in Texas. What unites the Black Church is the religious insight available to those who are black in the United States. African Americans have access to a special religious perspective that flows from two sources: one obvious that touches all African Americans; one more subtle that reaches many but not all. African Americans know the religious insight that comes from their near-universal experience of racial exclusion and prejudice in the United States. The ceaseless attempts to limit and marginalize African Americans have challenged nearly every black individual to find ever-deeper personal resources of affirmation and compassion. African Americans have been challenged to become a new people, a "great nation" in the biblical phrase, and the struggle toward this destiny has given them a unique and profound understanding of God and his works.

The more subtle strain informing the Black Church comes from its more distant roots in the spirituality of ancestors brought over from Africa. Africa has given the Black Church a way of worship through music, movement, and ecstatic experience. What might seem to outsiders to be mere "motor behaviors" remembered from Africa are actually expressions of a dynamic, incarnated spirituality which is found throughout the diaspora.[4] This way of worship, of course, is not found in every form of the Black Church, but the diasporan perspective that we have been developing allows us to see it spread very far and wide.

Stressing the continuities among the expressions of this diasporan spirituality allows us to bring together these twin features of the Black Church. The Black Church is both "black" in its independent wisdom arising from its exclusion from white America, and it is "African American" in its development of a spirituality born in Africa. Stressing its continuities with vodou, candomblé, santería, and Revival Zion requires a certain level of generalization and ahistoricism. Certainly the community of the Black Church is not one but many; its services, not one but many. But what of its spirit? In this chapter we explore what the Black Church of the United States shares with other diasporan religious traditions: how the spirit of the Black Church in the United States arises out of the service of its community.

COMMUNITY

Africans were present on the earliest Spanish voyages to the Americas. Ivan van Sertima makes a fascinating case that African ships made regular voyages to Central America in the centuries before Columbus.[5] Africans, free and bound, were important figures in the Spanish explorations of the South, Central, and North American interior. The presence of Africans in the developing pattern of enslavement and forced immigration that would characterize colonial North America can be traced to Jamestown where twenty Africans were transported and sold in 1619. By the end of legal slavery in 1865, nearly 600,000 Africans had been carried to North America, and it is likely that tens of thousands more were brought after the Civil War, even into the twentieth century.[6] Most would work and die as agricultural laborers, isolated from each other on small farms.

The ethnicities of the people carried from African to North America show the same range of distribution, but not the same kinds of concentrations, as those of other diasporan communities. Africans from Gambia to southern Angola survived the passage, and a variety of African languages were spoken in the American South.[7] Yet the relatively low number of Africans brought into colonial North America compared to the number taken to the Caribbean and Brazil, combined with the suppression of the American slave trade beginning in 1808, made for an accelerated development of uniquely African American institutions. Without the numbers and concentrated populations, the African "nations" of the Caribbean and Brazil were not reconstituted in North America.

Sterling Stuckey has shown how the national identities of enslaved Africans in North America were brought together in the pan-African ceremony of the "ring shout."[8] Citing African precedents from Upper Guinea, Dahomey, and Kongo-Angola, he finds the ring shout a synthesis of African styles of ancestor invocation. The ring shout is a well-known religious service that has been observed throughout the American South from the eighteenth century up to the present. Whether in the open spaces of plantations or within church buildings, African Americans have gathered to worship by forming a circle, calling songs, and moving counterclockwise while stamping their feet in rhythm. Harriet Ware, an abolitionist teacher from Boston who came to the recently federalized Sea Islands of South Carolina in 1862, described a ring shout she witnessed:

> . . . a true "shout" takes place on Sundays or on "praise" nights through the week, and either in the praise-house or in some cabin in which a regular religious meeting has been held. Very likely more than half the population of the plantation is gathered together . . . But the benches are pushed back to the wall when the formal meeting is over, and old and young, men and women, sprucely dressed young men, grotesquely half-clad field hands, the women generally with gay handkerchiefs twisted about their heads and with short skirts, boys with tattered shirts and men's trousers, young girls barefooted, all stand up in the middle of the floor, and when the "sperichil" is struck up, begin first walking and by-and-by shuffling around, one after the other, in a ring. The foot is hardly taken from the floor, and the progression is mainly due to a jerking, hitching motion, which agitates the entire shouter, and soon brings out streams of perspiration. Sometimes they dance silently, sometimes as they shuffle they sing the chorus of the spiritual, and sometimes the song itself is also sung by the dancers. But most frequently a band, composed of some of the best singers and tired shouters, stand at the side of the room to "base" the others, singing the body of the song and clapping their hands together on their knees. Song and dance alike are extremely energetic, and often, when a shout lasts into the middle of the night, the monotonous thud, thud of the feet prevents sleep within half a mile of the praise-house.[9]

The necessity of the kinetic expression of this form of African American worship can be seen in number of places. Frederick Law Olmstead, during his travels in the South shortly before the war, met a slaveowner who told him that he was requested to remove the back rails from the benches of the plantation chapel because the slaves would not have "room enough to pray."[10] When A. M. E. bishop Daniel Alexander Payne traveled the South some ten years after the war he found the "heathenish" practice of the ring shout much in evidence. On one occasion he asked a pastor to stop a shout in progress and was informed by the "leader of the singing and clapping ring" that "sinners won't get converted unless there is a ring."[11]

The conversion that the shouters referred to seems to have involved something more than the ordinary white or white-trained Christian might expect. To become converted was to experience an extraordinary state of mind described as "getting the spirit," "getting happy," "getting over," or during its first occurrence, "coming through." Clifton Furness, a traveler to South Carolina in the 1920s, felt himself the power of the spirit invoked by the community. At a service on a rural plantation he saw:

Several men moved their feet alternately, in strange syncopation. A rhythm was born, almost without reference to the words of the preacher. It seemed to take shape almost visibly, and grow. I was gripped with the feeling of a mass-intelligence, a self-conscious entity, gradually informing the crowd and taking possession of every mind there, including my own. . . . A distinct melodic outline became more and more prominent shaping itself around the central theme of the words, "Git right, sodger!" . . . Scraps of other words and tunes were flung into the medley of sound by individual singers from time to time, but the general trend was carried on by a deep undercurrent, which appeared to be stronger than the mind of any individual present, for it bore the mass of improvised harmony and rhythms into the most effective climax of incremental repetition that I have ever heard. I felt as if some conscious plan or purpose were carrying us along, call it mob-mind, communal composition, or what you will.[12]

Margaret Washington Creel in her study of the Gullah people of the Sea Islands, draws the parallel between the ring shout and the initiation ceremonies of the Poro and Sande societies of present-day Liberia and Sierra Leone.[13] The "conversion" that the ring occasioned was sealed by the descent of the spirit, overtaking the personality and body of the "sinner." Membership into the praise house was only open to the converted, and only members of the praise house could perform the shout.

African Americans looked to the Bible to describe and legitimate their experience of initiation into the life of the spirit. They saw in Christian baptism a framework to permanently convert or "sanctify" the neophyte. When Jesus was baptised in the river Jordan, the spirit was recognized to be "descending upon him."[14] John the Baptist says, "Upon whom thou shalt see the Spirit descending, and remaining on him, the same is he which baptizeth with the Holy Ghost."

Directed both by white missionary preachers and black pastors, African Americans went down to the rivers and streams of the South to be baptised. There they found occasion to seal the experience of new life with the extraordinary state of mind of spirit manifestation. Dorothy Scarborough describes a scene in the early twentieth century that might be witnessed in any Southern African American community before and since. She writes with condescension but telling detail of shouting at a river baptism:

> With each immersion the excitement grew, the shouting became more wild and unrestrained, the struggles of the candidate more violent. . . . The crowd surged back and forth, and as one bystander would rush to greet a candidate coming out of the water, shrieking forth joy and thanksgiving, the crowd would join in vehement song. Sometimes half a dozen shouters would be in ecstasy at once, each surrounded by a group of admirers trying to control him, or her— usually her. Each group would be a center of commotion in the general excitement.
>
> The shouter would fall on the ground, writhing about as if in anguish, tearing her hair, beating off those who sought to calm her.[15]

The connections between initiation and spirit manifestation suggest parallels throughout the African diaspora. By the time that the descriptions above were written, the language of the participants was English and the imagery Christian. Yet the connection between immersion and spirit manifestation in baptism suggests a symbiosis of religious experience of various origins. The ring shout redoubles this connection between initiation and spirit manifestation, now channeled for the inspiration of the community by rhythmic movement and song. The division of the ring shout into two parts, one hymns with benches arranged in lines, and the other with "room to pray," shows too a creative rearrangement of ritual structures to meet a new cultural environment. The ring shout moves from a service of the word, where Baptist and Methodist hymns were sung, to a communion of spirit, where only African American spirituals were performed.[16] In both baptism and the ring shout the biblical word is both juxtaposed and given expression in the incarnation of the African spirit.

Despite the accusations of heathenism from their white teachers, African Americans insisted on the essential Christianity of their way of worship. It became clear to both parties that there were important differences between Christianity as it was practiced among whites and Christianity as it was practiced among blacks. Many slaveholders paid white ministers to see to the religious instruction of the slaves. In antebellum South Carolina an English clergyman named Alexander Glennie was engaged by several plantation owners to preach and instruct in the slave quarters. His sermons reveal a good deal about the "two christianities" of plantation North America.

"Servants, be obedient to them that are your masters according to the flesh, with fear and trembling, in singleness of your heart, as unto Christ; not with eye service as menpleasers; but as the servants of Christ, doing the will of God from the heart. . . ." [Ephesians 6:5–6]. This passage from the Bible shews to you, what God requires from you as servants; and there are many other passages which teach the same things. You should try and remember these parts of the Bible, that you may be able "to do your duty in that state of life, unto which it has pleased God to call you." For although a bad servant may not wish to know what God requires of him, yet a Christian servant will desire to know this, and to do his will in every thing.[17]

This "highly selective form of Christianity"—in Charles Joyner's phrase—was rejected by African Americans for the opiate that it was intended to be. An unnamed black Virginian in 1870 described an exchange which occurred in a slave church when a white preacher was interrupted mid-sermon by an elderly Uncle Silas, "Is us slaves gonna be free in Heaven?" Uncle Silas demanded. The preacher attempted to continue the sermon, but Uncle Silas, once provoked, would not be silenced. "Old white preacher pult out his handkerchief an' wiped de sweat fum his face. 'Jesus says come unto Me ye who are free from sin an' I will give you salvation.' 'Gonna give us freedom 'long wid salvation?' ask Uncle Silas."[18]

White preachers in general were unprepared to answer that question, so black ministers spoke of a very different Christianity of black liberation. In independent African American urban churches as early as the close of the eighteenth century, and in innumerable "brush harbors" on country plantations and farms, the word came from the Bible of a chosen people in bondage who were delivered by God.[19] Inspired by the successful revolution in Haiti and the message of the righteous struggle of Samson against the Philistines, Gabriel Prosser organized a holy rebellion against slavery in Virginia in 1800. Twenty-two years later in Charleston, deacon Denmark Vesey's exposed conspiracy rested on Zechariah's vision of the gathering of all nations against corrupt Jerusalem.[20] Nat Turner in Virginia describes his vision: "And on the 12th of May, 1828, I heard a loud noise in the heavens, and the Spirit instantly appeared to me and said the Serpent was loosened, and Christ had laid down the yoke he had borne for the sins of men, and that I should take it on and fight against the Serpent, for the time was fast approaching when the first should be last and the last should be first . . ."[21]

Beside these desperate actions, there were many other forms of liberating African American theology. Frederick Douglass saw in the spirituals a multi-level call to liberation. He writes:

A keen observer might have detected in our repeated singing of:

> O Canaan, sweet Canaan
> I am bound for the land of Canaan,

something more than a hope of reaching heaven. We meant to reach the *North*, and the North was our Canaan.[22]

This lively double meaning of African American theology could be actualized in ceremonial contexts as well as armed resistance or escape. The freedom promised in the scriptures, the kingdom of God which is "already but not yet," could be entered in the ceremonial space of the "ring" or "camp meeting," the community in action.

> Going to moan and never tire,
> Moan and never tire,
> Moan and never tire,
> There's a great camp meeting in the promise land.[23]

The Black Church was a place where the power of the ancestors through the spirit could loose the bounds, drop the imposed limitations of the mask, and ignite the power of the people. Hagar Brown of South Carolina recalled the spirit-filled meetings of slavery days:

> Fire take the Church!
> Heart commence to turn over!
> Great Lord! The whole thing been jump![24]

The movements of the ring shout often repeated the actions of biblical figures. As the participants sang repeatedly, "We're traveling to Immanuel's land," they would move through the gestures of Joshua's army surrounding Jericho or the children of Israel leaving Egypt.[25] The construction of the sacred space of the ring allowed them to participate in the mighty events of liberation, to incarnate the successful struggles of the biblical ancestors into the harsh worlds of slavery and its aftermath. While this travel to the other world of the Bible has been interpreted as a flight from the reality of enslavement, it is also a commentary upon it.[26] The idea of freedom is made physically present in the bodies as well as the minds of the participants. Freedom from all the restraints of a false and contradictory existence could be directly experienced, if only temporarily. Ceremonial freedom was a release from enslavement, but it was something more as well, a pattern or archetype of liberation. The experience of the ring nurtured an interior freedom that could be maintained in this world until it could be fulfilled in one to come. In writing of the penultimate freedom of emancipation, W. E. B. Du Bois stresses the connection between ceremonial and historical freedom:

> In song and exhortation swelled one refrain—Liberty; in his tears and curses the God he implored had Freedom in his right hand. At last it came, —suddenly, fearfully, like a dream. With one wild carnival of blood and passion came the message in his own plaintive cadences:
>
> > "Shout, O children
> > Shout you're free
> > For God has bought your liberty."[27]

The ring shout is but one well-known feature of antebellum African American spirituality. Black Americans were responding to their social situations and interacting with the spirit in a great variety of ways, from the non-Christian spiritual manipulations of hoodoo medicine, to the great northern churches of Richard Allen, Absalom Jones, and Peter Williams.[28] Yet the shout forms a useful model for understanding a spirituality that is found throughout the Black Church. The construction of communion with the spirit through the rhythms of words and music, movement and prayer, became a distinctive feature of the African American Church experience. The spirituality of the Black Church is perhaps best understood when this ceremonial orientation to freedom is seen to reflect the general quest for the entire people's liberation. It is this isomorphism of experiences of freedom, already in liturgy and not yet in history, that has been carried from slavery to the not-yet freedom of the present day.

Franklin Frazier writes that the reorganization of African American life after the Civil War merged the "invisible institution" of slave religion with the institutional churches of African Americans who were free before the war.[29] Frazier observes: "The Negro masses were concentrated in the Methodist and Baptist churches which provided for a more emotional and ecstatic form of worship than the Protestant Episcopal, Presbyterian, and Congregational churches. But even in the Methodist and Baptist denominations there were separate church organizations based upon distinctions of colour and what were considered standards of civilized behavior."[30]

While the presence of class and color distinctions within the Black Church should not be overlooked, an emphasis on the connections between worship and theology is not misplaced. As the Southern Methodist and Baptist churches institutionalized the spirituality of the ring shout, the great migration of African Americans from South to North in the twentieth century brought that spirituality to every corner of the African American community in the United States.

Amid the diversity of the contemporary Black Church we might choose one or two examples that reveal the dynamic spirituality of the shout and still may be recognized across a broad spectrum of African American worship traditions. There is no "typical" church within the Black Church, but there are features which apply to a wide variety.[31] Despite the resistance on the part of what Frazier calls the "elite" toward the "emotionalism" of the "masses," the spirit of the rural black Southern churches has permeated "from below" the Black Church as a whole. It is a frequent lament among many members of the Black Church that the more urban and affluent its members become, the more they move away from the dynamic "old time religion" of the South. As African Americans moved North toward greater opportunities, a compromise between the staid, urban church and the enthusiastic down-home community could be found in the newly formed Pentecostal churches. A large urban, Pentecostal church provides a concrete example of the diasporan spirituality seen in the shout and now institutionalized in a contemporary African American community.[32]

The Church of God in Christ, incorporated in Memphis at the close of the nineteenth century, is the largest black Pentecostal church, today claiming four million members in over nine hundred congregations.[33] Its founder, Bishop Charles Harrison Mason, describes his personal experience of Pentecost in these terms:

The Spirit came upon the saints and upon me. . . . So there came a wave of glory into me, and all of my being was filled with the glory of the Lord. . . . When I opened my mouth to say Glory, a flame touched my tongue which ran down to me. My language changed and no word could I speak in my own tongue. Oh! I was filled with the Glory of the Lord. My soul was then satisfied.[34]

Bishop Mason's faith and energy inspired thousands of believers to receive the Holy Spirit and accompany migrants to the North to work among them. Though its roots and central temple are in the South, the majority of the congregations of the Church of God in Christ are in the North, and the Church took considerable pride in seeing African Americans through the difficulties of the migration. Bishop Mason's pacifism made him the object of police surveillance, and his interracial ordinations were the occasions for frequent harassment by the F.B.I. and local police forces during the most perilous days of segregationist retrenchment after World War I. The Church of God in Christ was at the center of the Memphis sanitation workers' strike in 1968 when Martin Luther King, Jr., was assassinated.[35]

The Church of God in Christ, like all congregations of the Black Church, has provided more than worship services for its congregation. During the difficult years of legal or de facto segregation, the church functioned as a full alternative society offering education, financial assistance, and health care to its members. It often gave members the only avenue toward justice in the wider society, and it provided the network, leadership, and ideology for the quest for civil rights. The "this-worldly" activities of the Black Church are not divorced from the "other-worldly" ones. Some internal critics may charge that some churches are "escaping" into spiritual experience, while other critics bemoan the "loss" of spirit in politically active churches. The harmony between "this-worldly" and "other-worldly" actions has always been the desideratum of the Church of God in Christ. Most studies of the contemporary Black Church have focused on its social and political activities, but I would like to reexamine these activities through the lens of the spirituality of the church service. The centrality of the service to the church's self-identity, and the spirit shared during its condensed time and space, reveal the model the church offers for the liberation of all of its people.

A 1978 study by Thomas A. Burns and J. Stephen Smith of an affiliate Church of God in Christ in Philadelphia gives us a structure for understanding the "old-time" spirituality in a contemporary urban setting.[36] The Church of God in Christ recognizes three phases of initiation into the community. An individual must first be saved, then sanctified, and finally filled with the Holy Spirit. To be saved is to experience Jesus Christ in one's life as one's personal savior and to accept baptism. To be sanctified is to bring the teachings of Jesus into every phase of one's life so that one is committed to never straying from them. When one is sanctified, one may receive the Holy Spirit into oneself and may share it with others by manifestation in services. To be filled with the Holy Spirit is to confirm the sanctification experience by the gift of "tongues." "Tongues," or glossalalia, is the momentary inspiration to speak a sacred language of spiritual praise, which, in the Church of God in Christ, corresponds to a special spiritual state of consciousness. Although it is the spirit who chooses who will be saved, sanctified, and filled with the Holy Spirit, each stage of initiation is recognized only by ceremonial offices within the church. Each church is under the authority of a single pastor for whom the church is his or her sole source of income, and who is likely to have inherited the mantle from his or her family. Technically the Church of God in Christ ordains only men to the pastorate, but increasingly its main seminary is training women for the post.[37] Though it is still relatively unusual, the pastor of the 1978 Philadelphia church was a woman. The pastor had received and announced her call to lead the church and had served as an assistant pastor before rising to her present role. To be promoted she had to demonstrate her skills in preaching, song, and healing.

Well over half of the small congregation of under a hundred persons in the Philadelphia church have official roles to play in the Sunday service. The pastor is aided by an assistant pastor, who is a sanctified elder man. He reads the scriptural lesson, supervises the collection, and leads the first part of the service. Together with the pastor and assistant pastor, a council of deacons and trustees supervises the operation of the church and the conduct of the service. These are senior men and women, "elders" and "mothers" who are at least sanctified and many of whom are filled with the Holy Spirit. Each service requires the attentions of a number of "nurses" who may or may not be filled with the Holy Spirit and who assist those who receive the spirit during the service. Indispensable to the service are musicians playing "gospel" instruments, organ, piano, and drums. Finally there are three choirs which reflect levels of seniority in the church: the Zionettes, composed of twenty young children; the Fellowship Choir of ten or so saved young adults; and the Memorial Choir of junior and senior sanctified mothers, deacons, and trustees.

Each member plays a part in the manifestation of the spirit within the body of the congregation. The saved move the spirit by sacred rhythms: swaying in place, singing, clapping, keeping time with tambourines and sanctioned instruments. The sanctified move through the church, pray with their palms raised, and manifest the spirit through emptying their consciousness of their own personalities. Those filled with the spirit speak the heavenly language of the spirit, putting into vocal forms the ineffable praise due the Holy Spirit. The pastor modulates the presence of the spirit through the rhythms of her speech, the musicians through the pitch of their instruments. The nurses seal the boundaries of the spirit's presence and protect those manifesting the spirit from the power that surges through their bodies.

With this overview of the relationship between human roles and the power and presence of the spirit, we can turn to a specific service of the Church of God in Christ offered in Washington, D.C.[38]

SERVICE

It is a gray January Sunday morning, just before the Clinton inauguration of 1993 and the Martin Luther King holiday. The church rises above a busy commercial intersection in a neighborhood of small, single-family, brick row homes. The building is new, high-ceilinged with large glass windows and gleaming wood paneling. Thick, sky-blue carpet is underfoot, and the rows of polished pews have plush blue cushions. The pews can hold at least three hundred people, a large vestibule in back can accommodate another hundred, and the wide side aisles probably a hundred more. At eleven o'clock only a few people stand in small groups chatting, but the large room is full of sound as the choir finishes its warm-ups.

Today the women's choir—twenty-five young women from their late teens to mid-thirties—will offer its service. They wear black dresses, similar though some are adorned with gold sequins or are cut in more stylish variations. The church boasts a Senior Choir of older men and women, and a junior choir of children and adolescents. There is also an usher's ensemble for younger men. Together with the musicians, nearly everyone in the church is involved in some way with the music ministry.

In twos, threes, and fours, people slowly enter the church as the choir takes its final break before the service opens. Everyone is impeccably dressed: men in conservative dark suits and ties; boys in white shirts and dark dress pants; young women in dresses of solid bright blue or green fabric; girls in ironed jumpers and kilts; and elder women in suits and wearing great ornamental hats. The clothes, the neighborhood, the furnishings of the new church show a prosperous, growing, and self-confident congregation. But times are hard, jobs insecure, and the awareness of the fragility of this modest rung of the American economic ladder is part of the fabric of the worship life of the community.

With some hundred people in their pews, the choir takes its place without ceremony on a dais to the right of the central pulpit and altar. Three deacons in long black cassocks walk to a semicircle of stately wooden chairs arranged around the pulpit. Mother Delores Hall in a stylish white suit and broad-brimmed sequined hat steps up to the pulpit and calls the community to worship. The organ swells, drums fall in, and the choir fills the church with the old spiritual:

> Everytime I
> Feel the Spirit
> Moving in my heart
> I will pray!

Twenty-five singers, an amplified organ, and driving drums quickly get the congregation moving. Choirmembers on the dais and elders in the pews take out tambourines in the midst of the song to bring the energy of the song yet higher. Some people are swaying, some clapping, some raise one hand high, waving to the spirit in praise. The song lasts ten minutes or so, and the organ gradually brings down the enthusiasm to the accompaniment of a few shouts of "Amen" and "Praise the Lord" from the congregation. Mother Hall leads the congregation in the creed of the Church of God in Christ which affirms belief in the infallibility of the Bible, the triune nature of God, the necessity of repentance and baptism, and the rapture of Christ at his return. The creed stresses the necessity for "regeneration by the Holy Ghost" for salvation, "by whose indwelling the Christian is enabled to live a holy and separated life in this present world." Finally the creed affirms that baptism in the Holy Ghost is found according to the story of the Pentecost in Acts 2:4 and "given to believers who ask for it."

From the recitation of the creed, Mother Hall requests the choir to sing the Lord's Prayer. The arrangement is slow, wistful, and the choir and the congregation sway slowly from side to side to the syncopated clap of hands. The choir brings the volume up to the heights when it trumpets the last verse "For thine is the kingdom and the power and the glory," and many hands follow the energy upward. Again the organ, with an occasional look or gesture from Mother Hall, will take the song and congregation down to a more contemplative yet pulsing plane. Mother Hall chants the Church of God in Christ national anthem, "Yes Lord." In a sure, husky voice she asks the congregation to affirm the wonders of creation, the saving deeds of Jesus, and the power of the spirit. With each pause the congregation affirms "Yes, Lord." As the enthusiasm grows, more and more people shout "Yes" and "Yes, Lord" as they feel moved. One woman comes out into the aisle to spin about with back bent, feet pumping in place, and hands raised high, fingers spread. "Oh Yes, Lord!"

The organ does not enter to maintain the manifestations of the spirit, and Mother Hall asks an elderly Senior Mother to the pulpit to offer the

General Altar Prayer. All the congregation kneels in place, somewhat awkwardly sideways in order to fit into the pews without kneelers. Kneeling silently with heads bowed, all are asked to pray for the sick, shut-in, those suffering in Africa, Asia, and Europe, for our leaders and for the pastor. All rise and the choir begins a rolling, joyous rendition of the old hymn:

> This is the day the Lord has made
> I will rejoice and be glad
> This is the day that the Lord has made.

Amid soaring organ, powerful handclaps from a church now filling with two hundred people, and quivering tambourines, the church once again lets the spirit move their bodies in place. The organ carries the feeling for a short time after the singers stop but drops the tempo for Mother Hall to introduce the lectors of the day's scripture readings. The first reader is a younger woman who reads with authority from Psalm 24. At the end of each verse, she returns to the psalm's refrain, "Who is this king of Glory?" Her deep voice rises in pitch and emphasis on every other word of the phrase:

> Who *is*
> This *king*
> Of *glo* ry?

With each repetition and increase in emphasis the congregation is moved to clap, raise hands, or shout "Amen," "Yes," "Praise the Lord." As these die down an older woman reads from Romans 8:33, "Who shall separate us from the love of Christ?" Her voice is less confident than the first reader's, and so the defiance of the verse does not move the congregation as before. However, the affirmations of her words offered by the congregation are sincere if subdued.

Mother Hall returns to the pulpit and introduces a male soloist, Brother Stubbs, to sing "I will bless the Lord." The choir carries the soft melody while the organ and drums follow in easy time. Brother Stubbs comes in after the second verse in a deep baritone and the choir raises the chorus an octave. "I." "*I will.*" "I will." "*I will bless.*" And then together: "I will bless the Lord!"

At the climax the organ drops out entirely and the voices of Brother Stubbs and the choir call, respond, and come together again and again. The organ returns with more power yet, and the congregation erupts into applause. Two women at the front of the church jump into the aisles and whirl in praise of the Lord. "Bless him, bless him, bless him, bless him!" the congregation shouts. "Praise him, praise him, praise him," they chant over and again. Fifteen or twenty people are in the aisles, some whirling, some leaping in place, some running up and down before the altar. All hands in the church are clapping in heightened double time. A number of people have come from the aisles to assist those manifesting the spirit. Sometimes three or four people will surround a person in the spirit, gently supporting him or her, and rocking in rhythm to the driving hand claps and the swelling, soaring organ. Brother Stubbs and the choir bring the song to a crescendo, both clear at the very top of their range.

Then, slowly, musicians and choir slow the tempo and drop the volume. Brother Stubbs sings each time more gently, plaintively, "I will . . . I will . . . I will . . ." The organ starts to bring the song to a close, but the congregation is not done. Mother Hall comes to the pulpit, nods to the organ, and shouts "Praise him! Praise him! Praise him! Alleluliah!" She begins to praise the spirit in tongues, and many in the congregation shout in tongues in return. Those not in the aisles leap in place. At last the organ changes the rhythm, Mother Hall returns to ordinary English and calls for the still spirit-filled congregation to welcome the pastor, Dr. Cecil Brown.

Dr. Brown enters from the rear amid the stamping, leaping, and tongue-speaking of his congregation. He wears a splendid velvet and brocade cloak, white with intricate grapeleaf designs on the exterior and lined in vibrant royal purple. He works his way swiftly through the joyous congregation shaking hands and shouting praises. He ascends the dais with a nurse in a starched white uniform and cap who takes his cloak and carefully spreads it across a vacant chair. She attends his every move, filling his water glass and wiping his brow as the service proceeds.

From now on the service belongs to the pastor, and the congregation is delighted to see him among them. Once again the organ is the instrument for slowing and cooling the manifestations of the spirit. Within a minute or two, all are back in their seats fanning themselves or being fanned with small paper fans provided by a local funeral home. Pastor Brown is a small, athletic man in his sixties. Despite his obvious pleasure in seeing the congregation whom he calls in gentle moments "my sweethearts," his face seems sad and drawn. Despite the cape, the excitement of his entrance, and the personal attendance of the nurse, there is nothing affected or grand about the personal manner of the pastor. He seems to work deliberately against any vanity with homey anecdotes and deflects adulation with repeated calls to the congregation to take responsibility for their own lives.

The melancholy of the pastor's expression may be due to sad news. "My burden is heavy this week," he tells the congregation. He has been to four funerals over the last seven days, the last the most difficult of all. A beloved bishop of the church passed away and was buried on Friday. "I know some people do, but I don't like funerals," he says, "but it's part of the job." "I must live," the pastor says with both force and resignation, and the congregation applauds him through the grief. He calls on the congregation to be thankful for their health, to visit the sick and shut-in, and to see for themselves the wonderful blessings of life that they enjoy.

He begins to tease the congregation a bit about a big football game to be played later in the afternoon. "What time is the game?" he asks. Everyone knows this is a trap. "Well we *might* be over in time for the game," he taunts. "Hey when I was coming up we didn't mention the game. If we were *going* to the game we didn't mention it . . . to anyone. Well, I'm not as traditional as that. I'll get you out of here in time."

He turns to the real heart of his message, one it seems that he repeats week after week, the power of God to solve problems. The organ begins to back up the pastor's soft words. "We live in a world of many, many, many, many problems," he says softly. "And these problems have to be addressed. You can't push them aside and pretend that they aren't there. You can bring them here, bring them to God and He'll give you the strength to know that everything is going to be all right. Everyone say: 'It's going to be all right!'" The congregation complies as they must do often, and the organ leads the choir into the pastor's song "I Will Serve Him Lord Jesus."

The song begins with a slow lilting melody from the choir, and a female soloist takes up the verses. The congregation sways slowly in place, spreading hands wide to clap on every fourth beat. But after two or three verses the tempo increases, the soloist's voice turns more hoarse as she seems to challenge the choir to pick up the beat. After five minutes or so, the beat changes entirely, hands are clapped in rapid five-on, one-off rhythm. The singer seems now to be spirit-filled herself, and she shouts the words over the driving beat of the choir and instruments. The congregation keeps the clapping at the fast pace, shouts praises, and waves hands on high, but people remain in their places in the pews. They will not again come out to move in the aisles though the pastor's words will continue to provoke manifestations of the spirit among them.

The song reaches its peak, the organ dips in and out of a short reprise, and the pastor begins to speak again of problems. "How many of you were sick and told that you were going to die?" he asks. "Stand up and praise the Lord for you are here by the power of God." Three or four people stand, and the congregation applauds heartily. The pastor calls for anyone who is sick or downhearted to come forward and be anointed. Some fifteen people come forward. He tells the congregation, "The Adversary Lucifer wishes to destroy you, to knock you from your stead-fastness. But . . . the day of the Lord is at hand! You have to save yourself! You have got to fight for yourself! You have got to fight for your own survival! Some time you are going to have to stop worrying about everybody else and save yourself." The pastor returns to his theme of the ubiquity of problems: no money, no job, sickness, frustration, the ingrat-itude of others. As he names each problem the congregation shows their experience of them with an "Amen."

"God is going to ease your oppression and your faith will set you free." As the organ begins the pastor says louder and louder "Set you free!" "God can . . . *drum slap* . . . set you free. God can . . . *drumsticks whack* . . . set you free. God can . . . He's never failed me yet . . . Set you free. God can . . . Jesus will break the chains . . . Set you free."

The choir takes the rhythm of the chant and begins a song of the triumph of God's healing power over evil, "Victory is Mine." With the help of the nurse and the three deacons, the pastor moves before the altar to anoint and lay hands on the people who have come forward for healing. Sometimes hands are laid on shoulders, sometimes an outstretched palm is placed on a forehead, sometimes oil is rubbed into the temples. As they finish with the last supplicant the pastor intones the healing power of Jesus through his spirit. "In the name of Jesus," he chants as the organ and the congregation immediately burst into response, "Amen." His voice becomes huskier, rising and falling more rapidly. He stretches out some words and runs through others to keep a beat which organ, drums, and handclaps punctuate. "In the name of Jesus—Amen, In the name of Jesus—Amen. Stop and deliver—Amen. Give us peace—Amen."

> Thank you Lord.
> Heal us and deliver, heal and deliver us.
> Bring down the Lord.
> We feel your presence.
> We feel the lightning.
> Bring down the Lord.
> Bring down the Lord
> Thank you Jesus, thank you Lord.

As the sounds die down from the anointing service, the pastor announces "Let's go to the Word." Today's lesson will come from several sources "all in the same pot:" Acts 27:31; Isaiah 59; and Psalm 124. "When I was coming up, we weren't rich. We'd all eat from the same pot. Get some greens, some green beans, cut yourself a thin slice of fat back, and cook it up in the same pot. Grab yourself a hunk of cornbread. You had hamhock you were doing good, you know . . ." "*Amen,*" the congregation knows. "Well today, I'm going to cook the scripture up in the same pot and there'll be enough for everybody."

He repeats slowly the sermon's central passage from Acts. "Except these that abide in the ship, ye cannot be saved." The ship, he says, is the church, and the port is heaven. "In the church you are able to *survive* the storms." There always will be storms and they just keep getting worse. "When you think that things are going to get better, all of the sudden, you're in a worse storm than the one you came out of." "*Amen.*" "All the difficulties are multiplied a hundredfold, our hopes and dreams and happiness are shipwrecked. But, in spite of the danger, ye shall not be *ashamed* of hope."

The congregation is fully with the pastor, reinforcing his every emphasis with a shout of "Amen" and "Yes, sir." He proceeds to tell them the story—"dramatize" it is his phrase—of Paul's shipwreck. Bound for Rome as a prisoner to stand trial for religious sedition, Paul warns his captors that the ship will be wrecked, but if the crew and passengers remain aboard they will survive the disaster. The pastor acts the parts of each of the characters. He moves about the dais, changing his voice to be the righteous Paul, the fearful crew, the officious Roman authorities, the greedy owners. As he comes to the fateful storm the pastor is in full voice, hoarse, shouting, like the waves and wind.

> They went from port to port,
> From port to port.
> They lost their course.
> They lost their course.
> They ran ashore, shipwrecked.
> *In* that storm,
> The worst storm they ever knew,
> Things got so bad on the journey,
> Things go overboard.

> Some things of this world,
> Not so valuable.
> Had to get rid of them to save their lives.

Organ bursts, drums, handclaps, and shouts punctuate the end of each line of this part of the sermon, just as they had when the Holy Spirit was invoked during the anointing earlier. Whenever the pastor particularly emphasizes a word, or trembles his voice in a harsh buzz, members of the congregation shout. The pastor returns to his theme of desperation and salvation, continuing his narrative in roaring chant:

> Things had gotten way way way way way off course,
> We ain't gonna survive.
> But our *Lord* is the master of the ship.
> Problems,
> Will make you forget everything.
> Problems,
> Will make you lose your head
> Problems,
> Will make you lose your equilibrium,
> But Problems,
> Will make you love your enemies.
> You you you got the Lord,
> It's going to be all right.
> If you abide in the ship,
> God will bring you out all right!
> God will bring you out all right!
> Because for God . . .
> It's not over until it's over.

The congregation is carried with the message now, allowing the spirit to have them stand, shout, clap, raise hands, and stamp in place. The nurse brings the pastor water and wipes his brow. He lets the enthusiasm settle and returns to his ordinary speaking voice. "You've got to stand up and say the storm is passing over, it's going to be all right. Everything is going to be all right, because God is going to save the ship. It ain't over until it's over. Listen, my message to you is: you've got to stay in the ship. It's not over until He says it's over."

The pastor steps back from the pulpit to great applause and is rerobed by the nurse. As the organ plays a gentle melody, he comes forward again to announce the "ministry of tithing." Three ushers bring a wooden box with electric flame bulbs to the front of the church. Gently, but persistently, the pastor calls upon the congregation to make good their tithes. He begins by calling those donating one hundred dollars. A few do and they receive the applause of the congregation. Then donors of twenty, thirteen, ten, seven, and five dollars are asked to stand, take their places in the aisles, and put their donations in the box. Before it is clear who is donating what, the pastor calls those who are unable to give anything to join in the line and silently pledge to give when they have the opportunity. The entire congregation now forms a single file in the central aisle moving forward to put their tithes in the box. Though the pastor has called for donations in such a way as to blur the amounts that individuals are giving, the ushers who stand before the box watch as each person puts in his or her tithe. Two large, young men stand at attention at the doors. When all the donations are made and the pastor has said a few words, the ushers count the money before the congregation and sign receipts for the count.

"Yes, we must pay our debts to the Lord and who knows what the end shall be," the pastor says. "It's not over until He says it's over. With this in mind we offer a tribute in honor of Martin Luther King's birthday. The choir with John Grant will sing the spiritual 'Done Made My Vow to the Lord.'"

The leader of the choir comes forward to introduce the hymn. "In memory of Dr. Martin Luther King this song will be performed today. His birthday will be celebrated tomorrow all across the country and the special thing about Dr. King was that he had a dream. And he would not let go of it. He pursued that dream with all of his heart, soul, and mind. And the dream cost him his life. Tonight the choir comes to encourage you, as recorded in the Word of the Lord, Psalm 76:11 'Vow and pay unto the Lord your God.' You have made a vow today, don't let go of it. Go on, and see what the end shall be."

A heavy-set young man comes forward to sing the spiritual with a powerful, operatic bass voice in the concert style of Paul Robison and the Fisk singers.

> Done made my vow to the Lord,
> And I'm never going to turn back,
> I will go,
> I shall go,
> To see what the end will be.
>
> Sometimes I'm up.
> Sometimes I'm down.
> Sometimes I'm level to the ground.
> If you get there before I go,
> Tell my friends I'm coming too.

With the sustained high note of the last word, the congregation applauds. The pastor speaks his final benediction, asking God to bless the memory of Dr. King, to bless the incoming president Clinton "who is to rule over our people," praying for special members of the congregation who could not be present, and for all gathered here. The people are in no hurry to leave, many turn to speak with neighbors or wave across the church to friends. Most will spend the rest of the afternoon in church activities, lunch, meetings, games, conversation, and they will gather again for an evening service. Their week will be filled with church projects. For now they are renewed by their contact with the spirit, pledged to pay Dr. King's vow. They are free for the moment of their burdens, abiding in the ship amid the storm.

SPIRIT

The spirit of the Black Church is the ceremonial experience of God's ultimate freedom in the body of the congregation. In word, song, music, and movement, the spirit is brought down to become incarnated in the very bodies of the devotees, showing them its power to sustain, heal, and liberate the community. As with other diasporan traditions, we are concerned, in our study of the Black Church, with the community's construction of ceremonial space and time. In ceremonies the community reveals its orientation to the African past, to the relationship between the human being and spirit, and to the sharing of the spirit among the community by manifestation in the human body.

Charles Long argues that the image of Africa "has been one of the primordial religious images of great significance" for African Americans "even if they had no conscious memory of Africa." Africa, for African Americans, "constitutes the religious revalorization of the land, a place where the natural and ordinary gestures of the blacks were and could be authenticated."[39]

Elias Farajajé-Jones has produced a powerful argument for the connection between the repatriation movements of the nineteenth century and the spirituality of the Black Church. He quotes an 1892 sermon from Solomon Buckaloo as rendered by the New York Sun: "We is de Lord's chillen of Israel of de nineteenth centery; der ain't no doubt at all about dat. . . . If we can't get to Liberia any oder way, de Lord He'll just open up a parf through the 'Lantic Ocean jes' as he did for dem oder chillen through the Red Sea. . . . De days ob miracles ain't done yet . . .[40]

The very events of the Exodus occurred in Africa, and in the Black Church the protagonists were seen as the ancestors of present-day people in bondage. While most interpreters saw the references to the "Promised Land," "Canaan," or a home "over Jordan" as references to the future heaven, they are just as much references to the homeland of the past. Farajajé-Jones shows how not only repatriation movements but also African American missionaries were inspired by biblical images of Africa. The past and future were brought together in the Exodus archetype. He writes:

Commentaries on Psalm 68:31 ["Princes shall come out of Egypt; Ethiopia shall soon stretch out her hands unto God."] along with the appropriation of the Exodus-event became the basis for explaining that which apparently had no explanation: why God had allowed the Blacks to be taken from Africa and sold into captivity and harsh labour in the Americas. A meaning was found in the light of a future filled with hope, a future in which they would be delivered and would bear the light of Christ into the ancestral continent. The future vocation explained the bondage and suffering of the past.[41]

The knowledge of freedom *in biblical Africa* became the archetype for freedom in North America. Three-quarters of a century after Solomon Buckaloo, Martin Luther King could say on the eve of his murder that he had been to the mountaintop and seen the promised land.

The once and future freedom of Africa could not only be imaged, but experienced, in the sacred time and space of the Black Church. Antebellum observers to the ring shouts noticed the relationship between the gestures of the dance and the events of the spirituals being sung. Laurence Levine writes: "The shout often became a medium through which the ecstatic dancers were transformed into actual participants in historic actions."[42] In the service of the contemporary Church of God in Christ, the pastor's "dramatized" oratory, powered with spirit-filled huskiness, brought the congregation "in the spirit" to the storm-tossed Mediterranean in the ship of the church. In the sanctuary, in the voice of the preacher, in the exclamations of the congregation, the sacred time of the Bible is made present to the experience of those in the spirit.[43]

From the orientations toward the timeless places and events of the promised land, we can see the spirit of the Black Church in the relationship cultivated between the individual and the spirit. African Americans of the antebellum period recognized the conversion from living as a sinner to becoming a saint with the extraordinary experience of "coming through," manifesting the spirit through one's body while one's consciousness was absent. A collection of the conversion experiences of Southern African Americans gathered during the nineteen-twenties sheds light on this extraordinary state of mind. Interviewees speak of a "little me" that travels on spiritual journeys while a "big me" is left to operate the body. The "little me," like the crucified Christ, dies, journeys to heaven and hell, and is reborn within the "big me" at the conclusion of the journey.[44]

In the Sea Islands, "coming through" involved an elaborate series of preparatory ceremonies where the individual was isolated from the community in "mourning." There followed several days of fasting and sleeplessness in isolation in the "wilderness." "Seekers" heads were wrapped, and on some occasions even shaved, as they prepared to receive baptism.[45] While many of these practices of "coming through" were not carried beyond the unique culture of the Sea Islands, we see examples throughout the South of shouting during baptism. It was recognized that this kind of contact with the spirit was one that symbolized the death of the "little me,"—the personality or consciousness of the convert—and its subsequent resurrection, "sanctified" in the spirit. This resurrection signaled the candidate's spiritual transformation as well as his or her admission into the hierarchy of the praise house or church. When we turn to the contemporary Church of God in Christ, we can see the same emphasis on a hierarchy based upon experience with the Holy Spirit as it is shown by spirit manifestation. Burns and Smith's study of the Philadelphia church shows that roles in the service, clothing, and even positioning in the church building rest upon one's experience of manifesting the spirit in ecstatic language and behavior. Speaking in tongues is both a sign of initiation into the spirit and a language of those initiated, a "secret" language which only initiates may employ or be gifted to understand.

Gospel music contains many references to ecstatic experience and initiation. Morton Marks writes that when Gospel singers recount the story of their conversion in song, they "relive the call" by changing the musical and vocal structure of the song. Marks writes:

Sermons and gospel songs mediate between trance enactment and trance induction. It is for this reason that the term "shouting" has a double sense. It describes both the individual trance that the preacher-singer achieves while performing, as well as the trance responses of the congregation. . . . While the call is being talked about, it is simultaneously re-lived. This re-living is signalled in speech by the appearance of trance-generated features, including glottal constrictions, increase in volume, elongated and wavering vowel sounds, rhythmic repetitions, and strongly marked hyperventilation preceding each utterance.[46]

These signs of spirit manifestation in performing the song are appropriate only to those who have undergone the ecstatic experience of conversion. No less a gospel authority than Willie Mae Ford Smith summarizes the initiatory quality of religious experience behind Gospel music by saying: "Holiness is like college, you need to become educated in God's ways."[47] Thus the development of the human person is linked to a special experience of the spirit revealing itself as a part of him or her. The "little me" that is displaced by the Holy Spirit becomes sanctified by its death and resurrection in Christ. It becomes a fluid vehicle for the inchoate, winged power of the Holy Spirit to allow the body to experience its true freedom in the promised land. The Holy Spirit is "located" in the body of the congregants and revealed when the actions of the community show it in the joyful speech and behavior of shouting.

In her study of "the sanctified church," Zora Neale Hurston says that shouting is "absolutely individualistic" and yet "a community thing."[48] Each individual manifests the spirit in his or her own individual way. One person will nearly always run, another hop on one foot, yet another fall to the ground. When one becomes familiar with the members of such a church, one will see each individual, in Farajajé-Jones's phrase, "manifesting a particular force which must be wedded to her or him."[49] Far from random "cathartic release," these behaviors are patterned according to a complex relationship between the spirit and the individual.

Yet while the individual manifests the spirit in predictable and recognized patterns, Hurston reminds us that this manifestation is "a community thing." The spirit moves individuals in particular ways, but never alone. The individual cannot manifest the spirit without the assistance of the community. The circularity of the ring shout was both a common memory of basic African ceremonial style and a symbol of a new community in the making. In the equidistance and ahistoricism of the ring, a common culture could be wrought. All sanctioned members contributed to the composition of the "sperichel" which became the rhythmic pulse for a new common consciousness. We have seen in descriptions of the Sea Islands ring shout the recognition of the connection between the song, movement, and altered states of consciousness among the participants. In Harriet Ware's account, a "band" of singers "base" the shouters, providing a counter rhythm to the thudding of their feet. The function of the music and dance, the "essence of religion" as Bishop Payne observed, was the creation of a shared consciousness born of their common trauma and troubles and communicated through the several rhythms of the song. While those who manifest the spirit shout out of the pain and fire and joy within them, they show the spirit to all the rest and so share it.

The contemporary Black Church still maintains the connection between worship and movement that required the ring shouters to demand "room enough to pray." The spirit moves the congregation not only in mind but in body. The movement is cued and controlled by a conversation among the aural elements of the service. Choir voices, organ swells, drums beats, hand claps, the tones of the preacher's voice, and the antiphony of exclamations of the congregation serve to "bring down" the spirit to bodies on earth. In the contemporary Black Church, the ring only briefly shows itself, when groups form around a particular individual manifesting the spirit. While this circling has the purpose of protecting the manifesting person from harm, those forming the circle are moving and shouting in time with the central figure. They are both protecting his or her spirit manifestation and partaking in it, "basing" the person as the power courses through his or her body.

Individuals offer their bodies to the spirit so that the community will be empowered by its presence. In the ceremonial space and time of the "boat" of the church, the Christian split between the body and soul is repaired and overcome. The incarnated spirit of the Black Church heals the split between heaven and earth and shows it in holy movement. The incarnated spirit heals the split between who the people really are, and who America has said they are.

The spirit of the Black Church can be shown to be present in *this* world as a sign of the world to come. Nearly every selection of the Church of God in Christ choir on that particular Sunday contained the phrase "I will." This is an extraordinary affirmation given the obstacles that members of the Black Church have had to overcome. "I *will* pray." "I *will* rejoice and be glad." "I *will* bless the Lord." "I *will* go, I *shall* go, to see what the end shall be." It shows the determination of the people to act freely and resolutely. It is also a future tense, showing that prayer, gladness, blessings, can only be fulfilled in a world that is not yet arrived. By dedicating the spiritual "Done Made My Vow to the Lord" to the memory of Martin Luther King, the church brought together the idea of "payment" in the tithing upon which the community depends, with the "payment" of one's dedication to the pursuit of Dr. King's dream. It is only when one has made this vow that one can see what the end will be. Here again the church has brought together the "other-worldly" interest of the spiritual with the "other world" of the future fulfillment of the dream, another world which depends upon action in this one. The ceremonial actions of the Black Church, the movements to incarnate the freedom of the spirit, realize the future and empower the congregation to fulfill it. As Pastor Brown chanted until the congregation could see this end, "It's not over until it's over."

7

Working the Spirit

In the preceding pages I have drawn portraits of five important traditions
of the African diaspora. These portraits of vodou, candomblé, santería,
Revival Zion, and the Black Church in the United States have been
designed to give a sense of both of the distinctiveness of each tradition
and the similarities among them. The strokes have been broad, the details
limited, and the focus rather narrow. By creating a separate portrait for
each tradition, I have attempted to make an image that stands on its own,
one which offers some basic information and a condensed impression of
the "spirit" of the tradition. By placing the portraits side by side, I hope to
have revealed relationships among the traditions which have not been
sufficiently emphasized or appreciated. For example, each portrait has
highlighted certain distinctive elements in the "spirit" of each tradition:
the revolutionary power of vodou, the prestige of African precedent in
candomblé, the multiple levels of meaning in santería, the deliverance
from evil in Revival Zion, and the freedom eschatology of the Black
Church. Once these elements are seen "side by side," they inform and
deepen our understanding of each of the other traditions. Our understanding of the biblical tradition of the Black Church is deepened when
we see it from the perspective of the ceremonial reenactments of the
Haitian revolution in vodou. And the drama of the vodou service is given

new meanings when seen from the point of view of the Black Church's prefigurative realizations of freedom in the ceremony of shouting.

By bringing the portrayed traditions together in one volume, I am invoking a principle of learning by comparison, adapting the famous dictum that "to know one tradition is to know none."[1] I have arranged the portraits around activities in the "service" of "spirit." All the members of the portrayed traditions would probably assent to this description of their central ceremonies, and so similarities might be found in their actions of "service" and in their ideas of "spirit." The purpose of this final chapter is to explore some of the more significant similarities and differences among the traditions portrayed. From these similarities and differences I wish to isolate the elements of a spirituality that runs through each of the traditions.

HEMISPHERIC PERSPECTIVES

The term "disaporan" to indicate the traditions that we have examined shows the issues of similarity and difference in historical and cultural contexts. Diaspora means "dispersion," and its first reference is to the Jewish cultures which flourished in the ancient Middle East and Mediterranean outside Judea. When Jerusalem was destroyed by Roman armies in 70 C.E. the term took on more vital significance as referring to communities in exile from a lost homeland. For nearly 1900 years the uniting force of the diaspora was the idea of a lost homeland, a mythic past that might be politically delivered to the people again and could be symbolically entered through the rites and rituals of the communities.

The use of "disaporan" to refer to the religions of peoples of African descent living in the Americas arises out of African Americans' profound identification with the biblical people of God in their enslavement, exile, and deliverance. An African diaspora connotes both one and several communities, separated by language and culture, but united in a similar past and future. Peoples of African descent in the Americas share a common history as Africans, and this identity has had to develop itself against crushing attempts to destroy it. Thus the traditions of the African diaspora are different because they come from very different sources in Africa and they have developed in very different societies in the Americas. Yet they are similar in that they are indeed out of Africa and forged in the fires of American slavery and racism.

"Diaspora" connotes both a dependence on Africa for its meaning and an independence from it. Our understanding of the religious traditions of the African diaspora continues to be illuminated by references to the meaning of contemporary or historical African beliefs and practices which might be their antecedents. Melville Herskovits blazed this path of interpretation, and it has been furthered in exciting ways by the work of Pierre Verger, Robert Farris Thompson, Kenneth Bilby, John Janzen, and Fu-Kiau Bunseki.[2] But I would also like to emphasize the independence of the traditions from Africa. While each traditions looks to Africa for its wellspring, each has also defined itself against Africa as a distinct community. For example, African precedent holds enormous prestige in Brazilian candomblé, yet Brazilians readily note when Africans have "lost" traditions that are current in Brazil.[3]

Over fifty years ago Herskovits argued that the African heritage of any diasporan community could not be understood without reference to the others.[4] In his study of antebellum slave religion in the United States, Eugene Genovese refers to a "hemispheric perspective" which would illuminate among the diasporan religions "the same creative impulse to blend ideas from diverse sources into the formulation of a world-view sufficiently complex to link acceptance of what had to be endured with a determined resistance to the pressures for despair and dehumanization."[5] Albert Raboteau surveys the "differing contexts" of the diasporan religions from a hemispheric perspective and concludes that the "character of the religious milieu, the average number of slaves on plantations, and the number of Africans in the slave population were all factors in the survival or loss of African culture."[6]

I can only mention here what the huge scope of the ethnohistorical project of Herskovits would entail. Each religious tradition of the African diaspora derives from many sources, including the African provenance of the tradition, the natural and social ecology of the environment in which enslaved Africans found themselves, and the history of each community in the national culture around it. Haitian vodou is different from Jamaican Revival because different numbers of Africans from different parts of the continent came to each island at different times. There they found similar but different plantation environments, economic systems, social stratifications, and European traditions. Haitians won their independence from France in 1804 and have struggled bitterly with isolation and political opportunism. Jamaicans were "emancipated" in 1834 and won independence in 1962. Were we to compare the details of these African heritages, social systems, and histories—together with those of Brazil, Cuba, and the United States—we would never allow ourselves to see important similarities in the religious life of each of these communities.

CEREMONIES OF THE SPIRIT

In the pages that remain I want to focus on these similarities, always bearing in mind and at times alluding to the all too important differences that distinguish them. The narrow focus in each of the portraits on the actions and meaning of "service" in each community places the emphasis for comparison squarely on the ceremonies of the traditions. The theme connecting the portraits is that the "spirit" of each tradition is shown and shared in the major ceremonies of the tradition. I believe that it is in the construction of the central ceremonies of the religious traditions of the African diaspora that the most significant similarities lie. The ceremonies show, in condensed form, both to the outsider and to the participants themselves, each community's fundamental self-understanding of its social identity and its role in the cosmic drama of which the social environment is a part. The focus on ceremony reveals important similarities of action within the boundaries determined by ritual time and space. I believe that I am being most true to the traditions by making actions the primary data of the portraits. In each tradition the people gather together to literally move, to "work" in their service of the spirit. In general the more vigorous the movement, the "hotter" the service, the more the spirit is served.

By now I hope that it is clear that the dynamism of diasporan ceremony is not only a cathartic release of tension—though of course it is that—but it is also a profound view of the relationship between human and spirit. Even to call it a "view" is mistaken. It is a refined orientation, an active spirituality, and "ideas" of the spirit grow from reflection on the movement of the spirit in ceremonies. Knowledge of the spirit, the *konesans* of the Haitian priest, can only come from action in ceremonies. The "college" of holiness that Willie May Ford Smith referred to offers its "courses" in spiritual experience generated by ceremonies. The theology of the religious traditions of the African diaspora grows out of the encounters between human being and spirit in ceremonies.

The focus on ceremonial spirituality reveals an interdependence of human and spirit. In the language of candomblé and santería, the spirit is "made" by human action. This means that the spirit is made present by gestural metaphors, and can be localized or "fixed" into physical objects and human bodies. But it also suggests that the spirit is manufactured by human action, "worked" from more basic spiritual force into the special force or personality to be reverenced. Its life as "a" spirit depends on the service of its devotees. A Yoruba proverb states this interdependence most emphatically: "Where there is no human being, there is no divinity."[7] The biblical traditions would not speak of a spirit "made" by human action, yet God "pours out of his spirit" (Acts 2:17) through human bodies at Pentecost. In Revival Zion and the Black Church this "pouring out" comes through the movement of the community as service to the spirit. Each of the diasporan traditions emphasize the necessity of this movement to "show" the spirit to themselves and others. It is this action which is condensed in space and time in the activity of ceremonies, the "work" or "service."

The priority and indispensability of ceremonial action for the diasporan traditions may also shed light on another vexing theological problem in comparing the traditions. So far we have been referring to "the" spirit in the singular, glossing over the significant point that *many* spirits are venerated in vodou, candomblé, and santería, while the Black Church speaks of *one* "Holy Spirit." This would seem to set the traditions into categories of difference centered on beliefs in "polytheism" or "monotheism." A reconciliation might lie in two directions: a comparison of beliefs and a comparison of rituals. First, theology is most adept in trying to reconcile the plurality and singularity of beliefs about spirit. Christianity, perhaps more than any other tradition, has attempted to explicate a complex relationship of participation between one God in three persons. If we apply some of these theological models to the problem of multiple or singular spirits in the traditions of the African diaspora, we may find similar reconciliations of seeming contradictions.

Each of the traditions speaks of one God who is the first principle of the universe: Vodou's Grand Maître or Bondye; Olodumare or Olorun in candomblé and santería; and God Almighty in Revival Zion and the Black Church. In each case the focus of the service is on the incarnation of one or more spirits which partake of the essence of the single, supreme being, but which also represent more localized or concretized forms of the abstraction. In explicating the relationship between the one God and the multiple spirits of veneration, members of the traditions have offered metaphors of electrical generators and receptors, or fragmentation of one being into many pieces, or sons and daughters of a single parent.[8] The Christian metaphors of several persons or hypostases of one God might be applied to diasporan ideas of spirit. In examining the problem of one and many gods in West Africa, Newell Booth quotes the Christian theologian Paul Tillich: "The concreteness of man's ultimate concern drives him toward polytheistic structures; the reaction of the absolute element against these drives him toward monotheistic structures . . ."[9]

From this point of view, belief in one and in many spirits among the diasporan traditions is not contradictory but rather a question of different emphases or contexts of theological reflection.

But even more fruitful than theological harmonies of diasporan beliefs is to focus on the ceremonies that have been constructed to incarnate the spirits. For though the ideas of relationship between the spirit and the one God might be expressed differently, there seems to be remarkable similarity in the ways in which the relationship between spirit and human being is acted out. From the ad hoc theologies of spirit that believers present, we may move to the more precise ways that the spirit is to be incarnated in the human community.

Wyatt MacGaffey, in his study of Kongo religion, speaks of the problem of attempting to interpret African traditions through Western theological categories. The Kongo idea of spirit is so fluid, he argues, that any typology or distinction is bound to fail. The baKongo do not care to discriminate among classes or types of spirits, but rather among the actions and actors that invoke them. He writes of "the impossibility of defining a nonliterate religion as a system of ideas and the possibility of defining it as a system of action."[10] Leaving aside for the moment whether the traditions of the African diaspora are "nonliterate," MacGaffey's study of the baKongo orients us toward comparing traditions by their organization of actions rather than by their organization of beliefs. We have seen in each of the traditions that spiritual growth is measured in experiences gained through ceremonial actions. Though the spirit "is" everywhere, the most valued encounter between humans and spirits occurs within the ceremonial confines of community action. Whatever one's personal experience of the spirit, through dreams, visions, or revelations, one grows in the spirit only when one shares it with others in ceremonies.

The fluid ideas of spirit held by the diasporan traditions when they are compared with the relatively specific means for manifesting the spirit suggest a high interdependency between the idea of spirit and the actions which incarnate it. In a sense the spirit *is* the action of the community. *Santeros* will say that a certain rhythm is Shango as easily as they will say that it is Shango's rhythm. For Revivalists, Jeremiah is the healing power of the leaves as much as the leaves "belong to" Jeremiah. The spirit can be conceived independently of human action, but it cannot be shared without it.

MacGaffey may be right that the key factor that distinguishes African from European theology is literacy or at least the literary exegesis of texts.

In the African diaspora the texts of the tradition—the songs, prayers, rhythms, gestures, foods, emblems, and clothing—have been transmitted orally and ceremonially. Even in the biblical traditions of Revival and the Black Church, the exegesis of the written text is to be found in the experience of the spirit that accompanies the Word's ceremonial performance. Eugene Genovese quotes an antebellum white preacher: "Many of the blacks looked upon the white people as merely taught by the Book; they consider themselves to be instructed by the inspiration of the Spirit."[11] Nearly every witness to African American preaching has tried to convey that it is the style of the delivery of the sermon as much as the content which is important to the congregation. The preference for ceremonial precision over systematic thought indicates an alternative spirituality. If the practice of this ceremonial spirituality has been carried on by poor folk, their commitment to it in the increasingly literate communities of the Americas shows that it is as much a choice as a limitation. By insisting on the oral interpretation of the actions of the spirit, devotees ensure that only sanctioned people will transmit the teachings and that the transmission will happen only in face-to-face encounters between initiates and novices. Oral and ceremonial transmission makes for a smaller, tighter community, which, for all its drawbacks, might have benefits not to be found in communities dependent on literary exegesis. The embrace of diasporan spirituality by middle classes who have been ambivalent toward it shows its vitality among lettered as well as unlettered people.[12]

In Jamaica and in Haiti Katherine Dunham discovered a concern on the part of her teachers for the ignorance of North Americans about their ritual obligations. She writes:

"When the stigma of being an American had worn off, there was a great and protective interest in the recognition of "Guinea" blood ties and great concern for my ancestors, who had not received the proper ritual attention because that group of slaves taken farther north had been cut off from their brothers in the Caribbean and had forgotten these practices. In some instances, as in that of the mambo Téoline at Pont

Beudet, it seemed that the welfare of the entire Negro race might be improved if these unfortunates to the north could be acquainted with the rituals of ancestor worship and the vodun.[13]

The importance of ceremonial action in diasporan religions can be stressed in one final way. Just as African traditions are best understood as systems of action rather than beliefs, so the adaptations carried out by Africans in the Americas were oriented toward effective action. The process of "syncretism" was not an accommodation among enslaved Africans to a set of universal African beliefs, a folk construction of a creed or a honing of rough ethnic and regional edges into a generalized African Sacred Cosmos. Rather it involved the gravitation to ritual specialists. Whether Africans were brought to colonies and nations with Catholic or Protestant traditions, they constructed new ritual systems from the variety of effective ritual actions which had landed with the specialists who learned them in Africa. It was the relationship of these actions with Catholic or Protestant traditions which formed the basis for the "syncretisms" or "reinterpretations" that each tradition developed. In general we might see the traditions of the Latin Americans: vodou, candomblé, and santería as developing alternative and complementary ritual systems *to* those of Catholicism. The traditions of British America, Revival Zion and the Black Church, on their part, developed alternative ritual forms *of* Protestant Christianity.

The focus on the ceremonies of the spirit in the African diaspora shows a broad commonality that distinguishes them from the European-derived traditions around them. For not only is the spirit "made" in ceremonies, it actually occasions a special state of mind. To be "in the spirit" is to actually bring the consciousness of the spirit into one's very own and to share it with others. Just as the presence of the spirit may be fixed into objects and shown through them, the spirit may manifest itself more or less fully in the bodies and minds of individuals. Some individuals have sufficient spiritual experience to manifest the consciousness of the spirit so fully that they lose their ordinary awareness, while others are touched by the spirit's consciousness while retaining something of their own. Whoever is empowered to manifest the spirit does so for the benefit of the community to allow others to share in the consciousness, either in dialogue or in identity with their own. In each tradition this path to shared consciousness is grounded in rhythm.

The complexities of the rhythms in each community's ceremonies represent a complexity of distinctions that each makes in recognizing spiritual presence. The three drums, bell, and voice of candomblé refine the presence of spirit into different distinctions than those achieved by the alternating volume, pitch, and glottal patterns of the Black Church preacher. It is not my purpose to argue whether these rhythms "cause" the special state of consciousness that usually accompanies them. While there may be neurobiological factors in generating spirit manifestation, they must be read against the cultural interpretations of the events. In the diasporan traditions the response to the rhythms is supposed to be conditioned upon initiation, yet often enough the rhythms fail to generate the state of mind in initiates while noninitiates may receive the spirit.[14]

Each tradition in its own way affirms that the first occasion of an individual's ceremonial manifestation of the spirit transforms the inner nature of the individual. To be mounted, crowned, or converted by the spirit is to die to a former life and be reborn into a new one "in the spirit." When an individual receives the spirit, a part his or her inner nature is also transformed to partake of the spirit's divinity. Their *gwo bònanj, ori,* "good shadow," or "little me" enters a cycle of spirituality so that it may exist independent of the body and be called upon eventually to manifest itself in others.

These beliefs about the spirit are all made intelligible through a focus on the ceremonies which "make" them. I have been particularly interested in seeing an interdependence among the ideas of spirit, the ceremonial construction of space and time, and spiritual states of mind. In the traditions of the African diaspora, the "spirit" is at once a divine personality, an intersection of humanly constructed coordinates, and a level of awareness. Diasporan spirituality can be recognized by its orientation to Africa, its reciprocity of spirit and human being, and its sharing of the spirit in the service of the community.

ORIENTATION TO AFRICA

Each community employs a variety of ceremonial means to align itself with its African ancestors. The boundaries of space and time constructed by the ceremony condense the experience of the community into a limited number of symbols so that the people can show themselves their part in the cosmic drama of the African people. In the construction of the space of the ceremony and in the limited time bounded by the ceremony's opening and closing, the people may enter an African space and time. The *peristil, terreiro, igbodu,* seal, or church can be recognized to be Africa. And the time which extends from rhythmic transition to the spirit's music to the final sounds that close the gate becomes the time of the ancestors who are contemporary in the bodies and minds of the people.

In vodou, the community orients itself toward Africa through the architecture of the *peristil*, centering on the great tree of the *poto mitan* which links the visible trunk and branches of Haiti with the roots in the invisible earth of Ginen. The life giving, invisible water of Ginen, particularized and personified as the *lwa*, is brought up the tree from below by the rhythms, songs, and dances of the people. From the transition from Catholic prayers to the opening of the gate by Papa Legba to the closure of the ceremony in Gede's cemetery, the community is brought to Africa. The fluid *lwa* incarnate themselves in all of the kinetic media and find their most complex incarnation in the bodies of the *ounsi*, where they interact with the human community as people themselves. Thus the Haitian community is made contemporary with the African ancestors who have become elemental powers.

In candomblé Nagô, Africa is less a location of "mystical geography" and more a historical memory. Africans came to Brazil in large numbers well into the late nineteenth century, and many Brazilians traveled back and forth across the Atlantic. The herbalism, cookery, musicianship, choristry, and dance of candomblé have always been aligned with African models. The purity of African heritage came to be seen as the highest mark of authentic practice, and all the actions of the candomblé are evaluated on their ability to cite African precedent.

This historical contact led to a distinctive orientation toward Africa in candomblé. The architecture of the *terreiro* with its central court and constellations of outbuildings reflects the ideal organization of the Nagô kingdoms. The *barracão* is the court of the king of the nation of the *terreiro*'s founder whether this is reckoned by blood descent or by initiation. Thus Ilé Axé Opô Afonjá is the court of Xangô at Oyo with his subordinate kings arranged around him. Within the *barracão* at Casa Branca, a center pole similar to the Haitian *poto mitan* can be found. This staff of Oranmiyan is not a tree but a phallus, linking the father of the Nagô at Ilé Ifé with his children in Brazil. By dancing around the staff, are the Brazilian children returning by a procreative link to the first kings of Nagôland and, like the *ounsi*, making themselves present with the African ancestors.

Perhaps the revolutionary heritage of Haiti, contrasted to the royal experiences of Nagô-Brazilians, is the factor that most informs different ceremonial visions of Africa. The *lwa* are "citizens" like their serviteurs. They are *kouzen*, country cousins, who are as bawdy and earthy as their human counterparts. The *orixás* of candomblé are remote royal personages, affectless in their procession before the community. While they offer the joy and healing of the royal touch, they embody more the national values of the people instead of the interpersonal triumphs and tragedies of the *lwa*. Yet in each case it is from Africa that the spirit arrives and it is to Africa that the community journeys by means of the "work" of "service."

For Cuban-American santería, Africa has been, in David Brown's apt phrase, "miniaturized" into the residences of *olorishas* in large urban centers. All the objects which act as media for the *orishas*' presence are contained in one room, the *cuarto de santo*. These may be still further reduced to the *canastillero*, a shelved armoire whose doors may be closed to conceal the holy objects from uncomprehending eyes. Yet the arrangement of objects reflects as much concern for African royal precedent as the more expansive sacred spaces of the candomblé *terreiro*. Obatala, the first king at Ilé Ifé, is placed above all others, royal *orishas* are raised on shelves or pedestals above the ground. Shango must sit on his royal mortar outside the hierarchy of the others, and the *orishas* of the forest, in their form as warriors are placed on the ground at the threshold of the residence.

The African royal themes of candomblé are paralleled in santería in the crowning of initiates as they "make the saint." A portion of the house become the *trono* where the initiate will remain isolated until presented in state. The symbolisms of rebirth and marriage are redoubled in that of African coronation as the crowned initiate receives a new African name, is marked with the signs of his or her African nation, and is taught Lucumi.

While the center pole of vodou and candomblé is not found in santería architecture, the space for the dancing is given the Lucumi name *igbodu* meaning sacred grove. In Africa the *igbodu* is a cleared area on the threshold between the town and the bush and so between the world of human beings and the spirits. By the rhythms, songs, and dances of the *igbodu*, the *orishas* are brought "half way" toward the human world while the human actors are brought half way to theirs. As with vodou and candomblé it is the living presence of the *orishas* which makes the community present with Africa. In the sacred actions and consciousness of the *bembé*, the community shares space and time with the royal ancestors of Africa.

The Cuban American *orishas* seem to occupy a "halfway" point between the down-to-earth Haitian *lwa* and the regal Brazilian *orixás*. When they are manifest in their human mediums, they can be as impetuous and bawdy as the *lwa* or as stern and stately as the *orixás*. This might, as with Haiti and Brazil, reflect the social organization of the community and its history with royalty both African and European. In any event as the Haitians see their africanity through the familiar lens of *kouzen*, and the Brazilians through the formal experience of courts, the Cubans find their orientation to Africa in the *igbodu* where *orishas* and humans meet.

For Revival Zion Africa may be found in the experience of the biblical ancestors in Zion. The sacred space of the yard and the sacred time of the service open up this experience to the children of Zion in Jamaica. Once again the central pillar plays a role in orienting the community to Africa. While each Revival Zion church may fashion its pole differently, the church in our portrait hung from theirs the red, gold, and green colors of Ethiopia. The spirits are said to come down the pole into the holy water sitting on a table at its foot, and then into the bodies of the dancers around the pole. The spirits are the angels, prophets, and evangelists of the Bible who dwell in Zion. All these spirits are subsumed in the Holy Spirit who "journeys" the children to Zion.

Zion is a different version of Africa than the Ginen or Ilé Ifé of vodou, candomblé, and santería. Zion is the Africa of the past where the ancestors lived and whose exploits are told in the Bible. Zion is the Africa of the present when the converted souls of the living are guided by those of the dead to lead the congregation on a journey to and from Zion within the boundaries of the sacred space and time of the service. And Zion is the Africa of the future when the great journey of God's people will be completed. This might be understood to happen to the individual in death when converted souls will join those of the ancestors in the holy city. But it will also happen in the fullness of time when God's people will be delivered to justice and righteousness.

The Africa of Revival Zion is understood through the images and historical vision of the Bible. But the world of the Bible is not an account of a remote people whose struggles have "relevance" to us today, but a living, creative world that is open to those who have the sight to see it. The cosmic drama of the enslavement and deliverance of God's children out of Africa is enacted in all its fullness in the special sight that is shared in the Revival service. Revival Zion adds to the orientation to Africa maintained by vodou, candomblé, and santería, a vision of destiny, the biblical history of promise and fulfillment for Africa's children.

As for the Black Church the significance of Africa is at once obvious and obscure. When the first independent churches named themselves "African" and "Ethiopian," they may be thought of as doing nothing more than choosing racial markers to distinguish themselves from the larger white churches that were so inhospitable to them. But these titles reflect a more profound identification between Africa and the events of the Bible than might be apparent. Like the Revivalists of Jamaica, African Americans saw the events of the Bible as taking place in Africa. The great biblical drama of God's deliverance from bondage was once played out in Africa, and as "Ethiopia shall soon stretch out her hands" it will be played out among Africans again.

The architecture of the Black Church, although in recent times images of a black Christ or hangings of African cloth may be displayed, offers us little of the ritual media familiar to us from the other traditions. True to the aniconic aesthetic of Methodist and Baptist Christianity, ceremonial attention is to be placed on the Word, the aural media of the spirit's presence, either in the sermon of the preacher or the music of the choir. Only when the spirit is "high" do we glimpse some of the spatial metaphors of the other diasporan traditions. In the ring shouts of the plantation churches of the South and the momentary rings that form around shouting congregants in the urban north, we see attempts to contain and localize the spirit that are similar to those of the circle dances of vodou, candomblé, santería, and Revival Zion. And the shared spirit of shouting, manifested through the various individual bodies of the congregants, allows the congregation as a whole to become contemporaries with the biblical figures. As with Revival Zion, the Black Church sees the struggles of God's people as their struggle. And as the mighty events once took place in Africa, they continue to take place when the congregation is brought to the biblical world in word, song, and movement.

RECIPROCITY OF SPIRIT AND HUMAN BEINGS

Each of the diasporan traditions seeks to develop an intimate relationship between individuals and the spirit. Through ceremonies of initiation, the spirit is recognized to be "fixed" or present within the person of the initiate so that his or her personality may become a vehicle for the manifestation of the spiritual personality. In each tradition the spirit calls the individual to its service through some disturbance in his or her life, usually a serious illness. This encounter with the borders of life and death opens up the experience of the individual to the reality of the spiritual world. In some cases the spirit may offer a covenant, an exchange of life for life. The spirit offers the individual a "return" to the human world in exchange for a life of service. Thus the individual will live in the spiritual world ceremonially and in abiding by the restrictions of a spiritual lifestyle instead of permanently through death.

The recovery from illness or grief or despair provides a natural model for the ceremonial transformation of initiation ceremonies. The individual is brought to a symbolic death and rebirth in the classic pattern of separation from the old life, liminal transition between spirit and human worlds, and incorporation back into ordinary life with a new identity and vision. In each of the diasporan traditions, an element of the person is brought through this passage through death and is reconstituted on a higher plane. The mark of this reborn self is the ability to "see" simultaneously the spiritual and human worlds. This sight allows the initiate to recognize the workings of the spiritual world within the human and to see the human actions within the greater context of the workings of the spirit. The initiate is also empowered to return to the spiritual world through ceremonies and show the actions of the spirit to the community.

In each of the diasporan traditions, the goal of the individual is to develop an inner relationship with the spirit so that one's body and mind might show and share it with others at ceremonies. The innermost nature of the individual "carries" the spirit so that he or she may become permeable to it and others might experience it. Through initiation the spirit is made an essential "part" of the person, a dimension in a constellation of elements that comprise a person. The spirit is not the conscious self, but something greater which may subsume the self, overcome its borders and direct the whole person. This relationship is the one that is fixed through the ceremonies of the African diaspora.

Vodou shows growth in the relationship between individual and spirit with ceremonies to prepare the head as a vehicle for spirit. The *lwa* call their serviteurs through illness or other persistent patterns of misfortune that awaken human beings to the limitations of their perspectives. In the *kouche* "flooring" ceremonies that make a *ounsi*, the soul of the novice, her or his *gwo bònanj* is brought below the waters to Ginen and resurrected to exist simultaneously in the pots of the temple and the heads of the *ounsi*. The death and rebirth of the *gwo bònanj* in its journey through Africa gives the *ounsi* a level of *konesans*, sacred sight to see Ginen in Haiti and Haiti in Ginen. The *ounsi* may be called to realize her or his *konesans* yet further, to take the *ason* or the *prix de yeux* and be able to shift to this sight at will. Maya Deren calls the wedding of *lwa* and human being an "amalgam," while Katherine Dunham sees *lwa* and serviteur as polar electrical currents. In each case the relationship is both one of identity and separation brought into focus by ceremonies of initiation.

In candomblé the same metaphors of chemistry and electricity might be used to describe the bond between human and *orixá*. The *iaô* is the "bride" of the spirit and remains so for seven years until she or he may be an *ebomin*, a "senior wife." As chemical reactions bind elements into amalgams, and positive and negative currents are bound into alternating cycles, so marriage is a binding of two persons in one flesh. Throughout the long seclusion in the *runkô* the *iaô*'s head is prepared to receive the *orixá* who has called the *iaô* often by an unfixed and therefore dangerous manifestation. Through blood, herbs, songs, and rhythms the *orixá* is literally placed inside the head of the *iaô* where it sits enthroned upon the transformed soul of the individual. As in Haiti the relationship is characterized as one between horses and riders, the *lwa* and *orixá* mount the *ounsi* and *iaô* to put them through their paces, directing the horses in service of their riders.

There does not seem to be the same emphasis in candomblé as there is in vodou concerning clairvoyance and extraordinary sight in the knowledge that the *iaô* gains by his or her intimate relationship with the *orixá*. Priestesses of the *orixás* receive the *búzios*, cowrie shells which may be read to reveal the actions of spirit in the world and the world in the spirit. Still, interpreting the shells requires a kind of *konesans* and the more senior the priestess, the more she may have internalized the signs of the shells so that she can see the spirit without them. Again, it may be that the formality and attention to orthodoxy in candomblé argue against the exercise of the more personal charisma of vodou and ground sacred knowledge more firmly in the learned behavior of the *terreiro*.

Santería shares a very similar African heritage with candomblé, and so its language of relationship between *orisha* and human being is nearly identical. *Iyawos* are "brides" of the *orishas* and, through their probationary status is much shorter lived than the *iaôs* of candomblé, they still act as horses to their spirit riders. Santería and candomblé look more to the institutions of divination than to the "sight" of the initiates in determining the nature of the spirit-*iyawo* relationship. In santería mastery of divination carries its own priesthood, the path of Orula. The *dilogun* shells received by the *iyawos* at initiation are considered to speak a "language with fewer letters" than the more complex Ifa. It is Ifa which determines which spirit a *iyawo* will receive upon and in her head. In *kariocha* the novice is crowned with the spirit, both upon his or her head in the symbolic placement of stones, and within it by the topical applications of water, herbs, and blood. The head of the devotee, his or her *ori* is cleansed and purified of the identities of the old life, to act as a seat for the enthronement of the *orisha*. The *orisha*, like its counterpart in Brazil and the Haitian *lwa*, is fixed into the head of the devotee, becoming a new element in the "amalgam" of individual and spiritual qualities. The *orisha* is the "owner" of an individual's head, its "mother" or "father," its spouse and, if vodou's image might be applied, its "mirror." The *orisha* is an image in an obscure mirror to the novice, an image that becomes progressively clearer as she or he grows *en santo*. And during the ceremonies of service to the *orishas*, the devotee becomes a mirror through which the congregation might see the *orisha*.

The spirit announces itself to the children of Revival Zion through a variety of extraordinary experiences of vision. As with vodou, candomblé, and santería, the spirit may first call the revivalist through a spontaneous manifestation at a ceremony. Or it may choose to reveal itself in the rare state of awareness brought on by serious illness. Yet the most persistently reported irruption of the spirit into human consciousness is through dreams. Here the spirit, in the personalities of biblical figures, or in the nonanthropomorphic force of the Holy Spirit demands that the novice join the "bands" to fulfill his or her journey in this life.

When the revivalist is baptized, the Holy Spirit comes to "dwell" in him or her and, in the immersion in and emergence from the baptismal waters, the "good shadow" of the individual dies and is reborn "in the spirit." This shadow self is now free to journey to Zion, to experience the scope of the cosmic drama unfolding in eternal time that impinges on the ordinary events of Jamaica.

It is possible that the revivalist's journey and drama of the soul, the "good shadow," in extraordinary states of mind—dreams, visions, and working with the "bands"—is a different kind of experience than the incorporation of the spirit known in vodou, candomblé, and santería. Jeremiah, Isaiah, and John the Evangelist act as guides for the soul, and when the "bands" journeys to Zion in ceremony it relays the messages of the guides to those less fully in the spirit. This relationship between the soul and its guides is not the same as the spirit mounting a bride, where the personality of the spirit overtakes that of the medium so that the spirit is incarnated in the *peristil, barracão,* or *igbodu.* Still through Revival Zion's baptism and the "tables" of initiation, the spirit becomes a dimension of action within the human person, more like Deren's amalgam or Dunham's polar current than not.

The same "fixing" of the spirit occurs in the baptisms of the Black Church. Either in the river baptisms of the old South or the Pentecostal baptism in the spirit, the soul of the saved is transformed by death and rebirth. The spirit comes to dwell in the body of the sanctified and as an outcome of this experience of coming through, one may be sanctioned to manifest the spirit in ceremonies. As in Revival Zion, this is not the kind of mediumship that manifests the spirit as a distinct personality. Rather the baptised gains the facility to let the nonanthropomorphic power that is the spirit show itself in the human body. As in the other diasporan traditions, the spirit is not the self, but the sanctified state that the self has experienced with the biblical ancestors in Africa and will enjoy to come in the promised land. The spirit is the divine freedom of God's promise that the sanctified come to know dwells within them.

SHARING THE SPIRIT

As the spirit is recognized to be permanently within a person through ceremonies of entry into service, so it may be brought out to serve the community in public ceremonies. By the work of rhythm, song, and movement, the spirit within the initiate is manifested through his or her body to gladden, guide, and heal the community. Linked by percussion the community shares the "sight" offered by the spirit, either in dialogue with an incorporated spiritual personality or swept together as a group by the experience of Holy Spirit.

In vodou the drums provide, in Maya Deren's image, the "pulse" for the personality of the spirit. The complex rhythms of the drums fine-tune the pulse to a variety of spiritual energies shared by the community as they move in time with its beats. The drums, then the songs, then the dances link the community through performance of its history. The community moves through its archetypal identities beginning with old Legba who opens the gate to Ginen, then through Danbala and his timeless course through the sky, Ogou in his political vainglory, Ezili, Agwé, and all the others, culminating in young Gede who keeps the cemetery and the keys to rebirth. When properly called the *lwa* will emerge in sequence, manifesting in the *ounsi* who have been prepared to receive them, and they serve the community with their particular energy, wisdom, and demands. Each *lwa* will speak or interact with the community, sometimes in Créole known to all and at other times in *langay* known only to initiates. The *lwa* offer insight and healing according to their different places along the spectrum of Haitian experience, making the story of African and Haitian ancestors alive to the present community. By working the spirit in rhythm, song, and dance, Haitian serviteurs bring the insight and healing of the *lwa* into the real world, into their very bodies. The presence of the ancestors, in all their vigor and tragedy, gives their serviteurs paths to survive the cruel history of Haiti and to work toward its revolutionary potential.

In candomblé and santería the drums are also the pathway for the manifestation of the spirit. The drums "call" the spirit and call the "head" of its children to let the spirit mount its human horse. The *iaôs* dance in a counterclockwise circle as the *ounsi* do in vodou, while each *santero* comes forward from a group to dance in place before the drums. In each tradition the dancer is mounted by her or his spirit as she or he dances before the drums, saluting them and the voice of the spirit that speaks through them. Cues of rhythm, melody, pitch, and body movement similar to those of vodou lead the initiate to her or his sacred state of mind. In candomblé, when each *iaô* has received her spirit, all are brought back to the *pegi*, adorned, and then returned in their regalia to process before the community. In santería, the dancer may also be led into another room to be vested in the *orisha*'s finery and returned to the *igbodu*, or perhaps just identified with a scarf or emblem as she or he dances.

While the work of the community to serve the spirits is equally energetic in vodou and candomblé, in vodou ceremonies the *manbo* and *oungan* seem to perpetually re-rhythmicize the surging energy of the *lwa* with their *ason*. In candomblé, the drums, bell, and songs, together with the support of the *ekedis*, ensure an orderly and more formal manifestation of the *orixás* into the *barracão*. The manifestation of the *orishas* in santería strikes a middle ground between vodou and candomblé, the *orishas* may be both imperiously formal and crudely earthy.

The same "motor behavior" at the onset of manifestation may be observed among the *ounsi, iaôs, and santeros*: trembling, undulating movements of the shoulders and back, strong shakings of the head from side to side and front to back, and full bending at the waist and sudden straightening. In all three traditions, the ministrations of helpers are required to prevent injury, adjust clothing, and settle the spirit by words, touch, and other techniques. Once the spirit is "fixed" in its incorporation, it acts in ways identifiable to its community. The *lwa* exhibit recognizable but unpredictable behavior. They take command of the service and they must be cajoled and enticed to act as the community wishes them to. The *orixás*, on the other hand, are affectless. They move as they are directed by the drums and the *ekedis*. The santería *orishas* seem less volatile than the *lwa*, yet they too dash about, parade before the community seeking its admiration, and often act aggressively and rudely.

Despite these differences in the tone of the services and the character of the spirits in manifestation, the rhythmic work of all the communities serves to allow the congregations to share the spirit. By showing the spirit in the human bodies of its initiates, the congregations of vodou and candomblé make it real and present for all to share. If the *lwa* are impetuous and the *orixá* formal, they are still the ancestors among us and—in the archetypal forms of vodou's serpents, generals, and lovers, or in the kings, queens, hunters, and warriors of candomblé and santería—show us as we really are to ourselves.

In Revival Zion the interpretations of this spirituality of working the spirit are grounded in the language and images of the Bible. Once again drums, songs, handclapping, and swaying are the media through which the spirit is worked to enter its human devotee. Throughout the service the presence of the spirit is maintained in its most diffuse form as the Holy Spirit by the careful arrangement of hymns, "lively choruses," and the exhortations of the preacher. When the small group of the "bands" is formed, all drum music ceases, a circle is formed, and the rhythm is driven by feet, handclaps, and the intake of air. This "trumping" of the "bands" journeys the entire congregation to Zion. Revival Zion is the only diasporan tradition that we have portrayed that ritualizes hyperventilation as a technique to achieve a spiritual state of mind, though it is likely that the breathing patterns of manifesting *ounsi*, *iaôs*, and *santeras* are different from those of ordinary congregants.

With the onset of trumping those in the spirit can see the sacred landscape while others rely on the journeyers' descriptions. The altered state of the "bands," as we have mentioned, is not so much their incorporation of the personalities of the spirit guides as it is a two-way journey. Their consciousness makes manifest the invisible world of the spirit. The cryptic messages of the spirit are plain to this sight as are the machinations of evil. The "bands" has *myal*, the sight to see the cosmic drama unfolding in the ordinary world. The initiates of the "bands" share this spiritual sight with the community, allowing it to see through them the "numbers and letters to be played" in the community's proximate and ultimate deliverance from evil.

The Black Church has used a variety of instruments to work the spirit. In the ring shout of the South witnesses attest to the effect of foot stomping on the boards of the meeting house to set a continuous rhythm. With handclapping, vocal antiphony, and ecstatic speech the basic rhythmic requirements for the manifestation of the spirit could be constructed. In contemporary urban churches, the "gospel" instruments of drums, guitar, piano, tambourine, and above all organ, provide the aural media to work the spirit. Together with these instruments, the spirit is worked by the songs of the choir, where variations in volume, pitch, and antiphony with soloists, carefully direct the presence of the spirit within the congregation. Finally the manifestation of the spirit requires the movement of the human body. The congregation needs "room to pray," and moves in swaying, handclapping and, once the spirit takes control, in shouting, shaking, and all the "motor behavior" of spirit manifestation. Specific spiritual personalities do not manifest themselves through the shouting congregants. Each person shouts "in his own way." The Holy Spirit drives the devotee to shout, but each manifestation is a specific "kind" or "way" that the Spirit descends.

The rhythm of the preacher's voice has received particular attention as a component of the Black Church's working of the spirit. The content of the sermon is the story of the struggle of God's people, but its performance in varying tone, pitch, glottal patterns, and volume make that struggle present in the spirit. For those who hear the sermon in ordinary consciousness, it is a dramatization of biblical stories. For those in the spirit, the sermon shows the stories to be present, in the church, in the bodies of the congregants, in the hard and real world of the United States. When the spirit fills the sanctified members of the congregation, they reenact the biblical dramas of deliverance, of passion and resurrection, and of freedom and fulfillment to come. They work the spirit to make the eschatological freedom of God's people present to their experience, in body and mind, "to see what the end shall be."

Albert Raboteau, in his study of slave religion in North America, emphasizes the differences between the theologies of the Protestant Black Church of the United States and those of diasporan traditions such as vodou, candomblé, and santería.

> While there may be similar effects—ego enhancement and catharsis, to name only two—on this level of faith event, there are major differences between spirit possession as it occurs in African and Latin American cults, on the one hand, and the ecstatic shouting experience of United States revivalism on the other. . . . The African gods with their myriad characteristics, personalities, and myths do not "mount" their enthusiasts amid the dances, songs and drum rhythms of worship in the United States. Instead it is the Holy Spirit who fills the converted sinner with a happiness and power that drives him to shout, sing, and sometimes dance.[15]

He speaks of the "death" of African gods in the development of African American Christianity and tempers Herskovits's bold assertions of the continuity of African and African American traditions in twentieth-century North America. Yet Herskovits' stress on their ceremonial similarities is equally significant. In his *Myth of the Negro Past*, Herskovits writes:

> . . . stress is laid on the outer forms of religious expression rather than on inner values and beliefs. For, as will be seen, while Christian doctrine by no means escaped change as it passed into Negro hands, the most striking and recognizable survivals of African religion are in those behavioristic aspects that, given overt expression, are susceptible of reinterpretation in terms of a new theology while retaining their older established forms.[16]

While the division between outer forms and inner beliefs should not be pushed too far, the importance of the ceremonial movement of North American (and Jamaican) black churches can not be undervalued. Through our portraits we have seen that the parallel movements among the ceremonies of the diasporan traditions reveal a spirituality of incarnation that runs through each of the traditions. The spirit is "worked" by rhythmic movement to enflesh itself in the bodies of sanctioned members of the community who share it with others. It is a spirituality that orients itself to the deeds of the ancestors in the mythic time and space of Africa. It reveals a special reciprocity of spirit and human being, recognizing the spirit to be a dimension of the eternal soul of the individual. And the spirituality of the African diaspora seeks to empower the community by making the spirit present in body and mind to all gathered in its service.

Though the differences in theology between the multiple and single spirits, or between ideas of spiritual personality and spiritual force, or between orientation to Ginen, to Ilé Ifé, Zion, or Canaan are significant and important, they also offer opportunities to explore further similarities. It has long been felt among members of the Black Church that theirs was a more authentic form of Christianity than that practiced by their oppressors. James Cone argues that it has been the task of African Americans "to create a new version of Christianity more consistent with its biblical origins."[17] This task has always been the mission of Protestant Christianity, but the search for authentic origins takes on new meaning in the light of the ceremonial spirituality of the African diaspora. Is this spirituality a recovery of the spirituality of the Bible, lost through two thousand years of European interpretation? Have diasporan communities, with their direct experience of enslavement, exile, and ghettoization, constructed a spirituality fully consistent with their biblical ancestors?

The juxtaposition of these portraits of diasporan traditions suggests, a relationship between ceremonial spirituality and eschatological freedom. Here the possible similarities between the nonbiblical and the biblical traditions begin to reflect each other. The spiritual state of mind shared between initiate and congregation is a prefiguration of the ultimate deliverance promised to God's people. In their different ways each tradition offers ceremonies of freedom. In the time and space of ceremony, diasporan communities are not only free from the restraints and indignities visited upon them by racist powers, but free to recognize themselves in the company of ancestors and saints.

Acknowledgments

A great number of people have given me help, encouragement and blessings as I have researched this book over the years. I want to thank each teacher, student, and colleague and to acknowledge their gifts, always remembering that the strengths of the book flow from them, while its weaknesses are mine. Modupé; Samuel Abegunde, Oba Oseigeman Adefunmi, Adetokunbo Adekanmbi, James Adelson, Antonio Maron Agle, Jenetta Alves, Laria Amador, Gabriel Andraos, Ajibola Isau Badiru, Leonard Barrett, Judith Bettleheim, George Bond, Pedro and Blanca Bonetti, Aida Borges, George Brandon, Lucy Bregman, David Brown, Karen McCarthy Brown, Raul Canizares, Isabel Castellanos, Luis Castro, Mãe Cleusa de Gantois, Donald Cosentino, Harold Courlander, Nicolas Creary, Mercedes Cros Sandoval, Portia Culley, Daniel Dawson, Constant Delfine, Leslie Desmangles, Juana Elbein and Didi Dos Santos, Margaret Thompson Drewal, Gregory Eck, Mãe Edelzuita, Martin Ellington, Maria José Espiritó Santo, Robin Evanchuck, Elias Farajajé-Jones, Edilson Fernandes de Souza, Carlos Fernández, Dorothy Flores, Sammy Flores, Alison Foley, Dalvadisio Fonseca de Melo, Fu-Kiau Bunseki, Cheryl Townsend Gilkes, Judith Gleason, John Gray, Johanna Green, Luysa Guercetti, Rosangela Guimarães, Rosalind Hackett, Jessica Harris, Lahela Hekekia, Jackie Henschke, Sherman Howard, Jay Jasper,

Jessy Jesse, Angela Jorge, Lynne Junker, Marcia Karasek, James Kennedy, Michael Kirwin, Karen Kramer, Michel Laguerre, Andrea Linthicum, Patricia Lorens, Wyatt MacGaffey, Antonio Carlos Magalhaes, Silvana Magda, Yvonne Maggie, Jeff Marcella, Morton Marks, John Mason, Elizabeth Mitchell, Lisa Moreno, Dikembe Motombo, Carole Myscofski, Nilo Neto, Rex Nettleford, Lucas Moreira Nevis, Dona Nirinha de Bogum, Mãe Nivalda da Pena Branca, Sergio Noronha, Obalumi, Mãe Olga dô Alaketo, Mikelle Omari, Richard Parker, Mario Passo, Luciana Patriota de Moura, Yaniya Pearson, John Pemberton, Daniel Philippon, Ernesto Pichardo, Angelina Pollak-Eltz, Emerante de Pradines, Albert Raboteau, Clea Rameh, Willie Ramos, Janet Redley, Antonio Moraes Ribeiro, Roger Rigaud, Kevin Roy, Alvaro Rubim de Pinho, Xavier Santiago, Ieda Santos, José Lauerano Santos, Ileana Scheytt, Courtney Smith Senise and Daniel Senise, Milton Sernett, Alain Silverio, J. J. Singleton, Gerard Sloyan, Hawthorn Smith, Juan Sosa, Janet Stanley, Mãe Stela de Opô Afonjá, Karen Stewart, Karla Sullivan, Mãe Tata da Casa Branca, Barbara Ann Teer, Robert Farris Thompson, John Thornton, Glicéria Vasconcelos, Marta Vega, Julio Velez, Pierre Verger, Gary Vessels, Antonio Viera, Jim Wafer, Sheila Walker, Lee Weinreb, Harold White, Susan Whitten, Vernel Williams, David Wood.

Finally a libation to the memories of Ifa Morote and Lydia Cabrera.

Notes

1. Introduction

1. See Melville J. Herskovits, *The Myth of the Negro Past* (Boston: Beacon Press, 1958), p. 33ff. for a discussion of the "baseline" of cultural similarities among the Africans taken to the Americas. See also careful generalizations of a common West African religious heritage in Mechal Sobel, *Trabelin' On: The Slave Journey to an Afro-Baptist Faith* (Westport, Conn.: Greenwood Press, 1979) and Sterling Stuckey, *Slave Culture: Nationalist Theory and the Foundations of Black America* (New York: Oxford University Press, 1987), especially the first chapter.
2. Herbert S. Klein, *Slavery in the Americas* (Chicago: University of Chicago Press, 1967), pp. 202, 236.
3. Most scholars of patterned, communal activity would distinguish between "ceremony" and "ritual," following Victor Turner's aphorism: "Ritual is transformative, ceremony confirmatory." *Forest of Symbols: Aspects of Ndembu Ritual* (Ithaca: Cornell University Press, 1967), p. 95. Bobby Alexander and Ronald Grimes see "ceremony" as a subset of "ritual" and link "ceremony" to demonstrations of "civil religion," where it is intended to confirm the authority of the state. "Ritual," on the other hand, is a much broader and more puissant category, with the more ambitious function of transforming the reality of the participants. Bobby Alexander, "Ceremony," in *The Encyclopedia of Religion*, edited by Mircea Eliade (New York: Macmillan, 1987);

Ronald L. Grimes, *Research in Ritual Studies* (Metuchen, N.J.: American Theological Library Association and Scarecrow Press, 1985).

While I am concerned with the relationship between human action and the experience of alternate realities, I frequently prefer the term "ceremony" to "ritual" for reasons of euphony. Though "ritual" is at times the appropriate word to use, at other times I find it off-putting, tainted by its usage by outsiders to describe the activities of others. I intend to employ the terms interchangeably, choosing their use by how they sound in their contexts.

4. On the generic qualities of the term *vodou*, see Harold Courlander and Rémy Bastien, *Religion and Politics in Haiti* (Washington, D.C: Institute for Cross-Cultural Research, 1966), p. 12, and Karen McCarthy Brown, "Voodoo," in *The Encyclopedia of Religion*, edited by Mircea Eliade (New York: Macmillan, 1987). On the varieties of traditions called *candomblé*, see Vivaldo da Costa Lima, "Nações-de-Candomblé," in *Encontro de nações-de-candomblé* (Salvador: Ediçoes Ianamá and Centro de Estudios Afro-Orientais, 1984).

5. The phrase "hemispheric perspective" for the study of African-derived religions in the Americas is Eugene Genovese's. See his detailed overview in *Roll, Jordan, Roll: The World the Slaves Made* (New York: Random House, 1972), pp. 168–183. This school of thought begins with Herskovits and is articulated today by Robert Farris Thompson's studies of the aesthetic philosophy of "atlantic" culture. See his *Flash of the Spirit: African and Afro-American Art and Philosophy* (New York: Random House, 1983).

6. William A. Wedneoja uses the term "ceremonial spirituality" in his description of Jamaican Revival, and I find it covers well the particular dimension of diasporan religion that I wish to examine. See his doctoral dissertation, "Religious Adaptation in Rural Jamaica" (Ph.D. dissertation, University of California, San Diego, 1978).

7. In one way or another, the central questions of all theology can be seen as the tension between the unity and multiplicity of the Divine and the participation of the human in that divinity. While these issues have been the quintessential Christian concerns of the nature of the trinity and the christ, they are important in every theistic tradition. The affirmation of the unity of God by Jewish and Muslim theologians has not impeded discussions about the relationship of God's name or

word to his divinity. In the diasporan traditions that recognize a multiplicity of spirits—vodou, candomblé, and santería—the spirits are all in some way "partaking" of each other and of a single, more transcendent spirit. These relationships might be conceived in terms of hierarchy or kinship or causal dependency, but there are clear notions of both unity and differentiation in the understanding of the spirit. In each of these traditions spirit and human being are also shown to be in a relationship of unity as well. In this book I will be looking closely at how each tradition understands the spirit to become "one" with the human person.

8. The difference between ritual behavior observed by the outsider and the participants interpretation of it in the African American context is well made by Albert Raboteau in his discussion of the category in spirit possession in Africa and the United States. See his authoritative *Slave Religion: The "Invisible Institution" in the Antebellum South* (New York: Oxford University Press, 1978), especially pp. 58–64.

2. Haitian Vodou

1. M. L. E. Moreau de St. Méry, *Description Topographique, Physique, Civile, Politique, et Historique de la Partie Française de l'Isle de St Dominque* (1797; Paris: Libraire Larose, 1958), pp. 65–69. I have relied on the translations of Ivor D. Spencer and of Selden Rodman in these extracts. See Spencer's translation, abridgement, and editing of Moreau de St. Méry which he had titled, seemingly without irony, *A Civilization that Perished: The Last Days of White Colonial Rule in Haiti* (Lanham, Md.: University Press of America, 1958;) and Rodman's *Haiti: The Black Republic* (Old Greenwich, Conn.: Devin-Adair, 1980).

   As for Moreau's description of vodou, most scholars have felt him to be reliable. The details and structure of his description seem to indicate direct observation of a vodou ceremony. Moreau's interpretations of vodou, of course, serve to reinforce colonialist claims of superiority and hegemony over the newly risen masses of Haiti. Alfred Métraux seems to accept Moreau's account as perhaps a description of a service to the serpent-spirit Danbala overgeneralized as the supreme being "Vaudoux." He argues that if the use of live serpents was a feature of eighteenth-century vodou, it is now defunct in the twentieth. See *Voodoo in Haiti* (1959; New York: Schocken Books, 1972), p. 38.

2. Moreau de St. Méry, *Description Topographique*, pp. 68–69.

3. Quoted by Harold Courlander, *The Drum and the Hoe: Life and Lore of the Haitian People* (1960; Berkeley and Los Angeles: University of California Press, 1985), p. 129.

4. A florid description of this rite is reproduced in Métraux's *Voodoo in Haiti*, pp. 42–43. Jean Price-Mars records the text of the oath in his *Thus Spoke the Uncle*, translated by Magdaline W. Shannon (1928; Washington, D.C.: Three Continents Press, 1983), pp. 47–48.

5. Métraux quotes a number of Haitian historians on the presence of vodou priests and symbols among the generals and troops of the revolutionary armies. See *Voodoo in Haiti*, pp. 43–49. Michel Laguerre argues forcefully that vodou "became the focus of political and underground activities and served as the channel to carry out the leaders' political ideology which was the total and unconditional liberation of Haiti from France." *Voodoo and Politics in Haiti* (New York: St. Martin's Press, 1989), p. 37. But compare Harold Courlander writing, "Vodoun and witchcraft undoubtedly lurked on the periphery of the conflict [the Haitian revolution] but they were not at its center as some European chroniclers suggested." Courlander, and Rémy Bastien, *Religion and Politics in Haiti* (Washington, D.C.: Institute of Cross-Culture Research, 1966), p. 18.

6. Métraux, *Voodoo in Haiti*, p. 49. Métraux points out that since Dessalines persecuted the vodou sects it is unlikely that he would care much for their twentieth-century descendants. It seems to me that to live forever in the spiritual lives of Haitians would be a destiny any emperor might assent to.

7. Michel Laguerre. *Voodoo Heritage* (Beverly Hills, Calif.: Sage Publications, 1980), p. 114.

8. Robert Farris Thompson, *Flash of the Spirit: African and Afro-American Art and Philosophy* (New York: Random House, 1983), p. 180. See also Maya Deren's characterization of the Petro rite as "cosmic rage" in *Divine Horsemen: The Living Gods of Haiti* (New York: Thames and Hudson, 1953), p. 62.

9. Laguerre, *Voodoo and Politics in Haiti*, p. 80.

10. James Leyburn, *The Haitian People* (New Haven: Yale University Press, 1941), p. 142. Leyburn's tone of regret that it was "too late" for the Church to eradicate vodou, tempers his sympathetic treatment of the tradition.

11. By "folk" I mean the bulk of the Haitian people who look to Africa for the organizing principle their cultural heritage. Selden Rodman estimates that some 60 percent of Haitians are active participants in vodou rites, while another 10 percent practice vodou from time to time. See Rodman, *Haiti: The Black Republic*, p. 61.

Don Yoder of the University of Pennsylvania defines folk religion as "the totality of all those views and practices of religion that exist among the people apart from and alongside of the strictly theological and liturgical forms of the official religion." See Yoder "Toward a Definition of Folk Religion," *Western Folklore* 33.1 (January 1974).

12. It could be argued that it is vodou which was the inspiration for the Negritude movement which galvanized Francophone Africans in their quest for independence. Jean Price-Mars looked to vodou in particular to articulate the values of Negritude and, with his wide influence on African intellectuals, one might see vodou behind the political philosophies of the independence era of mid-century Africa.

13. Quoted in and translated by Selden Rodman, *Haiti: The Black Republic*, p. 87.

14. Laguerre, *Voodoo and Politics in Haiti*, p. 120.

15. Rémy Bastien, "Vodoun and Politics in Haiti," in *Religion and Politics in Haiti* (Washington, D.C.: Institute for Cross-Cultural Research, 1966), p. 48.

16. See Amy Wilentz, *The Rainy Season* (New York: Simon and Schuster, 1989), for an account of the disturbances of post-Duvalier Haiti. Wilentz casts a jaundiced eye over the motivations of all the parties involved in the power vacuum of Haiti. Her portrait of the progressive elements of the Catholic Church make its support for the persecution of Duvalierist vodou priests something more or something less than a blow against tyranny.

17. Moreau de St. Méry, *Description Topographique*, pp. 64, 68.

18. See Suzanne Preston Blier, "Vodun: The Philosophical Roots of Art in Danhome," Paper presented at the National Museum of African Art, Washington, D.C., 1989.

19. See Philip Curtin, *The Atlantic Slave Trade: a Census* (Madison: University of Wisconsin Press, 1969), pp. 192–197. Curtin's data is derived from G. Debien et al., "Les origines des esclaves des Antilles," *Bulletin de l'IFAN*, série B, 1961–1967.

20. Courlander and Bastien, *Religion and Politics in Haiti*, P. 12. Katherine Dunham always speaks of the "Rada-Dahomey" rite as "true vodun" and distinguishes it from the Congo and the Petro rites. See *Dances in Haiti* (French ed., 1957; Los Angeles: Center of Afro-American Studies, University of California, 1983.

21. Melville Herskovits, *Life in a Haitian Valley* (New York: Knopf, 1937), p. 150. The nations recognized and honored by serviteurs seem particularly dependent on whom one asks. Each region, hounfor, and serviteur has its own constellation.

    Métraux names: Rada, Petro (which, he notes, in the north and northwest is called Lemba), plus Ibo, Nago, Bambara, Anmine, Hausa, Mondongue etc, plus Congo, Wangol (Angola), Siniga (Senegal, Caplau etc). Métraux notes the complexities of spirit classification by speaking of subgroups within nations, such as a distinction between Congo-du-bord-de-la-mer and Congo-savane. The Congo-savane are subdivided into families "of which the main members are: the Kanga, Caplau, Bumba, Mondongue and Kita." *Voodoo in Haiti*, pp. 86–87.

    Maya Deren in her famous chart of the spirits identifies eight nations, (Dahomey, Nago, Ghede, Juba/Martinique, Ibo/Kanga, Quitta/Simbi, Congo, Petro), with several "nationless" families included under the "petro rites." See *Divine Horsemen* pp, 82–83.

    Harold Courlander offers the most complete inventory of these "pantheons" and their members in *The Drum and the Hoe*, pp. 317–331.

22. Ira Lowenthal, "Ritual Performance and Religious Experience: A Service for the Gods in Southern Haiti," *Journal of Anthropological Research* 34 (1978): 393.

23. Deren, *Divine Horsemen*, p. 200. Price-Mars speaks of the "superstitious side of voodoo" which suggests a separability of vodou from what outsiders are calling superstition. *Thus Spoke the Uncle*, p. 148. Serge LaRose speaks of "serving Africa" as a moral lodestone among vodou priests. See "The Meaning of Africa in Haitian Vodu," in *Symbols and Sentiments: Cross-Cultural Studies in Symbolism*, edited by I. M. Lewis. (New York: Academic Press, 1977). Several authors note a distinction between service with the "right hand" and service with the "left hand." See Courlander, *The Drum and the Hoe*, p. 9.

24. The word *bosalle* is a reference to the status of African slaves newly arrived in the Americas. To a certain extent *bosalle* slaves became

Creoles by virtue of Christian baptism. In vodou the *bosalle* lwa is baptised by means of the serviteur's *lave tèt*.

25. Called "gripping of the eyes" by Métraux, *Voodoo in Haiti*, p. 69, and the "prize or price of eyes" by Katherine Dunham, *Island Possessed* (New York: Doubleday, 1969), p. 98.

26. See Deren, *Divine Horsemen*, pp. 73–74.

27. Dunham, *Island Possessed* p. 75.

28. Ibid.

29. On the cruelty of the lwa, see Dunham on the spirits' treatment of her fellow initiates Georgina and Mme. Soulouque in *Island Possessed*, pp. 80–81, 88–90.

30. Ibid., p. 78.

31. Ibid., p. 68.

32. Ibid., p. 108–109. See Métraux, *Voodoo in Haiti*, pp. 158–160, for the names of these gestures.

33. Deren, *Divine Horsemen*, pp. 24–33.

34. Dunham, *Island Possessed*, p. 62.

35. Ibid.

36. Deren calls this entity of the *pot tèt* an amalgam of the "cosmic loa and the immediate life essence of the person." *Divine Horsemen*, p. 221.

37. Dunham, *Island Possessed*, p. 106.

38. Ibid., p. 107.

39. Métraux, *Voodoo in Haiti*, p. 203.

40. Deren, speaking of kanzo, says that the *pot tèts* are not taken home, but kept by the initiator, since the soul of the individual is now part of the collective of the hounfor. Deren, *Divine Horsemen, p.* 222. Dunham tells us that she had long since lost her heat pot and is untroubled by the consequences. Dunham, *Island Possessed*, p. 104.

41. This abbreviated description is taken from Deren, *Divine Horsemen*, pp. 218–224, and Métraux, *Voodoo in Haiti*, pp. 195–219.

42. Deren, *Divine Horsemen*, p. 247.

43. Laguerre, *Voodoo Heritage*, p. 143–144.

44. Ibid., p. 169.

45. For a detailed discussion of the symbolism of the *vèvè* as sacred art, see Karen McCarthy Brown, *The Vèvè of Haitian Vodu: A Structural Analysis of Visual Imagery*. Ann arbor, Mich.: University Microfilms, 1975.

For a discussion of its African roots, see Thompson, *Flash of the Spirit*, pp. 188–191.

46. Laguerre, *Voodoo Heritage*, pp. 166–167.
47. Lowenthal, "Ritual Performance."
48. Laguerre, *Voodoo Heritage*, pp. 175–176.
49. Deren, *Divine Horsemen*, p. 250.
50. Ibid., p. 251.
51. Laguerre, *Voodoo Heritage*, p. 150.
52. Dunham, *Island Possessed*, p. 122.
53. Lowenthal, *Ritual Performance,"* p. 404n.
54. Deren, *Divine Horsemen*, p. 251–252.
55. Ibid., p. 252. Other descriptions of the yanvalou may be found in Courlander, *The Drum and the Hoe*, p. 42; Métraux, *Voodoo in Haiti*, p. 190; Dunham, in *Island Possessed*, p. 135, calls the *yanvalou* the "signature of vaudun."
56. Laguerre, *Voodoo Heritage*, p. 86.
57. Deren, *Divine Horsemen*, p. 254.
58. Laguerre, *Voodoo Heritage*, p. 171.
59. Deren, *Divine Horsemen*, p. 256.
60. Ibid., p. 257.
61. Ibid., p. 258–259.
62. Ibid., p. 260.
63. Laguerre, *Voodoo Heritage*, pp. 101, 100.
64. Courlander, *The Drum and the Hoe.* p. 22.
65. The notion of *poto-mitan* as center and *vèvè* as edge is taken from the work of Karen McCarthy Brown who demonstrates the spirituality of spatial arrangement. See *The Vèvè of Haitian Vodu*.
66. Antoine Gérard Bretous, "Le Poteau-Mitan," in *Cahier de Folklore et des Traditions Orales d'Haiti* (Port au Prince: l'Agence de Coopération Culturelle et Technique, n.d.), p. 133. This is a collection of student papers from the Faculté d'Ethnologie in the early 1970s under the direction of Max Benoit.
67. See Larose, "The Meaning of Africa," pp. 89–92.
68. Herskovits, *Life in a Haitian Valley*, p. 174.
69. Métraux, *Voodoo in Haiti*.
70. Courlander sums up the possibilities for this delineation of the lwa: "The 'surname' of a lwa can be a description of 'tribal' or 'national'

affiliation, regional provenience, character and temperament, or an indication of function." Courlander, *The Drum and the Hoe*, p. 26.

71. Karen McCarthy Brown, "Systematic Remembering, Systematic forgetting: Ogou in Haiti," in *African's Ogun: Old World and New*, edited by Sandra T. Barnes. (Bloomington: Indiana University Press, 1989) p. 78.

72. Dunham, *Island Possessed*, p. 128.

73. Deren, *Divine Horsemen*, p. 31.

74. Dunham, *Island Possessed*, p. 92.

75. Deren, *Divine Horsemen*, p. 249.

76. Deren, Ibid., p. 249.

77. Several writers have looked upon this as a problem of interpretation. See Laguerre, *Voodoo Heritage*, pp. 29–38; Métrau, *Voodoo in Haiti*, p. 187; and Courlander, *The Drum and the Hoe*, pp. 75–76.

78. Laguerre, *Voodoo Heritage*, p. 125.

79. Deren, *Divine Horsemen*, p. 235.

80. Dunham, *Island Possessed*, pp. 131–132.

3. Candomblé in Brazil

1. In Portuguese "candomblé" is ordinarily preceded by an article in both its generic and specific applications. In English we drop the article before generic nouns, and so refer to the tradition under investigation as "candomblé" without a "the" or "a" preceding it. In more specific contexts the article might be appropriate when referring to the physical site of the ceremonies or the community of devotees: "there is *a* candomblé in the Cabula neighborhood;" "*the* candomblé of Mãe Stela."

   A rough analogy might be found in the English word "church." We use the term "the church" in reference to both the building in which ceremonies are carried out and the community that performs them. If outsiders unfamiliar with Christianity were to refer to the entire tradition as "church," it would not be too different from the situation in Bahia.

2. Pierre Verger, *Bahia and the West African Trade: 1549–1851* (Ibadan: Ibadan University Press, 1964,), p. 31.

3. Philip Curtin, *The Atlantic Slave Trade: A Census* (Madison: University of Wisconsin Press, 1969), pp. 89, 268. Curtin estimates that 12.5 % of

all Africans carried to the Americas during the four hundred years of the slave trade went through Bahia.

4. Ibid., pp. 240–242. Curtin discusses the imprecision of the term "Mina," showing that it meant different things at different times to different people. For the use of the term among the Portuguese, see p. 186.

5. Verger, *Bahia and the West African Trade*, pp. 32–33.

6. Quoted in Robert Edgar Conrad, *Children of God's Fire: A Documentary History of Black Slavery in Brazil* (Princeton: Princeton University Press, 1983), p. 405. Islam played a key role in many of these revolts, and they seem to have been organized more on Islamic lines than on ethnic ones. The slaveholders' recognition of this led to attempts to exclude Muslim slaves from Brazil, and many Brazilian Muslims were deported. After the great rebellion of 1835 the chief of police in Bahia reported (ibid., p. 410):

> Generally speaking, almost all of them can read and write in unknown characters which are similar to the Arabic used among the Ussás [Hausa], who now evidently have made an alliance with the Nagós. The Ussás are the nation which in earlier times rebelled on several occasions in the province, having later been replaced in this by the Nagós. Teachers exist among them who give lessons and have tried to organize the insurrection, in which many free Africans, even rich ones, were also involved. Many books have been found, some of which, it is said, must be religious precepts derived from the mingling of sects, mainly the Koran.

The Islamic heritage is remembered in contemporary candomblé by the Yoruba word 'Malê [Islam] which is appended to some rites to indicate their origin among the community's Muslim forbearers.

7. Ibid., p. 403.

8. Ibid., p. 255.

9. Adèle Toussaint–Samson, writing in 1891, reproduced ibid., p. 86. Brazilian novelist Jorge Amado tells a story common in candomblé lore in which the African spirits, incarnated in their human mediums, physically battle and vanquish the police squadron intent on disrupting the candomblé. See his celebration of Afro-Bahian life, *Tent of Miracles* (original Portuguese ed., 1969; New York: Knopf, 1977).

10. Mikelle Smith Omari, *From the Inside to the Outside: The Art and Ritual of Bahian Candomblé* (Los Angeles: Museum of Cultural History,

UCLA, Monograph Series No. 24, 1984), p. 18.

11. See Raymundo Nina Rodrigues, *Os Africanos no Brasil* (1906; 2d ed., São Paulo: Companhia Editora Nacional, 1935); Arthur Ramos, *The Negro in Brazil* (Washington, D.C.: Associated Publishers, 1939); Donald Pierson, *Negroes in Brazil: A Study of Race Contact in Bahia* (1942; Carbondale and Edwardsville, Ill.: Southern Illinois University Press, 1967); Edison Carneiro, *Candombles da Bahia* (3d ed.; Rio de Janeiro: Conquista, 1961); Vivaldo da Costa Lima, "Nações-de-Candomblé," in *Econtro de Nações-de-Candomblé* (Bahia: Ianamá e Centro de Estudos Afro-Orientais, Universidade Federal da Bahia, 1984).

12. Pierre Verger, *Trade Relations between the Bight of Benin and Bahia from the* 17th *to the* 19th *Century* (Ibadan: Ibadan University Press, 1976); Pierson, *Negroes in Brazil*, pp. 239–244.

13. Pierre Verger, "Nigeria, Brazil and Cuba," *Nigeria* (October, 1960). In a personal conversation Didi Dos Santos told me of his mother, Mãe Aninha of Opô Afonjá, visiting Kêtu in post-emancipation times and arranging the passage of African priests back to Brazil.

14. Carneiro, *Candombles da Bahia*, pp. 61–62. See also Roger Bastide, *The African Religions of Brazil: Toward a Sociology of the Interpenetration of Civilizations* (1960; Baltimore: Johns Hopkins University Press, 1978), p. 165.

15. In the late 1930s the North American anthropologist Ruth Landes met a famous senior candomblé priest, Martiniano de Bonfim. Martiniano had been sent to Africa by his parents in fulfillment of their promise to the spirits to educate their son. Landes likens this exceptional, but well-understood, Bahian pattern of study to British colonials sending their children to Oxford and Cambridge. Ruth Landes, *The City of Women* (New York: Macmillan, 1947), p. 22.

16. See particularly Rodriques, *Os Africanos no Brasil*.

17. Pierson, *Negroes in Brazil*, p. 276.

18. Carneiro, *Candombles da Bahia*, p. 63.

19. While there are considerable differences of opinion about the relative merits of various houses, during my short visit to Bahia in 1991, these three were universally considered the most senior and authentic candomblé communities in the city. Mikelle Omari points out that there are other important Nagô lines in Bahia, particularly that of the

Alakêto house which claims a founding date of 1636. Omari, *From the Inside to the Outside*, p. 53n18.

20. Carneiro, *Candombles da Bahia*, p. 56. While Carneiro's União das Seitas Afro-Brasileiras da Bahia has not survived, a number of successor and rival organizations have arisen to carry on the same work. One national group that has been particularly generous to me in my research is the Instituto Nacional e Órgão Supremo Sacerdotal da Tradição e Cultura Afro-Brasiliera.

21. Claude Lepine, "Os Estereótipos da Personalidade no Candomblé Nagô," in *Olóòrisà: Escritos sobre a Religião dos Orixás*, edited by Carlos Eugênio Marcondes de Moura (São Paulo: Agora, 1981), p. 24.

22. Pierson, *Negroes in Brazil*, p. 276.

23. Landes, *City of Women*, p. 80.

24. Bastide, *The African Religions of Brazil*, pp. 113–119.

25. Roger Bastide writes: "I have observed over and over again that in northeastern Brazil these black brotherhoods are composed of the same individuals who frequent the *candomblés* and even hold high positions in them." Ibid., p. 54.

   Each of the three elite candomblés is dedicated to a Catholic saint and has the legal status of a Catholic brotherhood. For more information on these brotherhoods and sisterhoods, see Sheila Walker, "The Feast of Good Death: An Afro-Catholic Emancipation Celebration in Brazil," *Sage: A Scholarly Journal of Black Women* 3.2 (Fall, 1986); Luiz Cláudio Dias do Nascimento and Cristiana Isidoro, *Boa Morte em Cachoeira* (Cachoeira, Bahia: Centro de Estudos, Pesquisa e Ação Sócio-Cultural de Cachoeira, 1988); and A. J. R. Russell-Wood, *Fidalgos and Philanthropists: The Santa Casa da Misericórdia of Bahia, 1550–1775* (Berkeley and Los Angeles: University of California Press, 1968).

26. Ruth Landes tells us that Menininha of Gantois met the father of her children when he took sanctuary from the police in her candomblé. *City of Women*, p. 147.

27. Omari, *From the Inside to the Outside*, p. 17.

28. Meville Herskovits seems overly critical of Carneiro's and Landes's assertions about the prominence of women. While he rightly stresses the importance of *ogans* in the hierarchy of the candomblés, he does not offer any evidence to contradict the preeminent leadership of

women in the Nagô *terreiros*. See Melville Herskovits, "The Social Organization of the Candomble," in *The New World Negro*, edited by Frances S. Herskovits (Bloomington: Indian University Press, 1966), p. 230.

29. Landes, *City of Women*, p. 142. Sheila Walker refers to her teacher, Mãe Stela of Opô Afonjá, as Stela of Oxossi, after the priestess's patron *orixá*, Oxossi, the royal hunter of Kêtu. See "Everyday and Esoteric Reality in the Afro-Brazilian Candomblé," *History of Religions* 30.4 (1991) One of the characters in Jorge Amado's fictional homage a Afro-Brazilian culture, *Tent of Miracles*, is known throughout the novel as Rosa of Oxala.

30. Landes, *City of Women*, p. 36.

31. Ibid., p. 155.

32. Vivaldo da Costa Lima, "Os Obás de Xangô," in *Olóòrisà: Escritos sobre a Religião dos Orixás*, edited by Carlos Eugênio Marcondes de Moura (Sao Paulo: Agora, 1981), p. 92. See also Herskovits, "Social Organization of the Candomble," pp. 236–237.

33. Herskovits, "Social Organization of the Candomble," p. 234.

34. Landes, *City of Women*, p. 82.

35. Omari, *From the Inside to the Outside*, p. 24.

36. These are women of the candomblé who, for various reasons, are never called to become mediums for the *orixás* and, instead, serve the mediums as *ekedis*, literally "slaves" in Nagô. In her many conversations with candomblé women, Landes found that some of these attendants, far from feeling inferior to the *iaôs* who enjoyed the center stage of the liturgy, could be somewhat scornful of women who lacked the personal control to avoid trance. See Landes, *City of Women*, p. 42. Herskovits argues that the translation of *ekedi* as "slave" is unfortunate and finds the word to be derived from the Yoruba *akede* meaning "public crier, proclaimer, herald." See "Social Organization of the Candomble," pp. 239–240.

37. See Julio Braga, *O Jogo de Búzios: Un Estudo de Adivinhação no Candomblé* (São Paulo: Brasiliense, 1988).

38. Robert Voeks, "Sacred Leaves of Brazilian Candomble." *Geographical Review* 80.2 (April, 1990).

39. Walker, "Everyday and Esoteric Reality," p. 107.

40. Mãe Stela of Ilé Axé Opô Afonjá has become a public critic of the

mixing of Catholicism and candomblé, a leader of a purifying movement of *contrasincretismo*. Sheila Walker quotes from one of Mãe Stela's many newspaper interviews to say: "The period in which we had to hide our religion has now passed. Our ancestors were forced to syncretize the religion in order not to be massacred. We want to stop syncretizing." Ibid., p. 115.

41. Since the costs of the materials for initiation and the commitments of a new life of obligation are very dear, there are many stories of persons delaying their initiations, often with disastrous consequences. As might be expected, many people begin to think twice about promises made in the throes of illness or the heat of ceremonies.

42. *Iawo*. Directed by Geraldo Sarno. Produced by Sarue Films and Mariana Films, 1978. The film credits Juana Elbein Dos Santos's *Os Nàgô e a Morte: Pàde, Àsèsè e o Culto Égun na Bahia* (Petrópolis: Editora Voces, 1975), for its interpretations of the details of Nagô-Jeje initiation.

43. It is interesting to compare this metaphor of boat travel with Katherine Dunham's observation about the fellowship symbolism of her initiation. She wondered if the crowding of the initiates in their isolation reenacted the great ordeal of the Middle Passage in slave ships. This historical memory, shared by all African American peoples, would form a powerful model for rites of passage. See Dunham, *Island Possessed* (New York: Doubleday, 1969), p. 79.

44. It is this enormous investment in time which leads many researchers to explain the preponderance of women initiates in candomblé. It is argued by Pierson and Herskovits that men, since they are more likely to hold jobs outside the home, are both more socialized into Euro-Brazilian ways and less free to leave this work for candomblé obligations. Perhaps this may have been more true in the 1940s than today, although nearly all candomblé women seem to have been working outside the home then as they do now. Still they have most often been self-employed in their work. See Pierson, *Negroes in Brazil*, p. 285; and Herskovits, "Social Organization of the Candomble," pp. 230–231.

45. Jim Wafer says that this bell indicates "the initiand's prisoner-like status." It warns the *iyalorixás* if the *abian* tries to leave. See *The Taste of Blood: Spirit Possession in Brazilian Candomblé* (Philadelphia: University of Pennsylvania Press, 1991), p. 122.

46. Wafer refers to the *erê* as the infantile *orixá* within the neophyte which

is brought to maturity when it reveals its name in the public ceremony that closes the process. See ibid., p. 129. A long discussion of the idea of *erê* in various areas of Brazil and Africa is offered in Roger Bastide, *Le Candomblé de Bahia: Rite Nago*, (Pairs: Mouton & Co., 1958), pp. 179–202.

47. For a description of this "feeding of the head" see Pierre Verger, *Notes sur le Culte des Orisa et Vodun* (Dakar: L'Institut Français d'Afrique Noire, 1957), pp. 79–95. See also Jim Wafer's description of his own *bori* with his immediate reactions and later reflections in *Taste of Blood*, p. 149f.

48. Wafer writes of cuts in the Angola *nação* made at the top of head, the tip of tongue, the back, the upper arms, and the soles of feet. He notes that some houses cut the thighs and buttocks as well. See *Taste of Blood*, p. 144.

49. Margaret Thompson Drewal, "Projections from the Top in Yoruba Art," *African Arts* 9.1 (Fall, 1977).

50. Babalawo Funjiala of the Jeje tradition told me that the red feathers are a reference to a story of resolved strife between Oxala and Oxun. The feathers, *ekoijide*, refer to menstrual blood and female procreativity. Oxala transforms Oxun's menses into the feathers and so the newborn *iaô* is born of Oxala's sperm and Oxun's "blood."

51. Magnificent drawings of these initiation markings, costumes, and instruments can be found in Carybé, *Iconografia dos Deuses Africanos no Candomblé da Bahia* (São Paulo: Raizes, 1980). See also Carybé and Pierre Verger, *Orixás: 38 desenhos de Carybé, texto de Pierre Verger*. Coleção Recôncavo N. 10. (Bahia: Livraria Progresso Editora, 1955).

52. Wafer attended a ceremony of the "market" of the *iaôs* and speaks of the frivolity and cheer that attends the mock selling (and stealing) of wares. He notes that the *iaôs* were manifesting their *erês*, the child spirits of the *orixás. Taste of Blood*, p. 163.

53. Herskovits offers a sympathetic and detailed description of a *paná* in "The Panan, An Afro Bahian Religious Rite of Transition," in *The New World Negro: Selected Papers in Afroamerican Studies*. Edited by Frances S. Herskovits (Bloomington: Indiana University Press, 1966).

54. On the controls among the candomblé generations see Herskovits, "Social Organization of the Candomble" pp. 234–235.

55. See Roger Bastide, *African Civilisations in the New World* (New York: Harper and Row, 1972), p. 154.

56. Bastide identifies the Brazilian *irôkô* as the *Ficus doliara*, called *gameleira branca* in Portuguese. See *Le Candomblé de Bahia* p. 64. Botanical geographer Robert Voeks concurs, noting the substitution that Nagô-Brazilians made when the African species could not be transplanted. See "Sacred Leaves of Brazilian Candomble," p. 128. Orlando Espin presents an analysis of a myth of Irôkô in both Brazil and Cuba with an interest to "Yoruba-Christian dialogue." See "Iroko e Ará-Kolé: Comentário exegético a um Mito Iorubá-Lucumí," in *Perspectiva Teológica* 18 (1986).

57. For comparative data on Exu see: Donald Cosentino, "Who is that Fellow in the Many-colored Cap: Transformations of Eshu in Old and New World Mythologies," *Journal of American Folklore* 100, no. 397 (1987); Robert Farris Thompson, *Flash of the Spirit: African and Afro-American Art and Philosophy* (New York: Random House, 1983), pp. 18–33; Verger, *Notes sur le culte des Orisa et Vodun* pp. 109–140; Bastide, *Le Candomblé de Bahia*, pp. 148–172; Dos Santos, *Os Nágo e a Morte*, pp. 182–199.

    Wafer notes that Exu, more than any other spirit, is approached "in terms of metaphors of inducement." *Taste of Blood*, p. 15. The status of Exu among the *orixás* is ambiguous for on some occasions he can be seen as an *orixá* along side the others and at other times as an aspect of an *orixá*. It is said that each *orixá* has his or her own Exu, sometimes referred to as a "slave" or "child." Dos Santos argues throughout her construction of Nagô cosmology that Exu is a kind of dimension of matter, the creative origins of its force in the world. See *Os Nàgô e a Morte*, especially pp. 211–219.

58. Dos Santos, *Os Nàgô e a Morte*, p. 190, my translation and abridgement of Dos Santos's Portuguese.

59. Personal communication with José Laureano Santos, priest of Euá, 18 June 1991.

60. For a detailed article on the construction of Bahian drums in the 1940s, see Melville Herskovits, "Drums and Drummers in Afro-Brazilian Cult Life," *Musical Quarterly* 30.4 (1944).

61. A short, but detailed and informed description of Afro-Bahian dance may be found in Margaret Thompson Drewal's "Dancing for Ogun in

Yorubaland and Brazil," in *Africa's Ogun: Old World and New,* edited by Sandra T. Barnes (Bloomington: Indiana University Press, 1989).

62. See ibid., p. 220.
63. Verger, *Notes sur le culte des Orisa et Vodun,* pp. 175–206.
64. Landes, *City of Women,* p. 207.
65. Melville J. and Frances S. Herskovits, notes to record album "Afro-Bahian Religious Songs", *Folk Music of Brazil,* Album L-13, Collections of the Archive of Folk Song (1942), p. 13.
66. Subtitled text from film, *Iawo,* directed by Geraldo Sarno.
67. Bastide, *Le Candomblé de Bahia,* p. 23.
68. Bastide, *African Religion of Brazil,* pp. 247–248.
69. See Bastide, *Le Candomblé de Bahia* pp. 68–72; and Dos Santos, *Os Nàgô e a Morte,* pp. 65–67, 161–181. Bastide notes that the *poteau mitan* of vodou is sometimes called the *poteau Legba,* linking the phallicism of the penetrating spirit with the cosmic union of earth and sky.
70. Sung by José Laureano Santos, 18, June 1991.
71. Drewal, "Dancing for Ogun," p. 220.
72. Pierson, *Negroes in Brazil,* p. 281.
73. Landes, *City of Women,* p. 77, 95–97, 128.
74. Ibid., pp. 95–96.
75. For a systematic construction of Nagô psychology, drawing from African and Brazilian sources, see Dos Santos, *Os Nàgô e a Morte,* pp. 200–219.
76. Sheila Walker notes this interior dimension of the *orixá* when she writes: "Since the Orisha represents the deeper, transcendent self of the person, the Orisha is already present in the individual in a latent state. The initiation process serves to teach the person to manifest this level of his or her being, which corresponds to a specific form of higher reality or consciousness, when given the proper stimulus of particular drum rhythms played in the appropriate ceremonial context." "Everyday and Esoteric Reality," p. 120.
77. Landes, *City of Women,* p 96.

4. Cuban and Cuban American Santería

1. Most contemporary devotees of the Cuban tradition of the *orishas* seem to disapprove of the word *santería* as the appropriate term to comprehend the religion. They find it a colonial remnant that over-

emphasizes what they see as superficial European and Catholic elements of the tradition at the expense of a core that has remained true to its African roots. The word *santería*, they would argue, traps all conversation about the religion into discussions of syncretism and belies the fidelity of the tradition to Yoruba precedent.

Despite the rightness of these claims, I have decided to continue using the word *santería* for several reasons. It continues to be the term most often employed in scholarly literature; it has been accepted at least provisionally by members of the religion in their public struggle for free exercise before federal courts; it distinguishes the Cuban developments of Yoruba religion from other Yoruba traditions; the words *santero* and *santera* are in general usage without prejudice within the communities of worship; and I believe that the parallelism of the Catholic tradition is important in the development of the religion in Cuba.

2. Oba Oseigeman Adefunmi, in describing his journey to Yoruba religion, recalls his surprize when he was searching for an authentic African identity in America in the late 1950s and he discovered a "ready-made" African spirituality in the *santería* of New York. Unpublished paper delivered at the first International Congress of the Orisa Tradition, Ilé-Ifé, NIgeria, 1981.

3. The importance of this date is emphasized in Hugh Thomas's popular history *Cuba: The Pursuit of Freedom* (New York: Harper and Row, 1971).

4. Philip D. Curtin, *The Atlantic Slave Trade: A Census* (Madison: University of Wisconsin Press, 1969), pp. 31–40. Curtin's figures are often considered low. Manuel Moreno Fraginals estimates over one million Africans came to Cuba during the entire period of the slave trade. See "Africa in Cuba: A Quantitative Analysis of the African Population in the Island of Cuba," in *Comparative Perspectives on Slavery in New World Plantation Societies*, edited by Vera Rubin and Arthur Tudin (New York: New York Academy of Sciences, 1977).

5. Jorge Castellanos and Isabel Castellanos, "The Origin of Cuban Blacks," unpublished paper. These data and much more may be found in their (to-date) three-volume work *Cultura Afrocubana* (Miami: Ediciones Universal, 1989–1992). Cuban ethnographer Rafael López Valdéz speaks of over three hundred African ethnic groups represented

in Cuba. Personal communication, November 1992.

6.   Lydia Cabrera, *La sociedad secreta Abakuá* (Miami: Ediciones Universal, 1970), p. 9.

7.   See David H. Brown, "Garden in the Machine: Afro-Cuban Sacred Art and Performance in Urban New Jersey and New York" (Ph.D. dissertation, Yale University, 1989), p. 73ff.

8.   Hugh Thomas notes a frequently heard disclaimer, "Yo no creo pero lo repito" ("I don't believe, but I repeat the ritual"). *Cuba: The Pursuit of Freedom*, p. 1125.

9.   This preponderance of women has been explained from a variety of angles, ranging from I. M. Lewis's ideas about the compensation that economically deprived women seek in spirit possession to the *santeros'* explanation that women are more "open" to the spirit by virtue of their biology and psychology. See Lewis, *Ecstatic Religion: An Anthropological Study of Spirit Possession and Shamanism* (Baltimore: Penguin, 1971).

10. I've heard this notion of the "openness" of women's bodies to the spirit expressed several times by *santeras* in New York. The image of spiritual communion as sexual union seems a natural development of this emphasis on the significance of the body, but, either due to mutual reticence or my inadequate language skills, I've never been able to confirm this view.

11. For information on women *babalawos* in Nigeria, see Elizabeth M. McClelland, *The Cult of Ifa among the Yoruba* (London: Ethnographica, 1982), p. 88. Cuban *babalawos* have also insisted that the path of Ifa is only open to heterosexual men.

12. See Lourdes López, *Estudio del babalao* (Havana: Universidad de Havana, Departamento de Actividades Culturales, 1978).

13. There is a good deal of resistance on the part of many *santeros* toward the hegemony of *babalawos* in ritual and discipline. See David Brown's discussion of these competing claims of priestly authority in "Garden in the Machine," pp. 212–254.

14. Lydia Cabrera, *Koeko iyawo: aprende novicia* (Miami: Ediciones Universal, 1980) p. 162.

15. Brown, "Garden in the Machine," pp. 378–379.

16. Lydia Cabrera, *El Monte* (Miami: Ediciones Universal, 1975) p. 24. Cited by Brown, "Garden in the Machine," p. 379.

17. See Robert Farris Thompson, "The Sign of the Divine King: Yoruba Bead-embroidered Crowns with Veil and Bird Decorations," in *African Art and Leadership*, edited by Douglas Fraser and Herbert Cole (Madison: University of Wisconsin Press, 1972).

18. George Brandon speaks of the "themes" of *kariocha* as kingship, marriage, death and resurrection, and infancy. See "The Dead Sell Memories: An Anthropological Study of Santería in New York City." (Ph.D. dissertation, Rutgers University, 1983), p. 388.

19. *The King Does not Lie: The Initiation of a Shango Priest.* By Judith Gleason and Elise Mereghetti with the collaboration of Yermino Valdes Garriz and Marco Mensa. Distributed by Filmakers Library, New York, 1992. I am deeply indebted to Judith Gleason for her consultation in the preparation of this description of her work. Her advice on the inclusion of ceremonial details, Lucumi songs, and off-camera events proved invaluable.

20. The *kariocha* initiate will also receive the mysteries of other *orishas* to supplement the enthronement of the dominant *orisha*. Initiates are "children" of this *orisha*, but will sometimes say that they are children of a male/female pair of *orishas*. One might hear an initiate say that she is a daughter of the female *orisha* Oshun, and then say that Shango is her father.

    In addition to receiving a "master" (dueño) of the head, and a mother and father pair of *orishas*, the initiate also receives a cluster of spirits that are placed over and in her head. This core group are usually the most popular spirits: Obatala, Yemaya, Oshun, Shango, and sometimes Oya.

    Finally divination will reveal other *adimu orishas* which must be received outside the initiate's *kariocha* either as preparation for *kariocha* or following it. *Orishas* such as Olokun, Inle, Babaluaiye, the Ibeji, Orisha Oko, and Eleggua, Ogun, and Oshosi are "made" outside the crowning ceremony.

21. For a superb description and analysis of the ethnohistory and structure of Afro-Cuban thrones, see Brown, *Garden in the Machine.*

22. This translation of "*el monte*" as "wilderness" is taken from the work of *oriete* and scholar Ysamur Flores and his 1992 presentation to the American Folklore Society, "'El Monte' as Metaphor."

23. The usual practice in Cuban and Cuban American *santería* is for the

iyawo to have his or her head painted with four, or sometimes six, concentric circles coded to the colors of the cluster of orishas that he or she would receive: Obatala's white, Shango's red, Oshun's yellow, and Yemaya's blue. Also it is common for the face of the *iyawo* to be spotted with paste dots in the colors of the *orishas* of each of the attending *iyalorishas* and *babalorishas*. Judith Gleason says that the presiding priest in the film, Yermino "Chiqui" Valdes, has traveled to Nigeria, and having received some of his initiations there has been "re-Africanizing" some initiation practices. The limitation of colors to the patron *orisha* Shango and the leopard symbolism are examples of this departure from Cuban models.

24. Again this reception of the accompanying *orishas* on the occiput rather than on the crown of the head as is done in most Cuban and Cuban American *ilés* is a reform on the part of Yermino Valdes that reflects his African experience.

25. In a personal communication Judith Gleason writes: "If the *iyawo* becomes possessed under the canopy, then his tongue will be immediately cut with small incisions and a special sacrifice performed so that the *orisha* may speak subsequently through him. This 'opening of the mouth' ritual may be performed upon any subsequent occasion of possession by the head-ruling *orisha*."

26. Lydia Cabrera, *Yemaya y Ochún: Kariacha, Iyalorichas y Olorichas* (Miami: Ediciones Universal, 1980), p. 134.

27. See Brown's Garden in the Machine for documentation of an *ilé* in New Jersey that purchased a building solely for its own services.

28. Migene González-Wippler, *the Santería Experience*, (Englewood Cliffs, N.J.: Prentice-Hall, 1982), p. 125. She notes that the lavish decorations, the drummers and dancers, and the food for such a crowd might cost a thousand dollars or more.

29. This song is probably the best known opening song for Eleggua. This translation was furnished by Adetokunbo Adekanmbi.

30. González-Wippler, *Santería Experience*, p. 127.

31. Ibid., pp. 136–137.

32. Ibid., pp. 137–138.

33. From Gary Edwards and John Mason, *Black Gods: Orisa Studies in the New World* (New York: Yoruba Theological Archministry, 1985), p. 58.

34. Fernando Ortiz is the first to use the word "mosaic" to describe the

disposition to see the elegant cultural oppositions of Cuban society as one whole. See *Cuban Counterpoint* (New York: Knopf, 1949).

35. Roger Bastide, *The African Religions of Brazil: Toward a Sociology of the Interpenetration of Civilizations* (Baltimore: Johns Hopkins University Press, 1978), pp. 247–248. Cited by Brown, "Garden in the Machine," pp. 262–263. This passage is also cited in chap. 3 of this volume.

36. Brown, "Garden in the Machine," p. 263.

37. González-Wippler, *Santería Experience*, p. 142.

5. Revival Zion in Jamaica

1. Philip D. Curtin, *Two Jamaicas* (Cambridge, Mass.: Harvard University Press, 1955), p. 160. For African ethnicities of Jamaican slaves, see Orlando Patterson, *The Sociology of Slavery: An Analysis of the Origins, Development and Structure of Negro Slave Society in Jamaica* (Rutherford, N.J.: Fairleigh Dickenson University Press, 1969), pp. 113–134. Jamaican place names such as Accompong and Abeokuta indicate the memories of communities of people of Akan and Yoruba heritage. Most contemporary Jamaicans can identify at least one ancestor by African ethnic origins. For folk memories of African ethnicity, see Leonard E. Barrett, *The Sun and the Drum: African Roots in Jamaican Folk Tradition* (London: Heinemann, 1976). Monica Schuler's study of Central African indentured emigrants, *Alas, Alas, Kongo: A Social History of Indentured African Immigration into Jamaica, 1841–1865* (Baltimore: Johns Hopkins University Press, 1980), documents the importance of Kongo ancestry in the economic, social, and religious life of their contemporary descendants.

2. Curtin, *Two Jamaicas*, p. 233.

3. Bryan Edwards, who uses this report in his own 1794 work on West Indian history, attributes its authorship to Edward Long. This quote is from the *Report of the Lords of the Committee of the Council appointed for the consideration of all matters relating to Trade and Foreign Plantation*, London 1789. This work is quoted at length by Joseph J. Williams in *Voodoos and Obeahs: Phases of West Indian Witchcraft* (New York: Dial Press, 1932), p. 113.

4. Long in Williams, *Voodoos and Obeahs*, p. 111.

5. Alexander Barclay, *A Practical View of the Present State of Slavery in the*

West Indies (London, 1828), quoted in Williams, *Voodoos and Obeahs*, p. 188.

6. Our guide to Haitian vodou, Katherine Dunham, described a grave-side invocation of a deceased spirit performed on her behalf by *obeah* men in Accompong, Jamaica. The men commanded the *duppy* of Galileo, a deceased *obeah* man himself, "You know what mus' be done—Go an' do it! We wan' fer you 'tay wit' Missus. Stay with missus; what wan' fer she harm, you harm firs'. What wan' fer she he'p, you he'p. Trabble wit' Missus, go wit' missus." Katherine Dunham, *Journey to Accompong* (New York: Henry Holt, 1946), p. 157.

7. Edward Long, *History of Jamaica*, (London: T. Lowndes, 1774), 2: 416.

8. James M. Phillippo, *Jamaica: Its Past and Present State* (1843; London: Dawsons of Pall Mall, 1969), p. 248. Though long a resident of Jamaica, it seems likely that Phillippo's account is dependent on Long's. Still he confirms the earlier view. For another early view of *myal* as chiefly concerned with herbalist rites of death and resurrection, see Matthew Gregory Lewis, *Journal of a West India Proprietor* (London, 1834; New York: Negro Universities Press, 1969), pp. 354–356.

9. H. M. Waddell, *Twenty-nine Years in the West Indies and Central Africa* (1863; London: Frank Cass, 1970), p. 189.

10. Ibid., p. 190. From Waddell's account it seems that the *myal* people refused to break up the meeting because *obeah* was there, physically present and the service was designed to pull it. They were quite happy to have Waddell attend and even preach.

11. J. H. Buchner, *The Moravians in Jamaica* (London, 1854), pp. 139–140.

12. Given the propensity for nineteenth-century sources to freely use each others' accounts, the telling detail of the coffin to "catch" the shadow may be another instance of a widespread practice or it may simply be borrowed from Barclay's 1828 report of the *obeah* trial, *A Practical View*.

13. Thomas R. Banbury, *Jamaica Superstitions or The Obeah Book; A Complete Treatise of the Absurdities Believed in by the People of the Island, by the Rector (Native) of St. Peter's Church, Hope Bay, Portland* (Jamaica, 1894), quoted in Abraham I. Emerick, "Jamaican Mialism," *Woodstock Letters*, vol. 45 (1916), pp. 45–46.

14. Leonard E. Barrett, *Soul Force: African Heritage in Afro-American Religion* (Garden City, N.Y.: Anchor Press/Doubleday, 1974), p. 71.

15. See Schuler, *Alas, Alas, Kongo*, p. 76.

16. This contrast of *obeah* and *myal* was taken up rather relentlessly by Rev. Joseph John Williams in his studies of the history of Jamaican religion. Looking to Ashanti models to understand Jamaican witchcraft and religion, Williams concluded *obeah* to be an evil superstition and myal a genuine religious reaction. Williams argues that as legitimate worship among the slaves was suppressed by the authorities, witchcraft flourished unchecked. See his *Voodoos and Obeahs*. Donald Hogg finds in Williams's contrast an ethical dualism inappropriate to the Afro-Jamaican worldview. See his critique in his doctoral dissertation, "Jamaican Religions: A Study in Variations" (Ph.D. dissertation, Yale University, 1964), especially pp. 68–73. Orlando Patterson and Leonard Barrett take up the same contrast, but emphasize sociological interpretations in the private nature of *obeah* and the public dances of *myal*. See Patterson, *The Sociology of Slavery*, especially pp. 186–188, and Barrett, *Soul Force*, pp. 63–68.

    H. M. Waddell as early as 1863 called *obeah* and *myal* "corresponding parts of one system." *Twenty-nine Years*, p. 187.

    Katherine Dunham witnessed what was called a *myal* dance in Maroon country in the mid-twentieth century. She describes the focus of the dance as a contest between an old man and old woman. "The old man took the part of the myal 'doctor' and the dance was to entice into his power an evil spirit, the 'duppy' of some dead worker of black magic." See *Journey to Accompong*, p. 134ff.

17. Monica Schuler terms *myal*, "social control by and for the enslaved." See *Alas, Alas, Kongo*, p. 34.

    Of course there were and are Jamaicans who define *obeah* precisely as this illegitimate, antisocial activity, private sorcery to do nothing but harm. It would be difficult to imagine anyone, save a genuine sociopath, claiming to practice *obeah* with this definition in mind. Most people have no problem with the idea of using the medicines "for good." *Obeah* is thus the use of spiritual force which the community does not sanction.

18. Neither Long (*History of Jamaica*) nor Lewis (*Journal*), both of whom were writing prior to 1841, make a connection between *myal* and Christianity. It could be that they did not happen to observe it, or that *myal* became Christianized or took on Christian images in the inter-

vening period. It could also be that the definition of *myal* changed from a non-Christian dance to the special spiritual sight attained in Afro-Jamaican services which was referred to by contemporary *kumina* initiates.

19. Quoted by Phillippo, *Jamaica*, p. 278.

20. Lisle's letter of 1790 is reproduced in *Afro-American Religious History: A Documentary Witness*, edited by Milton C. Sernett (Durham: Duke University Press, 1985), pp. 45–46.

21. Curtin, *Two Jamaicas*, p. 168.

22. Phillippo, *Jamaica*, pp. 270, 273. See Waddell, *Twenty-nine Years*, pp. 661–663, for a more detailed contemporary critique of the Native Baptists. A fine summary is provided by Curtin, *Two Jamaicas*, pp. 32–34, 163–165.

23. William James Gardner, *A History of Jamaica from Its Discovery by Christopher Columbus to the Year* 1872 (1873; London: T. Fisher Unwin, 1909), p. 357.

    Monica Schuler provides evidence for Gardner's association of the Native Baptist movement with *myal*. In examining the St. James parish mission of Moses Baker, one of Lisle's most energetic preachers, she shows that the "geographical limits of Baker's following coincide almost exactly with the core area of an aggressive myal movement of the 1840s." Schuler, *Alas, Alas, Kongo*, p. 34.

24. Schuler cites an "apocalyptic mood" in 1860s Jamaica and provides the text of a newspaper article written by a "Son of Africa" which sees Jamaica as engulfed in the ultimate confrontation with the biblical forces of imperial evil, Gog and Magog. That very year eastern Jamaica would erupt in a bloody rebellion which is remembered today as a critical defeat for Jamaica's "sons and daughters of Africa." See *Alas, Alas, Kongo*, pp. 97, 105.

25. Gardner, *History of Jamaica*, p. 465.

26. Martha Beckwith, *Black Roadways* (Chapel Hill: University of North Carolina Press, 1929), p. 169.

    For a study of Bedward contemporary with the prophet see A. A. Brooks, *The History of Bedwardism or the Jamaican National Baptist Church* (Kingston, 1917).

27. Though the causal relationship that he draws between Bedward and revivalism may seem reversed, Abraham I. Emerick is recognizing the

reciprocal influence between the prophet and the tradition that preceded and followed him. Emerick writes: "Bedwardism seemed to have
had a parental affinity to Revivalism which is now rampant in Jamaica
and which is nothing but Mialism pure and simple under a new name."
"Jamaican Mialism," p. 48.

28.   See Edward Seaga, "Revival Cults in Jamaica," *Jamaica Journal* (June,
       1969). See also Martha Beckwith's rendering "Pukkumerians" in *Black
       Roadways*, p. 176.

29.   An index of the stigma of the label of *pocomania* is that in recent
       censuses of Jamaican denominationalism only a tiny fraction (0.01) of
       the Jamaican population publicly identifies itself with *pocomania*. Yet
       every researcher indicates that among the working and unemployed
       classes of Jamaican society, who make up the majority of the Jamaican
       population, *pukkumina* and other revival traditions can claim more
       adherents than all the mainstream traditions combined. It is likely that
       most members of revival churches identify themselves as Baptists. see
       Seaga, "Revival Cults in Jamaica," p. 5.

30.   George Simpson speaks of "alleged differences" between *pocomania*
       and Revival Zion by constructing a "continuum of demonstrative-
       ness" in religious expression. The spectrum runs from *pocomania* as
       the most enthusiastic tradition through Revival Zion through
       American-derived Churches of God to the mainstream denomina-
       tions with their centers in Europe and the United States. See Simpson,
       "Jamaican Revivalist Cults, *Social and Economic Studies* 5 (1956): 401–
       402.

31.   Joseph G. Moore, "The Religion of Jamaican Negroes: A Study of
       Afro-American Acculturation" (Ph.D. dissertation, Northwestern
       University, 1953), p. 69.

32.   See Seaga, "Revival Cults in Jamaica," p. 8, for a succinct listing of the
       varieties of revival ecclesiology.
           In the same volume of *Jamaica Journal* Rex Nettleford writes of his
       childhood memories of revival religion in Jamaica's Cockpit country.
       He attributes the relative simplicity of revival clothing in his home
       district to the dominance of Baptist churches and contrasts this cloth-
       ing with the rather lavish, "episcopalianesque" vestments he has seen
       elsewhere. See "Pocomania in Dance Theatre," *Jamaica Journal* (June,
       1969).

Barry Chavannes notes the incorporation of many revival churches in Jamaica into the organization of the African Methodist Episcopal Church of the United States. He argues that this organizational change will herald doctrinal and liturgical changes and that traditional Jamaican revival will disappear. See Chavannes, "Revivalism: A Disappearing Religion," *Caribbean Quarterly* 24. 3–4 (September–December, 1978).

33. Seaga identifies three major groups of revival rituals: prayer meetings; street meetings; and rituals for specific purposes such as feasting tables or duties; altars; or baths. Seaga, "Revival Cults in Jamaica," p. 9. Simpson lists the occasions for the "table" feasts as: thanksgiving, uplifting (deliverance), mourning (memorial service for dead family member), money raising, annual "sacrifice," and "destruction." Simpson, "Jamaican Revivalist Cults," p. 371.

For diagrams showing the sacred geometry of revival tables, see Moore, "Religion of Jamaican Negroes," pp. 64 and 75.

34. Beckwith, *Black Roadways*, p. 163. Mrs. Imogene Kennedy told Monica Schuler in the 1970s about her call to *kumina*. "In the night, in the cotton tree coming like it hollow, and I inside there . . . and at nighttime I see the cotton tree light up with candles; and I resting now, put my hand this way [under her head] and sleeping. And I only hear a little voice come to me and them talking to me. But those things is spirit talking to me, and them speaking to me now, and say: 'Now, you is a nice little child, and you going to get you right up now in the African world, because you [have] brains, you will take something. So therefore we going to teach you something.'" Schuler, *Alas, Alas, Congo*, p. 74. With the substitution of "spiritual" for the explicit reference to the "African" world of *kumina*, this could be a Revival Zion testimony.

35. The psychologist Madeline Kerr spoke of a revivalist identified as Dinah who told her that "she did not have to go to the meeting and jump to get the spirit, it came to her in her own bed." *Personality and Conflict in Jamaica* (1952; London: Collins, 1963), p. 125.

36. Kerr offers a very brief summary of a revival conversion experience. She was told, "Me lay on me back fe 21 days under de spirit and not a ting but cole water pass me mouth." *Personality and Conflict in Jamaica*, p. 125.

Simpson has a short description of a "rising table" in "Jamaican Revivalist Cults," pp. 375–376. Compare Hogg, "Jamaican Religions," p. 248.

37. Moore, "Religion of Jamaican Negroes," p. 77.
38. Simpson writes that no two revivalists will produce the same list of "angels," "protectors," or "messengers." He offers a list including the angels Michael and Gabriel, Old Testament prophets, New Testament saints, the Trinity, the Mother of Jesus, Satan, Rutibel, beings from the de Laurence books of magic, and sometimes the dead. See "Jamaican Revivalist Cults," p. 344. Seaga organizes the revival spiritual world into three categories of supernatural powers: (1) heavenly spirits: including the triune God, archangels, angels, and saints; (2) earthbound spirits: the satanic powers (fallen angels), biblical prophets, and apostles; and (3) ground spirits: all the human dead except those mentioned in the Bible. See Seaga, "Revival Cults in Jamaica, p. 10.

   All Zionists would categorically deny "working with" Satan, the de Laurence spirits, or any other entity associated with *obeah*.
39. Moore, "Religion of Jamaican Negroes," p. 76.
40. Beckwith, *Black Roadways*, p. 164.
41. This service was witnessed by the author and David Wood in June of 1976. The names of the church and its members have been changed.
42. This and the hymns that follow may be found in any number of collections of "Sankey" hymns. These are to be found in a volume entitled *Redemption Songs*, published in London by Pickering and Inglis in 1891.
43. This distinction seems to refer both to the history of Jamaican revival and certain patterns of service. In the historical interpretation, the numbers after the word revival are said to be the years of the Great Revival that the church looks to as the historical origins of its particular charisms. Thus Revival 60 and 61 would refer to the founding of their spiritualities in 1860 and 1861. The ritual meaning of the distinction can be found in the pattern of "trumping" or spiritual dance employed by each church.

   Barry Chavannes argues that the label of "61" is always an accusation of working with fallen spirits and all Revivalists would claim to be "sixty." See "Revivalism: A Disappearing Religion," p. 4.
44. Moore, "Religion of Jamaican Negroes," pp. 76, 78.

45. The equation of biblical Zion with geographic Africa is a major theme of Rastafarianism which is usually viewed as wholly distinct from the revival tradition because of the Rastas's impatience with the "other-worldliness" of revival eschatology. Yet this identification of biblical figures with African ancestors, and the understanding of the Bible as a guide to the black experience has a long history in Revival Zion, including an eschatological militancy toward the sinners against Africa. It would be worth investigating whether Rastafarianism owes more to the revival tradition than is usually thought. Note Simpson's contrast of revival and Rastafarian "utopias" in "Jamaican Revivalist Cults," p. 411. Barrett sees all "Afro-Christian cults" as characterized by "latent militancy." *Soul Force*, p. 126.

46. This is a generalization of a widespread view of the human person among Jamaicans drawn principally from Moore "Religion of Jamaican Negroes," pp. 33–34 with Beckwith, *Black Roadways*, pp. 97–98, and Kerr, *Personality and Conflict*, p. 131. A good summary of the literature on *duppies* is provided by Patterson, *Sociology of Slavery*, p. 203ff.

    This study of the spirit of Revival Zion is much indebted to William A. Wedenoja's superb taxonomy of revival spirits in his 1978 paper for the Society for the Scientific Study of Religion, "The Cultural Construction of Altered States of Consciousness." For the most thorough study of Jamaican revival, see his doctoral dissertation, "Religious Adaptation in Rural Jamaica" (Ph.D. dissertation, University of California, San Diego, 1978).

47. Beckwith offers an outstanding description of the neutralization of a *duppy* by a revivalist in *Black Roadways*, pp. 173–74.

48. Moore, "Religion of Jamaican Negroes," pp. 76–77.

6. The Black Church in the United States

1. The coinage of the term "Black Church" to highlight the unity within the diverse institutions of African American religious experience probably rests with G. Carter Woodson in his pioneering work: *The History of the Negro Church* (Washington, D.C.: The Association for the Study of Negro Life and History, 1921). E. Franklin Frazier cemented the term though in his classic sociological treatment, *The Negro Church in America* (New York: Schocken Books, 1964). The importance of Fra-

zier's work was underscored when it was brought out in a 1974 edition joined with a one-hundred-page essay by C. Eric Lincoln called, "The Black Church Since Frazier." Lincoln and Lawrence Mamiya have once again looked to Frazier in titling their monumental 1990 study, *The Black Church in the African American Experience* (Durham: Duke University Press, 1990).

2. Lincoln and Mamiya, *Black Church in the African American Experience*, p. 1.

3. Joseph R. Washington applies the classic typology of "church," "sect," and "cult" to African American religion in his survey of the latter two categories, *Black Sects and Cults* (Garden City, N.Y.: Doubleday, 1972), pp. 1–18. Hans A. Baer makes a convincing argument against "stereotypes about the alleged uniformity of Black religion" in *The Black Spiritual Movement: A Religious Response to Racism* (Knoxville: University of Tennessee Press, 1984), p. vi. He prefers to move away from the classic categories toward a "sectarian" typology for African American religion in four categories: (1) mainstream or established sects; (2) messianic-nationalist sects; (3) conversionist sects; (4) thaumaturgical/manipulationist sects (see p. 8ff). Baer and Merrill Singer apply this typology to a wide variety of African American religious traditions in *African American Religion in the Twentieth Century* (Knoxville: University of Tennessee Press, 1992), pp. 55–64.

4. Albert Raboteau emphasizes the differences between African and African American theology as it applies to ecstatic religion among African Americans. I examine his argument in chap. 7. See his *Slave Religion: The "Invisible Institution" in the Antebellum South* (New York: Oxford University Press, 1978), pp. 55–75.

5. Ivan van Sertima, *They Came Before Columbus* (New York: Random House, 1976).

6. See Robert William Fogel and Stanley L. Engerman, *Time on the Cross: The Economics of American Slavery* (Boston: Little, Brown, 1974), vol. 2, pp. 28–31.

7. Peter Wood, *Black Majority: Negroes in Colonial South Carolina from 1670 through the Stono Rebellion* (New York: Alfred A. Knopf, 1974), pp. 167–191. Mechal Sobel offers a fine overview of the dependence of slavers on black linguists. See *Trabelin' On: The Slave Journey to an*

Afro-Baptist Faith (Westport, Conn.: Greenwood Press, 1979), pp. 30–31.

8. Sterling Stuckey, *Slave Culture: Nationalist Theory and the Foundations of Black America* (New York: Oxford University Press, 1987), pp. 10–17.

9. Elizabeth Ware Pearson, ed., *Letters from Port Royal Written at the Time of the Civil War* (Boston: 1906), p. 27. Cited in Washington, *Black Sects and Cults*, p. 75, and in Raboteau, *Slave Religion*, pp. 70–71.

10. Frederick Law Olmstead, *A Journey in the Seaboard Slave States* (New York, 1856). Cited in Raboteau, *Slave Religion*, p. 68.

11. Daniel Alexander Payne, *Recollections of Seventy Years* (1886; New York: Arno Press and the New York Times, 1969). Cited in Raboteau, *Slave Religion*, p. 69.

12. Clifton Joseph Furness, "Communal Music among Arabians and Negroes," *Musical Quarterly* 16 (1930). Cited by Lawrence W. Levine, *Black Culture and Black Consciousness: Afro-American Folk Thought from Slavery to Freedom* (New York: Oxford University Press, 1977), p. 27.

13. Margaret Washington Creel, *"A Peculiar People": Slave Religion and Community-Culture Among the Gullahs* (New York: New York University Press, 1988), pp. 296–302.

14. Matthew 3:16; Mark 1:10; Luke 3:22; John 1:33.

15. Dorothy Scarborough, *On the Trail of Negro Folk Songs* (Hatboro, Pa.: Folklore Associates, 1963), pp. 14–16.

16. Creel, *"A Peculiar People"*, p. 298.

17. Glennie cited by Charles Joyner, *Down by the Riverside: A South Carolina Slave Community* (Urbana and Chicago: University of Illinois Press, 1984), p. 156.

18. Works Progress Administration, Workers of the Writers' Program in the State of Virginia, *The Negro in Virginia* (New York, 1940), p. 109. Cited by Levine, *Black Culture and Black Consciousness*, p. 46.

19. See Edward D. Smith, *Climbing Jacob's Ladder: The Rise of Black Churches in Eastern American Cities, 1740–1877* (Washington: The Anacostia Museum of the Smithsonian Institution, 1988).

20. See Levine, *Black Culture and Black Consciousness*, pp. 74–76. For a full treatment of the theological dimensions of these actions, see Gayraud S. Wilmore, *Black Religion and Black Radicalism* (2d ed.; Maryknoll, N.Y.: Orbis Books, 1985).

21. *The Confessions of Nat Turner . . . As Fully and Voluntarily Made to Thomas R. Gray.* Cited by Levine, *Black Culture and Black Consciousness,* p. 77.
22. Douglass cited by Raboteau, *Slave Religion,* p. 247.
23. John Wesley Work, *American Negro Songs and Spirituals: A Comprehensive Collection of 250 Folk Songs, Religious and Secular* (New York: Bonanza, 1940), p. 45. I am indebted to Georgetown students Lahela Hekekia, Elizabeth Michell and Daniel Philippon, all of the class of 1990, for their outstanding research on the spirituals and African American religion.
24. Cited by Joyner, *Down by the Riverside,* p. 160.
25. See Levine, *Black Culture and Black Consciousness,* pp. 37–38.
26. Frazier writes of the postemancipation Black Church: ". . . on the whole the Negro Church was not a threat to white domination and aided the Negro to become accommodated to an inferior status. The religion of the Negro continued to be other–worldly in its outlook, dismissing the privations and sufferings and injustices of this world as temporary and transient." *The Negro Church in America,* p. 46.
27. W. E. B. Du Bois, *The Souls of Black Folk* (1903; New York: New American Library, 1969), p. 47.
28. It is not within our scope to review anything like the full variety of religious beliefs and practices among African Americans. Suffice it to note that alongside and within Christianity a number of religious ideas and actions from Africa and elsewhere have been important to many African Americans. Charles Joyner organizes the spirituality of African Americans in antebellum South Carolina into three areas: (1) spirit possession "merged" with Christianity; (2) belief in hags and other spirits alongside Christianity; (3) conjure, a tradition of herbal and verbal healing and harming, as an underground alternative to Christianity. *Down by the Riverside,* p. 142. For more on conjure or hoodoo, see Newbell Niles Puckett, *The Magic and Folk Beliefs of the Southern Negro* (Chapel Hill: University of North Carolina Press, 1926); Zora Neale Hurston, "Hoodoo in America," *Journal of American Folklore* 44 (1931). For a suggestive interpretation of some aspects of African American hoodoo in the light of Kongo *minkisi,* see Robert Farris Thompson, *Flash of the Spirit: African and Afro-American Art and Philosophy* (New York: Random House, 1983), pp. 117–131.

Another, under-recognized element in the religious heritage of African Americans is the presence of Islam brought to the American South by many Africans. For a poignant profile of five prominent African muslims in America, see Allan D. Austin, *African Muslims in Antebellum America (New York: Garland, 1984)*.

29. Frazier, *The Negro Church in America*, p. 29ff.

30. Ibid., pp. 30–31.

31. See a defense of this generalization in Lincoln and Mamiya, *The Black Church in the African American Experience*, pp. 6–7.

32. Lincoln and Mamiya maintain that the "holy dance" of the shout has been abandoned in all but the Pentecostal and Holiness sects of the Black Church, *The Black Church in the African American Experience*, p. 354. But see Sonja H. Stone on the maintenance of a "facsimile" of possession spirituality in "sophisticated" black churches in "Oral Tradition and Spiritual Drama: The Cultural Mosaic for Black Preaching," *The Journal of the Interdenominational Theological Center* 8.1 (Fall, 1980).

   On the relationship between the spirituality of the Holiness and Pentecostal churches and that of the Baptists and Methodists, Joseph Washington, in *Black Sects and Cults* (p. 79), has this to say:

   > In time, what was the special creation of Pentecostals and Holiness black sects became contagious among all lower class black congregations. The black Holiness people left the Baptist and Methodist churches because they could not exercise therein their gifts of the spirit, but their spirited ways returned to dominate the scene to the extent that black Baptists and Methodists now claim this heritage as their very own, failing to credit the special gifts of Pentecostals and Holiness types.

33. Wardell J. Payne, *Directory of African American Religious Bodies* (Washington, D.C.: Howard University Press, 1991), p. 92.

34. Elder Mason cited by Lincoln and Mamiya, *The Black Church in the African American Experience*, p. 81.

35. Ibid., p. 83.

36. Thomas A. Burns and J. Stephen Smith, "The Symbolism of Becoming in the Sunday Service of an Urban Black Holiness Church," *Anthropological Quarterly* 51.3 (July, 1978). A full sociological treatment of an affiliate Church of God in Christ can be found in Melvin D. Williams, *Community in a Black Pentecostal Church* (Pittsburgh: University of Pittsburgh Press, 1974).

37. Lincoln and Mamiya, *The Black Church in the African American Experience*, pp. 89–90.
38. This service was witnessed by the author and Dr. Jane Hurst of Gallaudet University in January of 1993. The participants are given pseudonyms.
39. Charles H. Long, "Perspectives for a Study of Afro-Americans Religion in the United States," in *Significations: Signs, Symbols, and Images in the Interpretation of Religion* (Philadelphia: Fortress Press, 1986), p. 176.
40. Elias Farajajé-Jones, *In Search of Zion: The Spiritual Significance of Africa in Black Religious Movements* (Bern: Peter Lang, 1991), p. 33.
41. Farajajé-Jones, *In Search of Zion*, p. 40.
42. Levine, *Black Culture and Black Consciousness*, p. 31.
43. Henry H. Mitchell, a scholar and a preacher himself, summarizes the sacred time dimension of the sermon in the Black Church when he writes that "black Bible stories are to be relived, not merely heard." *Black Preaching* (Philadelphia: Lippincott, 1970), p. 139.
44. A. P. Watson and Clifton H. Johnson, *God Struck Me Dead: Religious Conversion Experiences and Autobiographies of Negro Ex-Slaves* (Philadelphia: Pilgrim Press, 1969). This material is ably summarized by Sobel, *Trabelin' On*, pp. 108–112.
45. Elsie Clews Parsons, "Folk-lore of the Sea Islands of South Carolina," *Memoires of the American Folk-lore Society* 16 (1923, p. 204; Raboteau, *Slave Religion*, p. 73; Creel, *"A Peculiar People"*, pp. 278–300.
46. Morton Marks, "You Can't Sing Unless You're Saved: Reliving the Call in Gospel Music," in *African Religious Groups and Beliefs: Papers in Honor of William R. Bascom*, edited by Simon Ottenberg (Meerut, India: Archana Publications, 1982), pp. 310, 313.
47. Willie May Ford Smith in Tony Heilbut, *The Gospel Sound: Good News and Bad Times* (New York: Simon and Schuster, 1971), p. 209.
48. Zora Neale Hurston, *The Sanctified Church* (Berkeley: Turtle Island, p. 91.
49. Elias Farajajé-Jones, personal communication, April, 1991.

7. Working the Spirit

1. See an illuminating discussion of the comparative method in the study of religion in William E. Paden, *Interpreting the Sacred: Ways of Viewing Religion* (Boston: Beacon Press, 1992). Paden cites the nineteenth-

century German comparativist scholar Max Müller for the application of this quote to the study of religion. Max Müller himself was paraphrasing Goethe who intended it to refer to the study of language.

2. Melville J. Herskovits, *The Myth of the Negro Past* (1941; Boston: Beacon Press, 1990; Pierre Verger, *Notes sur le Culte des Orisa et Vodun* (Dakar: L'Institut Français d'Afrique Noire, 1957); Robert Farris Thompson, *Flash of the Spirit: African and Afro-American Art and Philosophy* (New York: Random House, 1983); Kenneth Bilby and Fu-kiau Bunseki, *Kumina: A Kongo-based Tradition in the New World* (Brussels: Centre d'Etude et Documentation Africaines, 1983); John Janzen, *Lemba, 1650–1930: A Drum of Affliction in Africa and the New World* (New York, Garland, 1982).

3. I don't mean to imply that this isn't true. Herskovits again recognized that African Americans had maintained many traditions that could provide clues to the history of African practices. See "The Contribution of Afroamerican Studies of Africanist Research," *American Anthropologist* 50.1 (1948).

4. Melville J. Herskovits, *The Myth of the Negro Past*, (Boston: Beacon Press, 1990), pp. xxvii; "Problem Method and Theory in Afroamerican Studies," *Afroamerica* 1 (1945).

5. Eugene Genovese, *Roll, Jordan, Roll: The World the Slaves Made* (New York: Random House, 1972), p. 183.

6. Albert J. Raboteau, *Slave Religion: "The Invisible Institution" in the Antebellum South* (New York: Oxford University Press, 1979), p. 92.

7. E. B. Idowu, *Olodumare: God in Yoruba Belief* (London: Longmans, 1962), p. 63.

8. Laureano Santos, in Bahia in 1991, gave me the electrical generator-receptor metaphor, complete with intermediate relays and capacitors, to explain the relationship between Olorun, the *orixás*, and human beings. Maya Deren seeks to explain the mystery of two and one in vodou's veneration of twins; see *Divine Horsemen: The Living Gods of Haiti* (New York: Thames and Hudson, 1953), p. 38–41. I have constructed a santería theology around the progressive personalization of the abstract notion of power, *ashé*. See *Santería: African Spirits in America* (Boston: Beacon Press, 1988), pp. 130–134.

9. Paul Tillich, *Systematic Theology*, vol. 1 (Chicago: University of Chicago Press, 1951), p. 211. Cited by Newell S. Booth, "God and Gods in

West Africa," in *African Religions: A Symposium*, edited by Newell S. Booth (New York: NOK Publishers, 1977), p. 176. Booth's article shows how the creative application of Western theological categories can illuminate a great deal about African ideas of God.

10. Wyatt MacGaffey, *Religion and Society in Central Africa* (Chicago: University of Chicago Press, 1986), p. 8. See also his "African Religions: Types and Generalizations," in *Explorations in African Systems of Thought*, edited by Ivan Karp and Charles S. Bird (Washington, D.C.: Smithsonian Institution Press, 1987).

11. Genovese, *Roll, Jordan, Roll*, p. 214.

12. In each of the five diasporan communities we may find as much evidence in the late twentieth century that educated people are "returning" to these traditions as mid-century accounts spoke of them "dying out."

13. Katherine Dunham, *Dances of Haiti* (Los Angeles: Center for Afro-American Studies, University of California: 1983), p. xxiv.

14. See Sheila Walker, *Ceremonial Spirit Possession in Africa and Afro-America* (Leiden: Brill, 1972), and Gilbert Rouget, *Music and Trance: a Theory of the Relations between Music and Possession* (Chicago: University of Chicago Press, 1985).

15. Raboteau, *Slave Religion*, p. 64.

16. Herskovits, *The Myth of the Negro Past*, p. 214.

17. James Cone, "Black Worship," in *The Study of Spirituality*, edited by Cheslyn Jones, Geoffrey Wainwright, and Edward Yarnold (New York: Oxford University Press, 1986), p. 486.

Glossary

The definitions below are intended to give only the sparest meanings for the terms listed. The lowercase letters in parenthesis following each term refer to the traditions which employ the term: (c) Candomblé; (rz) Revival Zion; (s) Santería; (v) Vodou. Candomblé and Santería share many Yoruba terms, and their differences in spelling are only the result of local orthographies. I have indicated common usage in both traditions with (c, s). It is likely that many more terms than I have chosen are in use in both communities.

abébé (c). Metal fan sacred to female *orixás* Iemanjá and Oxun.
abian (c). Novice undergoing initiation.
acarajé (c). Fried bean cake sacred to Iansá.
actions de grace (v). Catholic prayers introducing a ceremony.
adarun (c). Drumbeat intensified in order to bring on spirit manifestation.
adja (c). White metal bell with clapper.
agôgô (c, s). Iron bell hit with stick.
Agwé (Agoué) (v). *Lwa* of the sea.
alua (c). Fermented beverage sacred to Oxossi.
amaci (c). Herbal preparation.
Aña (s). Foundation spirit of the drum.
apón (akpon) (s). Song leader.
apotí (s). Mortar throne upon which initiate is crowned.
Arada (v). Senior nation of Vodou.

ashé (axé, aché) (c, s). Divine power, objects chaneling divine power.

asiento (s). "Seating" ceremony of initiation.

ason (v). Rattle of the *manbo* or *oungan* that directs the energy of the ceremony.

assentametos (c). Objects consecrated to the altar of the *orixás*.

atabaque (autabaquis) (c). Cone-shaped drums.

axé (aché, ashé) (c, s). Divine power, objects chaneling divine power.

axôgún (c, s). Priest who holds the knife of Ogun, official sacrificer.

axoxô (c). Corn cooked with coconut, sacred to Oxossi.

Ayida (Aida, Aida Ouédo) (v). Danbala's consort, the rainbow.

ayugbona (yubona, yugbona) (s). Sponsor and attendant at *asiento*.

babalawo (s). "Father of the mystery," priest of Ifa.

babalorisha (babalocha, babalorixá) (s, c). "Father of the spirit," male priest.

Babaluaiye (Obaluaiye, Omulu) (s, c). *Orisha* of the transformative power of disease.

banda (v). Bawdy dance beloved of Gede.

bands (rz). Initiated dancers.

barracão (c). Dance court.

bata (s). Double-headed drums, sacred to Shango.

batea (s). Wooden bowl holding the fundamental symbols of Shango.

bembé (s). Drum dance.

Bois Caiman (v). Site of revolutionary vodou oath, 1791.

bosalle (v). "Unbaptised" spirit, African-born.

boule zen (brulé zin) (v). "Burning pots"; *kanzo* initiation.

búzios (c). Cowrie shells for diviniation; cf. *dilogun*.

cabildo (s). Nineteenth-century "assembly" of free and enslaved Afro-Cubans.

caboclo (c). Brazilian Indians and Indian spirits.

camino (s). "Way," "path," or "road"; initiation track or kind of spirit manifestation.

canastillero (s). Shelved cabinet holding *orisha* stones.

candomblé (c). Afro-Bahian religious tradition.

casa (s). "House," the fundamental social unit of santería, *ilé*.

catulagem (c). Ceremonial cutting of the novice's hair.

chekere (shekere) (s). Beaded rattle.

coronación (s). "Crowning" initiation into santería priesthood.

cundiamore (s). Herb sacred to San Lazaro.

Dahomey (v). Ancient African kingdom; Africa in general.

Danbala (Damballah) (v). Senior *lwa*, serpent.

deixaram o cargo (c). Releasing the charge of leadership.

deká (c). Seventh-year initiation.

Dessalines (v). Revolutionary general and emperor of Haiti.

dilogun (s, c). Divination with sixteen cowrie shells.

djèvo (v). Seclusion area for initiates.

duppy (rz). Restless spirit of the dead, unconverted soul, poltergeist.

ebo (s, c). "Work" in the spirit, sacrifice.

ebomin (egbomin) (c). Senior wife of the *orixá*.

ebori eleda (c). Work for the head.

efun (s, c). Ritual chalk made from dried egg whites.

ekedi (c). Attendant to dancers.

Eleggua (s). *Orisha* messenger, trickster, opener of paths; cf. *Exu, Legba*.

en santo (s). "In the spirit."

entoto (c). Aperture in *terriero* floor containing *axé* of community.

erê (c). Child-spirit accompaning patron *orixá*.

ewe (s, c). Medicinal leaves and herbs.

ewo (s, c). Lifestyle restrictions related to the initiate's *orixá*.

Exu (c). *Orixá* messenger, trickster, and opener of paths; cf. *Eleggua, Legba*.

eya aranla (s). Second drum cycle of *bembé* accompanied by drumming and
    singing.

Ezili (Erzulie) (v). *Lwa* of eroticism and protection.

Féray (v). Title of Ogou.

Festa dos Orixás (c). "Feast of the *orixás*," ceremony.

féy (feuillages) (v). Medicinal leaves and herbs; cf. *ewe*.

fundamentos (s). Foundation altar objects; cf. *assentamentos*.

gardes (v). Charms.

Gede (v). Hungry trickster *lwa* of the cemetery.

Ginen (Guinée) (v). Africa.

govi (v). Earthenware containers of spiritual presence.

guiro (s). Musical instrument, notched gourd scraped with stick.

gwo bònanj (gros bon ange) (v). Personality or soul of an individual.

heritage (v). Ancestral lands and lines.

Iansá (Iansan) (c). *Orixá* of winds, woman warrior; cf. *Oya*.

iaô (c, s). Bride of the *orixá*, new initiate; cf. *iyawo, Iawo*.

Iemanjá (c). Maternal *orixá* of ocean waters; cf. *Yemaya*.

igbodu (igbodún) (s). Sacred grove, ritual space.

iko (c). Raffia fiber sacred to Omulu.

ilé (c, s). House, community, family.

inafa (s). Large beaded necklace.

irôkô (c). Tree spirit.

iruke (c, s). Horsetail scepter.

itá (s). Shell divination reading at initiation.

italero (s). One who reads shells.

itotele (s). Middle-sized bata drum.

iya basé (c). "Mother who cooks," priestess responsible for feast.

iyá (c, s). Mother, wife, primary term of relationship in community.

iyá kêkêrê (c). Little mother, chief assistant to head of house.

iyalocha (iyalorisha, iyalorixá) (c, s). Wife/mother of the spirit, priestess.

iyawo (c, s). Bride of the *orixá*, new initiate; cf. *iaô*.

Jeje (Gege) (c). Dahomean candomblé.

jogo de búzios (c). "Play of the cowries, divination; cf. *dilogun*.

Juida (Ouida, Whydah) (v). City in southern Benin.

kanzo (canzo) (v). Rite of initiation.

kariocha (s). "To place the *orisha* on the head," initiation rite.

kele (c). Necklace sacred to an *orixá*.

konesans (connaisance) (v). "Knowledge," spiritual insight, extrasensory perception.

kouche (v). "To be laid on the floor," initiation rite.

kumina (rz). Kongo-Jamaican religious tradition.

lakou (v). Family compound.

langay (langage) (v). Secret African language of the *lwa*.

la place (v). Ritual assistant to *oungan* or *manbo*.

lave tèt (v). "Washed head," initiation.

lê (c). Smallest of three conical drums.

Legba (v). Old man, trickster, opener of the gate; cf. *Exu, Eleggua*.

Loko (v). Tree spirit; cf. *Irôkô*.

Lucumi (s). Yoruba of Cuba.

lwa (loa) (v). Spirit.

madrina (s). Godmother, *iyalorisha*.

mãe de santo (c). Mother, *iyalorixá*.

maman (v). "Mother," large drum.

manbo (mambo) (v). Priestess.

mariwo (c, s). Sacred palm fronds.

mèt tèt (maît' tête) (v). "Master of the head," personal *lwa*.

myal (rz). Sacred consciousness.

nação (c). Nation, or rite.

nación (s). Nation, or rite.

Nagô (c, v). Yoruba.

nangaré (s). Ritual meal of cornmeal and water.

Obatala (s). *Orisha* of white cloth, clarity, peace; cf. *Oxalá*.

obeah (rz). Sorcery.

obrigação (c). "Obligation," ritual work.

ocha (s). Spirit, *orisha*.

ode (c, s). Bow and arrow sacred to Oxossi.

ogan (c). Male "masters" of house.

ogan (v). Bell.

Ogou (v). *Lwa* of war, iron, politics.

Ogun (c, s). *Orisha* of iron and war.

okonkolo (s). Smallest *bata* drum.

olorisha (c, s). "Owner of the *orisha*," priest or priestess.

omiero (s). Herbal water to soothe the spirits; cf. *amaci*.

omo (c, s). Child, devotee.

ori (c, s). Head, soul.

oricha (s). Orisha.

orieté (oriaté) (s). Songmaster.

orisha (orixá) (s). Spirit.

oro de igbodu (s). Introductory song sequence of *bembé* ceremony.

Orula (s). *Orisha* of divination.

Osanyin (c, s). *Orisha* of forest leaves.

oshé (oxé) (c, s). Thunder axe of Shango.

Oshun (Oxun) (s, c). *Orisha* of cool water; luxury.

otanes (c, s). Stones carrying Orisha's presence.

ounfo (hounfor) (v). Temple, sacred space.

oungan (houngan) (v). Priest.

oungenikon (houngenikon) (v). Song leader.

ounsi (v). Priestess, dancer.

ounsi kanzo (v). Priestess who has undergone *kanzo* initiation.

ounsi lave tét (hounsi lavé tête) (v). Priestess whose "head has been washed."

Oxossi (Oshosi) (c, s). *Orisha* of the hunt, king of Ketu.

Oya (c, s). *Orisha* of winds, woman warrior; cf. *Iansá*.

Oyo (c, s). Yoruba kingdom, home of Shango.

padrino (s). "Godfather," priest and ritual sponsor.

padrino de Orula (s). Godfather in the path of divination.

pai de santo (c). "Father of the saint," male priest.

paná (c). "Market" ceremony in initiation cycle.

pano da costa (c). "Cloth of the (African) coast," torso wrap.

parada (s). Presentation ceremony in initiation cycle.

pegi (c). Altar, altar area.

peristil (peristyle) (v). Dance pavillion.

petit (v). Smallest of vodou drums.

Petro (v). Parallel ritual cycle to, or rite within, vodou.

pot tèt (v). "Head pot," containers for human spirit.

poto-mitan (v). "Center post," ceremonial focus of vodou dance.

prendición (s). "Surprise," element of initiation rite showing claim of spirit by sudden imposition of its necklace.

prèsavann (v). "Bush priest," responsible for Catholic liturgical elements of ceremony.

pukkumina (rz). "Smaller Kumina," possible etymology for popular term for enthusiastic revivalism, "pocomania."

pureza (c). "Purity," fidelity to African ritual precedent.

Rada (v). Dahomean rite, model for vodou.

raspagem (c). "Shaving," removal of hair for initiation.

regla (s). "Rule, "order," ritual path of a religious community.

la regla congo (s). "The path of the Kongo," the ritual system of the Cuban baKongo.

la regla lucumi (s). "The path of the Lucumi," the ritual system of the Cuban Yoruba.

roça (c). "Country," descriptive term for candomblé grounds, connoting peace and refuge.

rogación de la cabeza (s). "Prayer over the head," rite of purification.

rum (c). Largest conical drum.

rumpi (c). Middle-sized or smaller conical drum.

runkô (c). Initiation chamber.

santera (s). Priestess.

santería (s). "The way of the saints," popular term for the Cuban religion devoted to the orishas.

santero (s). Priest.

santo (s). "Saint," Spanish equivalent of *orisha*.

seconde (v). Middle-sized drum.

serviteurs (v). Those who serve the *lwa*.

Shango (s, c). *Orisha* of thunder, king of Oyo; cf. *Xango*.

societé (v). Vodou community.

sopera (s). Soup tureen, container of an *orisha*'s fundamental symbols.

terreiro (c). Building, grounds, community of candomblé; cf. *Ilé*.

travailing (rz). Working the spirit by dance and breathing.

trono (s). "Throne," sacred area for initiation.

trumping (rz). Breath and dance to incarnate the spirit.

vèvè (v). Ground drawings to bring *lwa* to ceremony.

wangas (v). Charms.

Xangô (c, s). *Orisha* of thunder, king of Oyo; cf. Shango.

xaxará (c). Broom sacred to Omolu.

xiré (c). Sequence of invocation songs to the *orixás*; cf. *oro*.

Yanvalou (v). Dance of vodou, particularly associated with Danbala.

Yemaya (s). *Orisha* of the seas; cf. *Iemanjá*.

Zaka (Azaka) (v). Peasant *lwa* of farming.

Select Bibliography

HAITIAN VODOU

Bastien, Rémy. "Vodoun and Politics in Haiti." In *Religion and Politics in Haiti*. Washington, D.C.: Institute for Cross-Cultural Research, 1966.

Blier, Suzanne Preston. "Vodun: The Philosophical Roots of Art in Danhome." Paper presented at the National Museum of African Art. Washington, D.C., 1989.

Bretous, Antoine Gérard. "Le Poteau-Mitan." In *Cahier de Folklore et des Traditions Orales d'Haiti*. Port au Prince: l'Agence de Coopération Culturelle et Technique, n.d.

Brown, Karen McCarthy. "Systematic Remembering, Systematic Forgetting: Ogou in Haiti." In *Africa's Ogun: Old World and New*. Edited by Sandra T. Barnes. Bloomington: Indiana University Press, 1989.

————.*The Vèvè of Haitian Vodu: A Structural Analysis of Visual Imagery*. Ann Arbor, Mich.: University Microfilms, 1975.

Cosentino, Donald. "Who is that Fellow in the Many-colored Cap: Transformations of Eshu in Old and New World Mythologies," *Journal of American Folklore* 100, 397 (1987).

Courlander, Harold. *The Drum and the Hoe: Life and Lore of the Haitian People*. Berkeley and Los Angeles: University of California Press, 1985.

Courlander, Harold, and Bastien, Rémy. *Religion and Politics in Haiti*. Washington, D.C.: Institute for Cross-Cultural Research, 1966.

Deren, Maya. *Divine Horseman: The Living Gods of Haiti*. New York: Thames and Hudson, 1953.

Dunham, Katherine. *Dances of Haiti*. Los Angeles: Center for Afro-American Studies, University of California, 1983.

———.*Island Possessed*. New York: Doubleday, 1969

Herskovits, Melville. *Life in a Haitian Valley*. New York: Knopf, 1937.

Laguerre, Michel. *Voodoo Heritage*. Beverly Hills, Calif.: SAGE Publications, 1980.

———.*Voodoo and Politics in Haiti*. New York: St. Martin's Press, 1989.

LaRose, Serge. "The Meaning of Africa in Haitian Vodu." In *Symbols and Sentiments: Cross-Cultural Studies in Symbolism*. Edited by I. M. Lewis. New York: Academic Press, 1977.

Leyburn, James. *The Haitian People*. New Haven: Yale University Press, 1941.

Lowenthal, Ira P. "Ritual Performance and Religious Experience: A Service for the Gods in Southern Haiti." *Journal of Anthropological Research* 34 (1978).

Métraux, Alfred. *Voodoo in Haiti*. New York: Schocken Books, 1972.

Moreau de St. Méry, M. L. E. *Description Topographique, Physique, Civile, Politique, et Historique de la Partie Française de l'Isle de St. Dominique*. Paris: Libraire Larose, 1958.

Price-Mars, Jean. *Thus Spoke the Uncle*. Translated by Magdaline W. Shannon. Washington, D.C.: Three Continents Press, 1983.

Rodman, Selden. *Haiti: The Black Republic*. Old Greenwich, Conn.: Devin-Adair, 1980.

Spencer, Ivor D., trans. *A Civilization that Perished: The Last Days of White Colonial Rule in Haiti*. Translation and abridgement of *Description Topographique, Physique, Civile, Politique, et Historique de la Partie Francaise de l'Isle de St. Dominique*. By M. L. E. Moreau de St. Méry. Lanham, Md.: University Press of America, 1985.

Thompson, Robert Farris. *Flash of the Spirit: African and Afro-American Art and Philosophy*. New York: Random House, 1983.

Wilentz, Amy. *The Rainy Season*. New York: Simon and Schuster, 1989.

BRAZILIAN CANDOMBLÉ

Amado, Jorge. *Tent of Miracles*. New York: Knopf, 1977.

Bastide, Roger. *African Civilisations in the New World*. New York: Harper and Row, 1972.

————. *The African Religions of Brazil: Toward a Sociology of the Interpenetration of Civilizations*. Baltimore: Johns Hopkins University Press, 1978

————.*Le Candomblé de Bahia: Rite Nago*. Paris: Mouton & Co., 1958.

Braga, Julio. *O Jogo de Búzios: Un Estudo de Adivinhação no Candomblé*. São Paulo: Brasiliense, 1988.

Carneiro, Edison. *Candombles da Bahia*. 3d ed. Rio de Janeiro: Conquista, 1961.

Carybé. *Iconografia dos Deuses Africanos no Candomblé da Bahia*. São Paulo: Raizes, 1980.

Carybé, and Verger, Pierre. *Orixás: 38 desenhos de Carybé, texto de Pierre Verger*. Coleção Recôncavo N. 10. Bahia: Livraria Progresso Editora, 1955.

Conrad, Robert Edgar. *Children of God's Fire: A Documentary History of Black Slavery in Brazil*. Princeton: Princeton University Press, 1983.

da Costa Lima, Vivaldo. "Nações-de-Candomblé." In *Encontro de Nações-de-Candomblé*. Bahia: Ianamá e Centro de Estudos Afro-Orientais, Universidade Federal da Bahia, 1984.

————."Os Obás de Xangô." In *Olóòrisà: Escritos sobre a Religião dos Orixás*. Edited by Carlos Eugênio Marcondes de Moura. São Paulo: Agora, 1981.

Dias do Nascimento, Luis Cláudio, and Cristiana Isidoro. *Boa Morte em Cachoeira*. Cachoeira, Bahia: Centro de Estudos, Pesquisa e Ação Sócio-Cultural de Cachoeira, 1988.

Dos Santos, Juana Elbein. *Os Nàgô e a Morte: Pàde, Àsèsè e o Culto Égun na Bahia*. Petrópolis: Editora Voces, 1975.

Drewal, Margaret Thompson. "Dancing for Ogun in Yorubaland and Brazil." In *Africa's Ogun: Old World and New*. Edited by Sandra T. Barnes. Bloomington: Indiana University Press, 1989.

————."Projections from the Top in Yoruba Art." *African Arts* 9.1 (Fall, 1977).

Espin, Orlando. "Iroko e Ará-Kolé: Comentário exegético a um Mito Iorubá-Lucumí." *Perspectiva Teológica* 18 (1986).

Herskovits, Melville. "Drums and Drummers in Afro-Brazilian Cult Life." *Musical Quarterly* 30.4 (1944).

————."The Panan, An Afro Bahian Religious Rite of Transition." In *The New World Negro: Selected Papers in Afroamerican Studies*. Edited by Frances S. Herskovits. Bloomington: Indiana University Press, 1966.

————."The Social Organization of the Candomble." In *The New World Negro*. Edited by Frances S. Herskovits. Bloomington: Indiana University Press, 1966.

Herskovits, Melville J., and Herskovits, Frances S. "Afro-Bahian Religious Songs." *Folk Music of Brazil*. Album L-13, Collections of the Archive of Folk Song, 1942.

Landes, Ruth. *The City of Women*. New York: Macmillan, 1947.

Lepine, Claude. "Os Estereótipos da Personalidade no Candomblé Nagô." In *Olóòrisà: Escritos sobre a Religião dos Orixás*. Edited by Carlos Eugênio Marcondes de Moura. São Paulo: Agora, 1981.

Omari, Mikelle Smith. *From the Inside to the Outside: The Art and Ritual of Bahian Candomblé*. Los Angeles: Museum of Cultural History, UCLA, Monograph Series No. 24, 1984.

Pierson, Donald. *Negroes in Brazil: A Study of Race Contact in Bahia*. Carbondale and Edwardsville, Ill.: Southern Illinois University Press, 1967.

Ramos, Arthur. *The Negro in Brazil*. Washington, D.C.: Associated Publishers, 1939.

Rodrigues, Raymundo Nina. *Os Africanos no Brasil*. 2d ed.; São Paulo: Companhia Editora Nacional, 1935.

Russell-Wood, A. J. R. *Fidalgos and Philanthropists: The Santa Casa da Misericórdia of Bahia, 1550–1775*. Berkeley and Los Angeles: University of California Press, 1968.

Thompson, Robert Farris. *Flash of the Spirit: African and Afro-American Art and Philosophy*. New York: Random House, 1983.

Verger, Pierre. *Bahia and the West African Trade: 1549–1851*. Ibadan: Ibadan University Press, 1964.

————."Nigeria, Brazil and Cuba." *Nigeria* (October, 1960).

————.*Notes sur le Culte des Orisa et Vodun*. Dakar: L'Institut Français d'Afrique Noire, 1957.

————.*Trade Relations between the Bight of Benin and Bahia from the 17th to the 19th Century*. Ibadan: Ibadan University Press, 1976.

Voeks, Robert. "Sacred Leaves of Brazilian Candomble." *Geographical Review* 80.2 (April, 1990).

Wafer, Jim. *The Taste of Blood: Spirit Possession in Brazilian Candomblé*. Philadelphia: University of Pennsylvania Press, 1991.

Walker, Sheila. "Everyday and Esoteric Reality in the Afro-Brazilian Candomblé." *History of Religions*. 30.4 (1991).

————."The Feast of Good Death: An Afro-Catholic Emancipation Celebration in Brazil." *Sage: A Scholarly Journal on Black Women* 3.2 (Fall, 1986).

CUBAN AND CUBAN AMERICAN SANTERÍA

Bastide, Roger. *The African Religions of Brazil: Toward a Sociology of the Interpenetration of Civilizations*. Baltimore: Johns Hopkins University Press, 1978.

Brandon, George. "The Dead Sell Memories: An Anthropological Study of Santería in New York City." Ph.D. dissertation, Rutgers University, 1983.

Brown, David H. "Garden in the Machine: Afro-Cuban Sacred Art and Performance in Urban New Jersey and New York." Ph.D. dissertation, Yale University, 1989.

Cabrera, Lydia. *El Monte*. Miami: Ediciones Universal, 1975.

————.*Koeko iyawo: aprende novicia*. Miami: Ediciones Universal, 1980.

————.*La sociedad secreta Abakuá*. Miami: Ediciones Universal, 1970.

————.*Yemaya y Ochún: Kariocha, Iyalorichas y Olorichas*. Miami: Ediciones Universal, 1980.

Castellanos, Jorge, and Castellanos, Isabel. *Cultura Afrocubana*. Miami: Ediciones Universal, 1989–1992.

Edwards, Gary, and Mason, John. *Black Gods: Orisa Studies in the New World*. New York: Yoruba Theological Archiminstry, 1985.

Fraginals, Manuel Moreno. "Africa in Cuba: A Quantitative Analysis of the African Population in the Island of Cuba." In *Comparative Perspectives on Slavery in New World Plantation Societies*. Edited by Vera Rubin and Arthur Tudin. New York: New York Academy of Sciences, 1977.

González-Wippler, Migene. *The Santería Experience*. Englewood Cliffs, N.J.: Prentice-Hall, 1982.

Lewis, I.M. *Ecstatic Religion: An Anthropological Study of Spirit Possession and Shamanism*. Baltimore: Penguin, 1971.

López, Lourdes. *Estudio del babalao*. Havana: Universidad de Havana, Departamento de Actividades Culturales, 1978.

McClelland, Elizabeth M. *The Cult of Ifa among the Yoruba*. London: Ethnographica, 1982.

Murphy, Joseph M. *Santería: African Spirits in America*. Boston: Beacon Press, 1992.

Ortiz, Fernando. *Cuban Counterpoint*. New York: Knopf, 1949.

Thomas, Hugh. *Cuba: The Pursuit of Freedom*. New York: Harper and Row, 1971.

Thompson, Robert Farris. "The Sign of the Divine King: Yoruba Bead-embroidered Crowns with Veil and Bird Decorations." In *African Art and Leadership*. Edited by Douglas Fraser and Herbert Cole. Madison: University of Wisconsin Press, 1972.

REVIVAL ZION IN JAMAICA

Banbury, Thomas R. *Jamaica Superstitions or the Obeah Book; a Complete Treatise of the Absurdities Believed in by the People of the Island, by the Rector (Native) of St. Peter's Church, Hope Bay, Portland*. Jamaica, 1894.

Barclay, Alexander. *A Practical View of the Present State of Slavery in the West Indies*. London, 1828.

Barrett, Leonard E. *Soul Force: African Heritage in Afro-American Religion*. Garden City, N.Y.: Anchor Press/Doubleday, 1974.

———.*The Sun and the Drum: African Roots in Jamaican Folk Tradition*. London: Heinemann, 1976.

Beckwith, Martha. *Black Roadways*. Chapel Hill: University of North Carolina Press, 1929.

Brooks, A. A. *The History of Bewardism or the Jamaican National Baptist Church*. Kingston, 1917.

Buchner, J. H. *The Moravians in Jamaica*. London, 1854.

Chavannes, Barry. "Revivalism: A Disappearing Religion." *Caribbean Quarterly* 24. 3–4 (September–December, 1978).

Curtin, Philip D. *Two Jamaicas*. Cambridge, Mass.: Harvard University Press, 1955.

Dunham, Katherine. *Journey to Accompong*. New York: Henry Holt, 1946.

Edwards, Bryan. *Report of the Lords of the Committee of the Council appointed for the consideration of all matters relating to Trade and Foreign Plantation*. London, 1789.

Emerick, Abraham I. "Jamaican Mialism." *Woodstock Letters* 45 (1916).

Gardner, William James. *A History of Jamaica from Its Discovery by Christopher Columbus to the Year 1872*. London: T. Fisher Unwin, 1909.

Hogg, Donald. "Jamaican Religions: A Study in Variations. Ph.D. dissertation, Yale University, 1964.

Kerr, Madeline. *Personality and Conflict in Jamaica*. London: Collins, 1963.

Lewis, Matthew Gregory. *Journal of a West India Proprietor.* New York: Negro Universities Press, 1969.

Long, Edward. "History of Jamaica. 3 vols. London: T. Lowndes, 1774; reprint ed., New York: Arno Press, 1972.

Moore, Joseph G. "The Religion of Jamaican Negroes: A Study of Afro-American Acculturation." Ph. D. dissertation, Northwestern University, 1953.

Nettleford, Rex. "Pocomania in Dance Theatre." *Jamaica Journal* (June, 1969).

Patterson, Orlando. *The Sociology of Slavery: An Analysis of the Origins, Development and Structure of Negro Slave Society in Jamaica.* Rutherford, N.J.: Fairleigh Dickenson University Press, 1969.

Phillippo, James M. *Jamaica: Its Past and Present State.* London: Dawsons of Pall Mall, 1969.

Schuler, Monica. *Alas, Alas, Kongo: A Social History of Indentured African Immigration into Jamaica, 1841–1865.* Baltimore: Johns Hopkins University Press, 1980.

Seaga, Edward. "Revival Cults in Jamaica." *Jamaica Journal* (June, 1969).

Sernett, Milton C., ed., *Afro-American Religious History: A Documentary Witness.* Durham: Duke University Press, 1985.

Simpson, George. "Jamaican Revivalist Cults." *Social and Economic Studies* 5 (1956).

Waddell, H. M. *Twenty-nine Years in the West Indies and Central Africa.* London: Frank Cass, 1970.

Wedenoja, William A. "Religious Adaptation in Rural Jamaica." Ph.D. dissertation, University of California, San Diego, 1978.

Williams, Joseph J. *Voodoos and Obeahs: Phases of West Indian Witchcraft.* New York: Dial Press, 1932.

THE BLACK CHURCH IN THE UNITED STATES

Austin, Allan D. *African Muslims in Antebellum America.* New York: Garland, 1984.

Baer, Hans A. *The Black Spiritual Movement: A Religious Response to Racism.* Knoxville: University of Tennessee Press, 1984.

Baer, Hans A., and Singer, Merrill. *African American Religion in the Twentieth Century.* Knoxville: University of Tennessee Press, 1992.

Burns, Thomas A., and Smith, Stephen J. "The Symbolism of Becoming in the Sunday Service of an Urban Black Holiness Church," *Anthropological Quarterly* 51.3 (July, 1978).

Cone, James. "Black, Worship." In *The Study of Spirituality*. Edited by Cheslyn Jones, Geoffrey Wainwright, and Edward Yarnold. New York: Oxford University Press, 1986.

Creel, Margaret Washington. *"A Peculiar People": Slave Religion and Community–Culture Among the Gullahs*. New York: New York University Press, 1988.

Du Bois, W. E. B. *The Souls of Black Folk*. New York: New American Library, 1969.

Farajajé-Jones, Elias. *In Search of Zion: The Spiritual Significance of Africa in Black Religious Movements*. Bern: Peter Lang, 1991.

Fogel, Robert William, and Engerman, Stanley L. *Time on the Cross: The Economics of American Slavery*. Vol. 2. Boston: Little, Brown, 1974.

Frazier, E. Franklin. *The Negro Church in America*. New York: Schocken Books, 1964.

Genovese, Eugene. *Roll, Jordan, Roll: The World the Slaves Made*. New York: Random House, 1972.

Heilbut, Tony. *The Gospel Sound: Good News and Bad Times*. New York: Simon and Schuster, 1971.

Herskovits, Melville J. *The Myth of the Negro Past*. Boston: Beacon Press, 1990.

———. "Problem Method and Theory in Afroamerican Studies." *Afroamerica* 1 (1945).

Hurston, Zora Neale. "Hoodoo in America." *Journal of American Folklore*. 44 (1931).

———. *The Sanctified Church*. Berkeley: Turtle Island, 1981.

Joyner, Charles. *Down by the Riverside: A South Carolina Slave Community*. Urbana and Chicago: University of Illinois Press, 1984.

Levine, Lawrence W. *Black Culture and Black Consciousness: Afro-American Folk Thought From Slavery to Freedom*. New York: Oxford University Press, 1977.

Lincoln, C. Eric. "The Black Church Since Frazier." In Franklin E. Frazier, *The Negro Church in America*. New York: Schocken Books, 1974.

Lincoln, C. Eric, and Mamiya, Lawrence. *The Black Church in the African American Experience*. Durham: Duke University Press, 1990.

Long, Charles H. "Perspectives for a Study of Afro-American Religion in the

United States." In *Significations: Signs, Symbols, and Images in the Interpretation of Religion.* Philadelphia: Fortress Press, 1986.

Marks, Morton. "You Can't Sing Unless You're Saved: Reliving the Call in Gospel Music." In *African Religious Groups and Beliefs: Papers in Honor of William R. Bascom.* Edited by Simon Ottenberg. Meerut, India: Archana Publications, 1982.

Mitchell, Henry H. *Black Preaching.* Philadelphia: Lippincott, 1970.

Parsons, Elsie Clews. "Folk-lore of the Sea Islands of South Carolina," In *Memoires of the American Folk-lore Society* 16 (1923).

Payne, Wardell J. *Directory of African American Religious Bodies.* Washington D.C.: Howard University Press, 1991.

Puckett, Newbell Niles. *The Magic and Folk Beliefs of the Southern Negro.* Chapel Hill: University of North Carolina Press, 1926.

Raboteau, Albert. *Slave Religion: The "Invisible Institution" in the Antebellum South.* New York: Oxford University Press, 1978.

Scarborough, Dorothy. *On the Trail of Negro Folk Songs.* Hatboro, Penn.: Folklore Associates, 1963.

Sertima, Ivan van. *They Came Before Columbus.* New York: Random House, 1976.

Smith, Edward D. *Climbing Jacob's Ladder: The Rise of Black Churches in Eastern American Cities, 1740–1877.* Washington, D.C.: The Anacostia Museum of the Smithsonian Institution, 1988.

Sobel, Mechal. *Trabelin' On: The Slave Journey to an Afro-Baptist Faith.* Westport, Conn.: Greenwood Press, 1979.

Stone, Sonja H. "Oral Tradition and Spiritual Drama: The Cultural Mosaic for Black Preaching." *The Journal of the Interdenominational Theological Center* 8.1 (Fall, 1980).

Stuckey, Sterling. *Slave Culture: Nationalist Theory and the Foundations of Black America.* New York: Oxford University Press, 1987.

Thompson, Robert Farris. *Flash of the Spirit: African and Afro-American Art and Philosophy.* New York: Random House, 1983.

Washington, Joseph R. *Black Sects and Cults.* Garden City, N.Y.: Doubleday, 1972.

Watson, A. P., and Johnson, Clifton H. *God Struck Me Dead: Religious Conversion Experiences and Autobiographies of Negro Ex-Slaves.* Philadelphia: Pilgrim Press, 1969.

Williams, Melvin D. *Community in a Black Pentecostal Church.* Pittsburgh:

University of Pittsburg Press, 1974.

Wilmore, Gayraud S. *Black Religion and Black Radicalism.* 2d ed.; Maryknoll,
N.Y.: Orbis Books, 1985.

Wood, Peter. *Black Majority: Negroes in Colonial South Carolina from* 1670
through the Stono Rebellion. New York: Knopf, 1974.

Woodson, G. Carter. *The History of the Negro Church.* Washington, D.C.: The
Association for the Study of Negro Life and History, 1921.

Work, John Wesley. *American Negro Songs and Spirituals: A Comprehensive
Collection of 250 Folk Songs, Religious and Secular.* New York: Bonanza,
1940.

Index

WORKING THE SPIRIT